GW01606541

# VICTORIAN & EDWARDIAN PAINTINGS

## IN THE LADY LEVER ART GALLERY

VICTORIAN & EDWARDIAN PAINTINGS
IN THE NATIONAL MUSEUMS & GALLERIES ON MERSEYSIDE:
VOLUME 1

# VICTORIAN & EDWARDIAN PAINTINGS

## IN THE LADY LEVER ART GALLERY

*British artists born after 1810*
*excluding the early Pre-Raphaelites*

**Edward Morris**

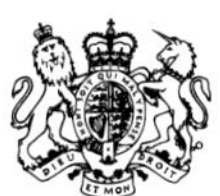


NATIONAL MUSEUMS & GALLERIES
· ON MERSEYSIDE ·

LONDON: HMSO

*ISBN 0 11 290530 7*

*British Library Cataloguing in Publication Data*
*A CIP catalogue record for this book*
*is available from the British Library*

*Design by HMSO*

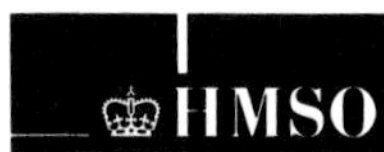


**HMSO publications are available from:**

**HMSO Publications Centre**
(Mail, fax and telephone orders only)
PO Box 276, London, SW8 5DT
Telephone orders 071–873 9090
General enquiries 071–873 0011
(queuing system in operation for both numbers)
Fax orders 071–873 8200

**HMSO Bookshops**
49 High Holborn, London, WC1V 6HB
(counter service only)
071-873 0011 Fax 071-873 8200
258 Broad Street, Birmingham, B1 2HE
021-643 3740 Fax 021-643 6510
33 Wine Street, Bristol, BS1 2BQ
0272 264306 Fax 0272 294515
9–21 Princess Street, Manchester, M60 8AS
061-834 7201 Fax 061-833 0634
16 Arthur Street, Belfast, BT1 4GD
0232 238451 Fax 0232 235401
71 Lothian Road, Edinburgh, EH3 9AZ
031-228 4181 Fax 031-229 2734

**HMSO's Accredited Agents**
(see Yellow Pages)

*and through good booksellers*

*Printed in the United Kingdom for HMSO*
*Dd 294240 C15 5/94*

# Contents

# FOREWORD

The Lady Lever Art Gallery has long been a mecca for all those interested in Victorian painting. Even when the taste for all things Victorian was at its lowest ebb, the Lady Lever Art Gallery remained one of the few places where great Victorian paintings could be seen. The wheel of fashion has now turned full circle. Victorian pictures change hands at auction for high prices and many public galleries have brought their Victorian paintings out of storage and put them back on show. But the Lady Lever still retains its pre-eminence in the field with an incomparable group of key pictures by some of the greatest Victorian masters. These include two of Lord Leighton's finest works, *The Daphnephoria* and *The Hesperides*, Herkomer's affecting piece of social realism *The Last Muster*, and a major group of paintings by Burne-Jones.

The Lady Lever Art Gallery is a monument to the personal taste of its founder, the first Lord Leverhulme, and it is dedicated to the memory of his wife. Originally run by a private trust, its transfer to the public sector, and then its move from local to national status, first to the Merseyside County Council and now to the National Museums and Galleries on Merseyside, have given the collections access to modern standards of curatorship and scholarship. The early Pre-Raphaelite pictures at the Lady Lever Art Gallery have been included in an exemplary catalogue by Mary Bennett. Now it is the turn of the other Victorian pictures in the collection. The present volume is the work of Edward Morris, who has already compiled the catalogue of the Foreign Schools at the Lady Lever Art Gallery. We would like to thank him for his very full and fascinating entries, which provide insight into the original context, meaning and critical reception of these paintings. His work will enable future generations of scholars, curators and visitors to gain a deeper understanding of the collections, thus furthering the aims of the Trustees of the National Museums and Galleries on Merseyside to promote the public enjoyment and understanding of art.

Richard Foster
*Director, National Museums and Galleries on Merseyside*

Julian Treuherz
*Keeper of Art Galleries*

# *Preface*

This catalogue contains all the oil paintings in the Lady Lever Art Gallery by artists born after 1810 except works by foreign artists (including foreign artists working in Britain) and works by the early Pre-Raphaelites (that is, J.E. Millais, F. Madox Brown, F. Sandys, D.G. Rossetti and W. Holman Hunt). These can be found in the *Lady Lever Art Gallery, Catalogue of Foreign Paintings, Drawings, Miniatures, Tapestries, Post-Classical Sculpture and Prints* by Edward Morris and Mark Evans published in 1983 and in the *Artists of the Pre-Raphaelite Circle: The First Generation: Catalogue of Works in the Walker Art Gallery, Lady Lever Art Gallery and Sudley Art Gallery* by Mary Bennett published in 1988. Some Victorian paintings by artists born on or before 1810 are therefore excluded while the small group of paintings done after 1910 are all included. Unattributed paintings imitating pre-Victorian styles do not appear in this catalogue even if it is likely that their unidentified artists were born after 1810; these paintings will be catalogued alongside the works which they imitate. Two important groups of paintings dominate the catalogue: first there are the late Pre-Raphaelite and classical revival works of Frederic Leighton, Edward Burne-Jones, J.W. Waterhouse and others; then there are the late Victorian and early 20th-century paintings bought directly from the artists, including an interesting group purchased to be used as advertisements by Lever Brothers. In addition, however, there is a more varied collection of mid-Victorian and late Victorian masterpieces cumulatively making the Gallery one of the most important centres for the study and appreciation of this phase of British art.

# Acknowledgements

The compiler is very grateful to Sandra Penketh for preparing the lists in the appendices to this catalogue. He has also received assistance from a wide variety of scholars, curators, archivists and private individuals whose names are recorded throughout the catalogue; to these he extends his thanks. Susan Fox and her colleagues at the Port Sunlight Heritage Centre, together with Jeannette Strickland at the Unilever Historical Archives, Port Sunlight, have always been most helpful. Lynda Rea typed the final draft of this catalogue with her usual efficiency and accuracy. The Friends of the Courtauld Institute generously awarded the compiler a bursary towards the costs of his research in London at the Institute and elsewhere; for this he was most grateful.

# *Explanatory Notes to the Catalogue*

All unpublished manuscripts, typescripts, letters, inventories lists, etc. are in the Lady Lever Art Gallery unless otherwise stated. All dimensions are in centimetres unless otherwise noted. Against the title of each painting are given both the current inventory number (prefixed LL) and the old inventory number(s) (prefixed WHL, TM, LP, H or HH). All the paintings in this catalogue acquired by Lever in or before 1922 were presented by him to the Lady Lever Art Gallery in 1922 except those that passed to Lever Brothers at his death; the paintings acquired by him after 1922 were presented to the Gallery very shortly after their purchase. All exhibitions and sales took place in London unless otherwise stated. Exhibitions that took place before each picture entered the Lady Lever Art Gallery are listed in full; later exhibitions are listed selectively. The only reproductions of each painting specifically mentioned are those made very soon after it was painted; they are in black and white unless otherwise stated. Italics are used in inscriptions, labels, etc. to indicate *verbatim* wording.

# *History of the Collection*

The Lady Lever Art Gallery was built and nearly all its collections were assembled by one man, William Hesketh Lever, later the first Lord Leverhulme, who will, for convenience, be referred to throughout this catalogue as Lever.[1] He was born at Bolton in 1851, the son of a prosperous Bolton wholesale grocer, and was educated locally but left school at the age of sixteen to join the family business which he greatly expanded. In 1886 the firm, Lever Brothers, diversified into soap manufacture, at first in Warrington and then from 1888 on a green-field site at Port Sunlight in Cheshire.

In 1887 he started to buy notable contemporary British paintings for use as soap advertisements (fig. 1). His expertise lay in marketing rather than in manufacture and he was eager to follow the example of his competitor T.J.

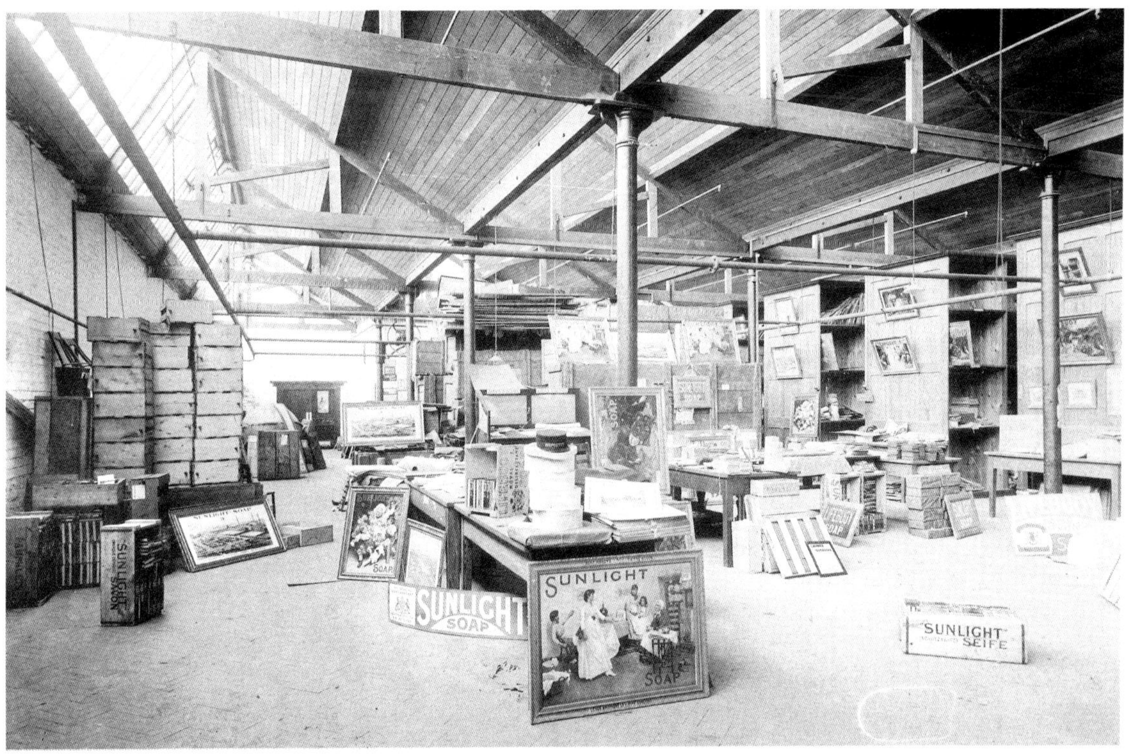


*Fig. 1 Warehouse at Lever Brothers factory, Port Sunlight, containing framed advertisements, some made from paintings now in the Lady Lever Art Gallery (photo: Port Sunlight Heritage Centre)*

Barratt of A. and F. Pears who, a little earlier, had pioneered this particular form of advertisement.[2] Some ten paintings acquired by Lever for this purpose survive in the Gallery, which also contains three paintings purchased by Barratt for reproduction as soap advertisements (see pp 22, 85). These paintings passed to Lever in 1916 following his take-over of A. and F. Pears and, like those he himself collected, were presented to the Gallery by Lever Brothers in 1983. Lever was looking for cheerful peasant, or at least lower middle-class, figures set in authentically humble interiors, as the expanding soap market lay in this direction rather than at the luxury end: it was natural, therefore, that he should buy works of the Newlyn School, or at least paintings by artists indirectly inspired by contemporary French naturalism (see pp. 1, 111). In this sense his taste as an advertiser was more 'progressive' and adventurous than his taste as a collector – and certainly more rewarding than Barratt's rather predictable enthusiasms (see pp. 22, 85). Some artists understandably objected to the use of their paintings as soap advertisements (see pp. 38, 105) and Lever gradually ceased literally reproducing their paintings with the name of his company printed over them as advertisements (fig. 2). Instead he bought pictures usually of a rather higher class (by contemporary standards) and issued high quality colour reproductions of them as prizes for collecting a large quantity of soap wrappers or in the context of similar advertising campaigns. These paintings tended to emphasize the importance of good clothes, personal appearance and cleanliness generally but the message was now more oblique and the purchasing parameters much wider (see pp. 33, 41).

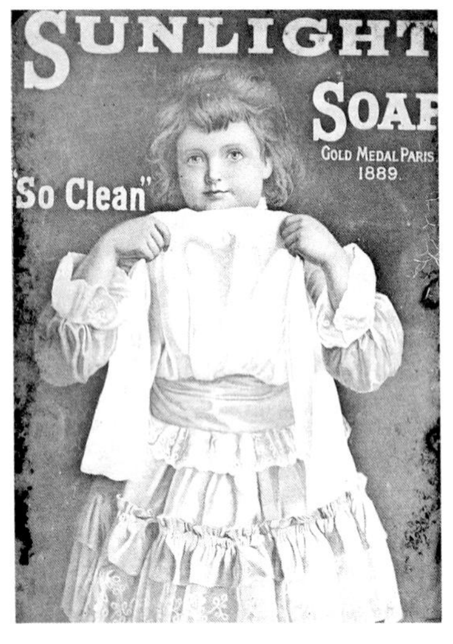


*Fig. 2 Advertisement made from Frith's* New Frock *by Lever Brothers in 1889 (photo: Port Sunlight Heritage Centre)*

About six years after he began buying paintings for Lever Brothers in order to advertise their soap, he started to assemble a private collection for his home, Thornton Manor, some 5 miles from his factories at Port Sunlight

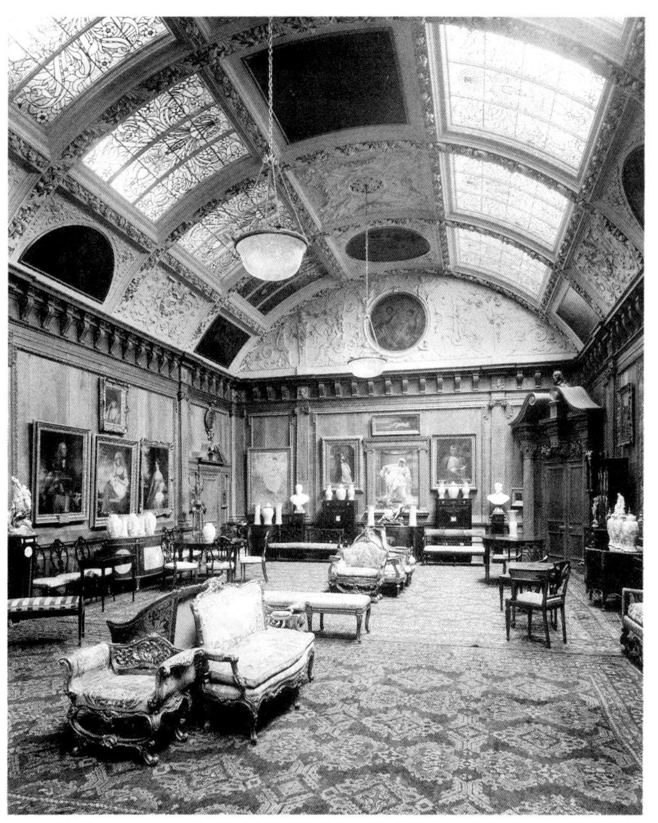

*Fig. 3 The Music Room, Thornton Manor, about 1903 (photo: Royal Commission on the Historical Monuments of England)*

(fig. 3). He bought Frederic Leighton's *Psamathe* (see pp. 68) of 1879–80 from a Liverpool dealer in 1893 and he knew that it had been owned by the Rathbones, a prominent Liverpool family; this seems to have been his first major purchase but thereafter he relied for some years on the leading London dealers, Thomas Agnew and Son; from them he bought Leighton's *Fatidica* of 1894 (see p. 75) in 1895 and during the following two years Agnew's supplied him with major works by E.J. Poynter, J.E. Millais, J.W. Waterhouse, and L. Alma-Tadema among others. He very rarely bought directly from leading artists partly because he believed that such artists inflated their prices and partly – probably – out of shyness. However, most of these paintings were at most ten or fifteen years old when Lever bought them and so he fits neatly into that well-known category – the relatively ignorant industrialist buying contemporary British paintings which he could understand rather than old master paintings which he could not appreciate. But Lever learnt quickly and he soon acquired a very knowledgeable if slightly dangerous mentor, James Orrock.[3] In 1896 Lever bought four paintings by William Etty and one by Thomas Lawrence from Orrock, whose greatest enthusiasm lay with British art of about 1770 to 1850, for which he campaigned tirelessly. Orrock did, however, appreciate some rather old-fashioned Victorian artists notably John Phillip, Henry Dawson and Edwin Hayes (see pp. 103, 23, 49) and works by these artists were included in the very large number of paintings which Lever acquired from him between 1904 and 1913.

Despite Orrock's influence and despite the mania for late 18th-century British portraits and landscapes to which Lever and many other British collectors succumbed around 1900, Lever continued to collect both contemporary paintings and 'classic' Victorian paintings right up to his death in 1925. He bought little of any description between 1906 and 1911 because the collapse of his proposed 'soap trust' severely reduced the profits of Lever Brothers but in 1913 the collection of George McCulloch came on to the market. McCulloch was the greatest single collector of that type of Victorian art fostered by the Royal Academy, and Lever, always anxious for a good provenance for his pictures, bought avidly (see pp. 27, 33, 62, 71, 84); he had begun his career as a serious collector with Leighton and it was under Leighton's *Daphnephoria*, acquired from McCulloch, that his body lay in state on 10 and 11 May 1925 (fig. 4) immediately after his death. The arrival in Port Sunlight of the great McCulloch pictures must have convinced Lever that if he was to display his collection to the public a new purpose-built art gallery was necessary – until then he had been relying on Hulme Hall, a redundant canteen for female factory staff. The unexpected death of his wife in the same year suggested to him that this new art gallery might be an appropriate memorial to her and when it was completed in 1922 Lever's Victorian masterpieces dominated the great central hall, the climax of the building (fig. 5). Even after this gift of many of his 19th- and 20th-

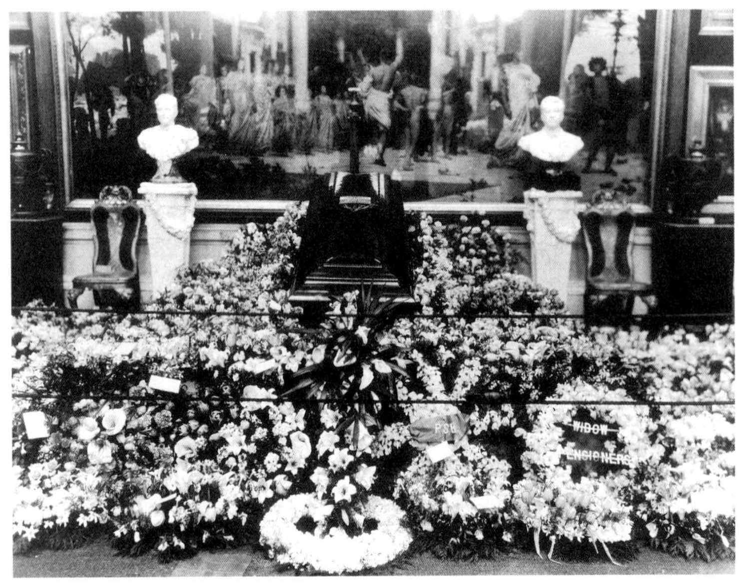

*Fig. 4 The body of W.H. Lever, first Lord Leverhulme, lying in state at the Lady Lever Art Gallery 10–11 May 1925 (photo: Port Sunlight Heritage Centre)*

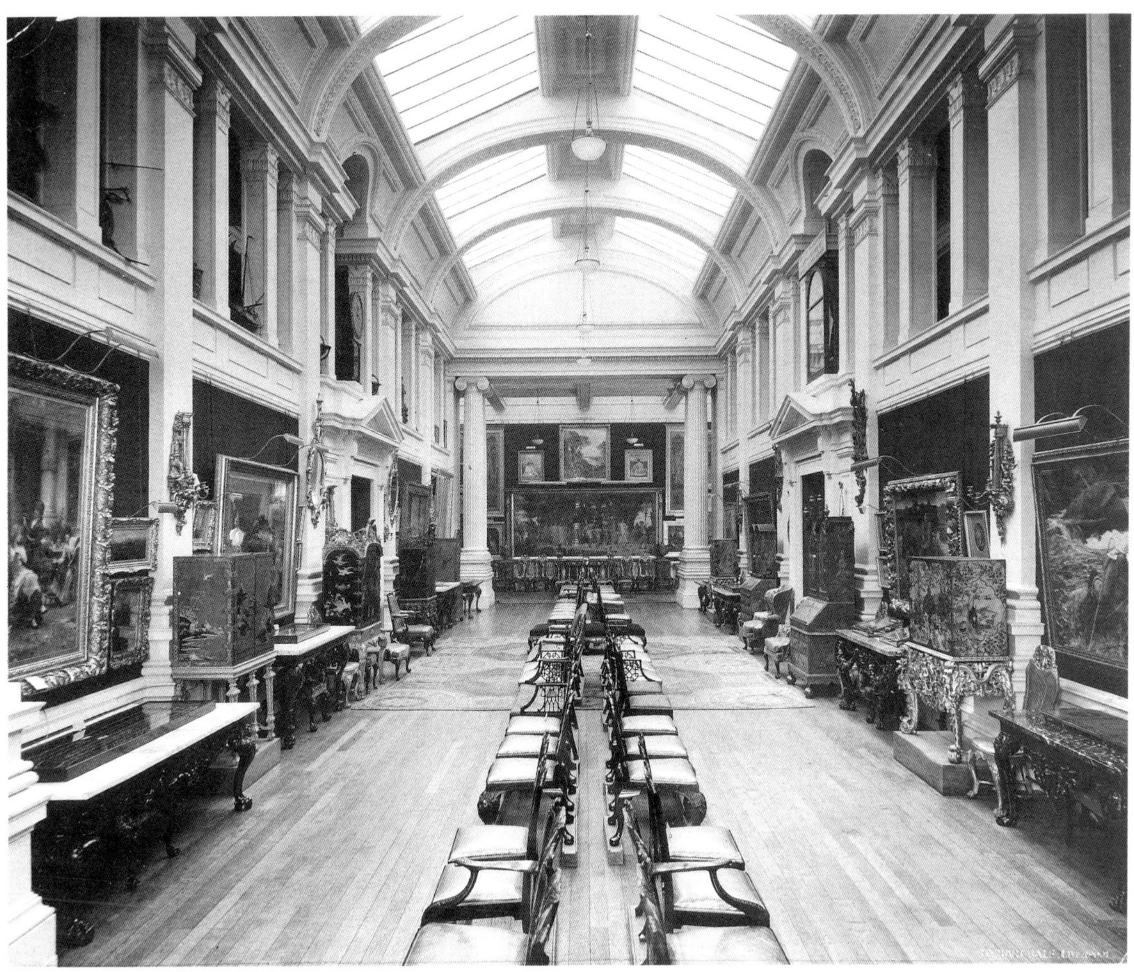

*Fig. 5 The Main Hall, Lady Lever Art Gallery, about 1930*

century paintings to the new Lady Lever Art Gallery in 1922, Lever still needed more space for his later pictures and around 1924 a new modern picture gallery was added to his London home, The Hill, at Hampstead (fig. 6).

Indeed, many of Lever's greatest Victorian paintings were acquired during the last ten years of his life; a large number of his speeches at this time were given at art gallery openings and in them he insisted on the social and moral value of art for the community and on the obliga tions on the leaders of industry to provide uplifting art for this purpose to the public.[4] 'We have here in Great Britain all the best traditions of Art . . . but Art for Art's

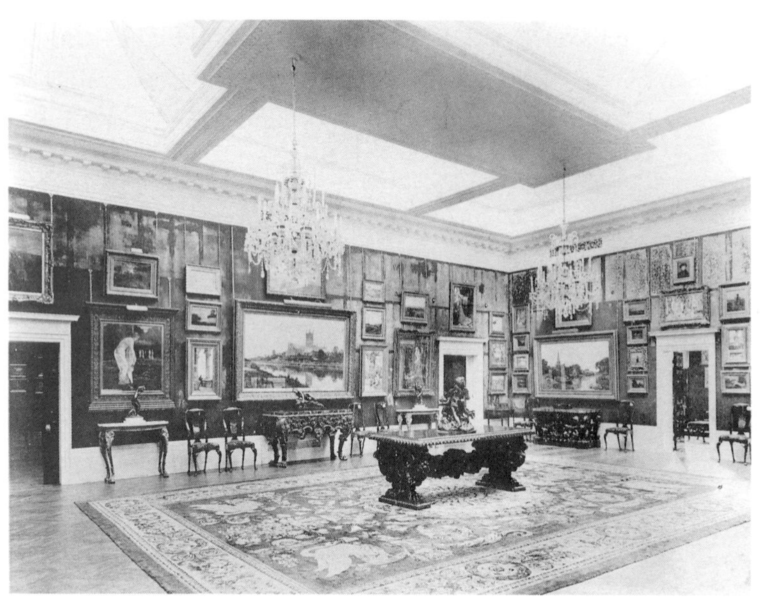

*Fig. 6 The Modern Picture Gallery, The Hill, Hampstead about 1924 (reproduced from Anderson Galleries sale catalogue 17–19 February 1926)*

sake is meaningless. Art for the service of humanity and for the people is a great and inspiring ideal.' Venice, he declared, should inspire Britain: 'All the beauty of Venice, all the art of Venice was the result of the fore sight and energy of her merchants; it was not the result of an idle wealthy class. If the merchants and manufacturers of Lancashire had done as the merchants of Venice did and introduced art at the same time as they carried on their industries I venture to say our industries would have benefited as well as our towns and cities.' Lever emphasized classical theories of art against which his enthusiasm for Leighton, Waterhouse and Burne-Jones (see pp. 62–78, 121–4, 7–18) and his repudiation of realism can be assessed. 'Art and the beautiful raise up in mind and soul an association of ideas and experiences suggesting prophecies of the ideal and the beautiful in conduct or character. The harmony in art and the beautiful suggest, again silently and with extreme sensibility, the ideal for conduct in our daily life. Art and the beautiful civilize and elevate because they enlighten and ennoble.' During the last years of his life Lever was delegating many of his business responsibilities – a process encouraged by his increasing deafness and by some disastrous new commercial ventures. This left him more time for art and its pursuit and his financial reverses deterred him from buying for only about a year in 1921.

To some extent his purchases reflected personal friendships with Luke Fildes, David Murray and Alfred East among painters (see pp. 33–7, 92, 30). During the last twenty years of his life he gave each year a lunch or dinner party to the members and associates of the Royal Academy on the occasion of their exhibition. Murray in particular was a determined opponent of modernism of any type and these social contacts probably encouraged Lever's artistic conservatism – notably his refusal in 1918 to assist the progressive artists associated with the Bluecoat Chambers in Liverpool to set up an art centre there. He did, however, play a leading part in establishing the Faculty of Arts which in 1921 opened in London as an arts centre for exhibitions, conferences, lectures, receptions and dinners related not just to fine art but also to music, drama, craft and literature. The Faculty of Arts was intended to give artists the same recognition and status accorded to other professions and was one of many such bodies set up in the early 20th century to encourage patronage of contemporary art – the Contemporary Art Society founded in 1910 and the London Artists' Association established in 1925–6 were two other examples but the Faculty of Arts was intended to embrace both conservative and more advanced styles.

Lever's status as a patron of contemporary art was seriously damaged by his mutilation of Augustus John's portrait of him in 1920. John's portrait was uncompromisingly realistic and Lever, who had been hoping for something more formal, cut out the head in order to conceal it in his small safe. The rest of the portrait was accidentally returned to the artist, who publicized the incident. The affair was however very untypical of Lever, who could, after all, have simply destroyed the whole portrait. He had little sympathy with naturalism or realism however defined – except in the narrower context of pictures to be used as advertisements – but he was a perceptive and generous patron both of mid-Victorian paintings and of the art of his own day.

On Lever's death in 1925 those paintings which he had not already presented to the Gallery were sold by his executors (see Appendix I) but after his death the Trustees of the Gallery were able to continue buying paintings with the generous endowments Lever had provided. They followed, like Lever himself, a conservative policy, acquiring principally new paintings which had been well received at the Royal Academy summer exhibitions including works by Brockhurst, Laura Knight and Campbell Taylor (see pp. 4, 59, 112), but they also bought earlier paintings by a slightly older generation of contemporary artists notably Harcourt and Brangwyn (see pp. 47, 3). Between 1958 and 1961 a considerable number of paintings owned by the Gallery were sold by the Trustees (see Appendix 2).

## Notes

1 The literature on Lever is enormous but the biography by his son Viscount Leverhulme, *Viscount Leverhulme*, 1927 has not been replaced. Many of his speeches were printed in *The Six-Hour Day and other Industrial Questions*, edited by Stanley Unwin, 1918. For Lever as a collector see particularly the series of essays published in 'Art and Business in Edwardian England: The Making of the Lady Lever Art Gallery', *Journal of the History of Collections*, 1992, vol. 4, and in Royal Academy, *Lord Leverhulme*, 1980.

2 For the influence of advertising on Lever's collecting policy, see Edward Morris, 'Paintings and Sculpture' in Royal Academy, *Lord Leverhulme*, 1980, pp. 14–16, Edward Morris, 'Advertising and the Acquisition of Contemporary Art', *Journal of the History of Collections*, 1992, vol. 4, pp. 195–200 and Charles Wilson, *The History of Unilever*, 1954, vol. 1, pp. 39–43.

3 See Alex Kidson, 'Lever and the Collecting of Eighteenth Century British paintings', *Journal of the History of Collections*, 1992, vol. 4, pp. 201–9.

4 W.H. Lever, *Art and Beauty and the City*, 1915, pp. 18, 21, 6.

# CATALOGUE

## BACON, John Henry Frederick
(1866–1913)

### *The Wedding Morning*

LL 3124 (WHL 4378)
Canvas: 118 × 163 cm
Signed: *John H. Bacon / 92*

M.H. Dixon[1] noted that this painting was in effect an 'essay in lighting' with the 'contre jour' arrangement so popular with the Newlyn School. The critic of the *Athenaeum*[2], however, argued that 'Mr. Bacon has adopted a hackneyed if artistic French motive at second hand and has so to say translated it into English.' The same critic went on to praise both the design and the faces and figures of the bride's companions and dress maker.

REPR: *Royal Academy and New Gallery Pictures*, published by Black and White, 1892, p. 104; *Royal Academy Pictures*, 1892, p. 137.

PROV: Bought by Lever[3] from the 1892 Royal Academy private view; presented by Mrs. James Darcy Lever, Lever's sister-in-law, 1922.

EXH: Royal Academy 1892 (423).

1 M.H. Dixon, 'Our Rising Artists: John H. Bacon', *Magazine of Art*, 1902, p. 196.

2 *Athenaeum*, 21 May 1892, p. 671. Similarly *The Times* critic (21 May 1892) found LL 3124 'no better and no worse than a hundred other renderings of precisely the same subject'.

3 Lever's diary published in the *Liverpool Echo*, 22 September 1952. Lever went on to note that LL 3124 was 'only a moderate picture but very suitable for a soap advertisement'. His advertisement based on it is reproduced in Leonard de Vries, *Victorian Advertisements*, 1968, p. 58 (taken from the *Illustrated London News*, 21 January 1893) and there is another example of the advertisement in the Port Sunlight Heritage Centre. In the advertisements, bars of Sunlight Soap have been substituted for the clock on the mantelpiece and for the cup and saucer on the table. For further details of Lever's use of paintings in advertisements see p. xiii.

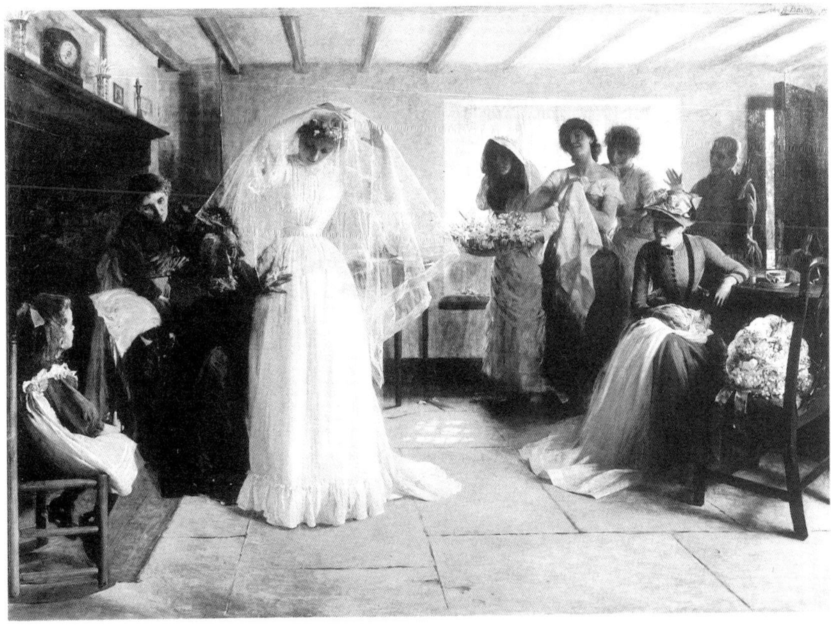

*The Wedding Morning*
LL 3124

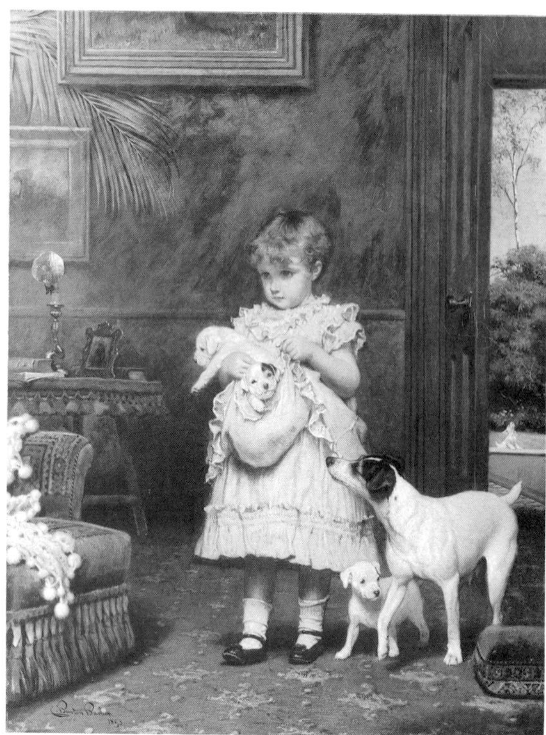

*Girl with Dogs* LL 3418

**BARBER, Charles Burton** (1845–1894)
***Girl with Dogs***
LL 3418
Canvas: 91.5 × 71.5 cm
Signed: *Burton Barber 1893*

One of many child and dog paintings done by Barber towards the end of his life; they were very popular with the dealers and were often reproduced as chromolithographs.[1]

PROV: Purchased by Lever Brothers before 1901;[2] presented by Lever Brothers 1983.

1 Harry Furniss, *Charles Burton Barber*, 1896, pp. 10–12.

2 The first Lever Brothers advertisements incorporating LL 3418 seem to have appeared around 1901 (Ailsa Bowers, letters to the compiler, 5 and 12 January 1987). There are examples of these advertisements in the Port Sunlight Heritage Centre. In these advertisements LL 3418 was entitled *The Family Wash* and it was stated that Lever Brothers had purchased the painting. For Lever's use of paintings in his advertisements see p. xiii.

**BELL, Robert Anning** (1863–1933)
***A Spring Revel***
LL 3150 (WHL 2892)
Canvas: 76.5 × 183.5 cm
Signed: *Rt. An. Bell 16*

The critic of the *Connoisseur*[1] noted that *A Spring Revel* was 'conceived in a decorative spirit, and has something of the feeling of a Greek frieze translated into pigment. It pulsates with joyous movement, and the colour is fresh and glowing.' The *Studio*[2] similarly found it 'vivacious'. *The Times* critic[3] was less impressed: 'This is a Bacchanalian scene but the Bacchanals seem a little too conscientious in their abandonment, as if they had been very well taught. They remind one, in fact, of Chelsea young ladies performing a morris dance. It is very well done but there is a fatal taint of unreality about it.' A sketch in tempera (33 × 43 cm) for the right-hand half of the composition is now in a British private collection;[4] it is signed and dated 1917 but certainly seems to be a sketch for the Lady Lever Art Gallery painting rather than a later version of it.

REPR: *Royal Academy Illustrated*, 1916, p. 61.

PROV: Bought by Lever from the artist August 1916 (£262.10*s*.).

EXH: Royal Academy 1916 (349).

1 *Connoisseur*, 1916, vol. 45, p. 125. When the sketch for LL 3150 was exhibited in 1917, however, the *Connoisseur* critic was reminded of 'the full and sumptuous life of the Italian Renaissance' (*Connoisseur*, 1917, vol. 49, p. 237).

2 *Studio*, 1916, vol. 68, p. 40.

3 *The Times*, 29 April 1916.

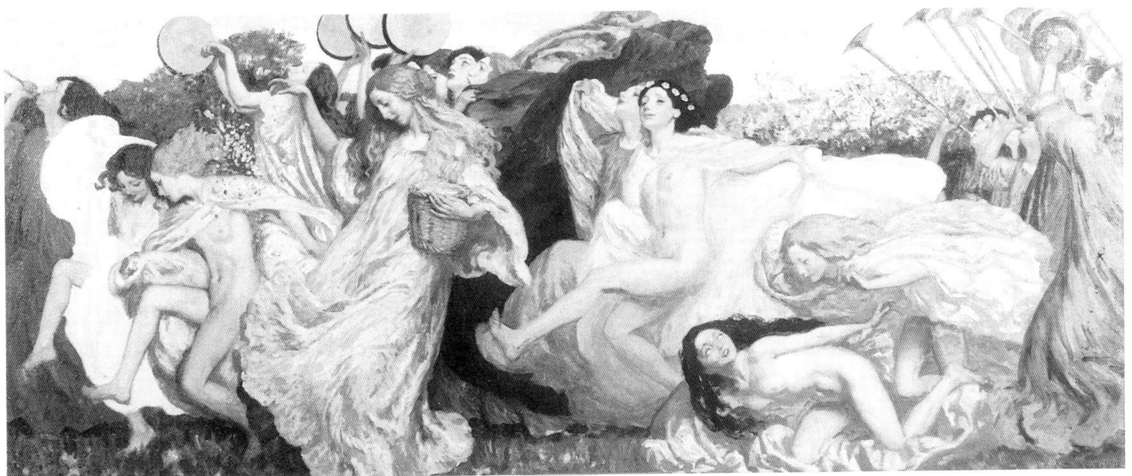

*A Spring Revel* LL 3150

4 It was probably exhibited at the Royal Water Colour Society 1917 (1) and possibly at the Fine Art Society 1934 *Robert Anning Bell* retrospective exhibition (75) as *Sketch for the Triumph of Spring*.

**BRANGWYN, Frank** (1867–1943)
***The Shipbuilders***
LL 3910 (LP 34)
Canvas: 92.1 × 203.5 cm.

This painting is closely related to Brangwyn's *Building the Frigate*, one of the colour illustrations in the 1911 edition of Robert Southey's *Life of Nelson*, for which John Masefield wrote an introduction.[1] For this reason it has been entitled *The Building of the Frigate*[2] and it has been dated probably rightly to 1910.[3] It can be seen in the context of Brangwyn's large decorative paintings of historical subjects for Venice and the Leeds City Art Gallery (1905), for the Royal Exchange (1906), for the Skinners' Hall (1904–9) and for the new court house at Cleveland, Ohio (1912–14).[4]

PROV: Sir Arthur Du Cros sale, Craigweil House, Aldwick, Sussex, Knight, Frank and Rutley 2 August 1932, lot 914, bought Barbizon

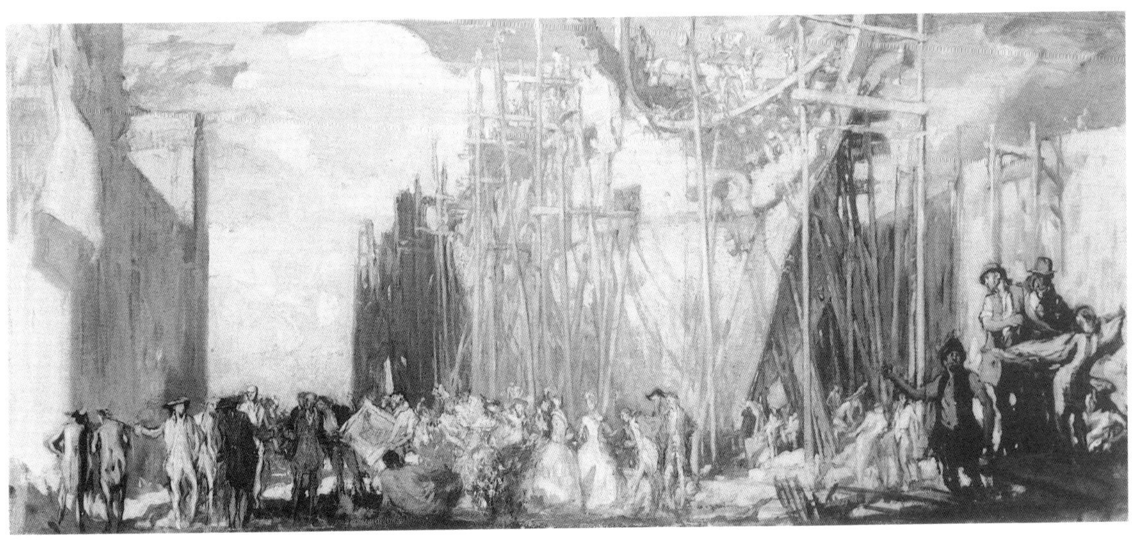

*The Shipbuilders* LL 3910

House (£630) for the Lady Lever Art Gallery (£661.10*s*).[5]

1 Reproduced on page 2. Brangwyn's illustration seems to have no reference to Southey's text unless it relates to Nelson's attack on extravagance in naval dockyards; W. Shaw Sparrow, *Prints and Drawings by Frank Brangwyn*, 1919, p. 219, describes the subject of the illustration as 'An officer and his friends, women and men gaily dressed, visit the frigate'. V. Galloway, *The Oils and Murals of Sir Frank Brangwyn*, 1962, nos. 107 and 108, p. 24, describes Brangwyn's original painting for the illustration as the sketch for LL 3910; he did not however know where that original painting was to be found and probably had never seen it.

2 Galloway, *op. cit.*; Herbert Furst, *The Decorative Art of Frank Brangwyn*, 1924, p. 18 called LL 3910 *The Building of the Ship*; Shaw Sparrow, *op. cit.*, p. 216 described it as *An Old-Time Shipyard*.

3 Galloway, *op. cit.*; *Barbizon House Record*, 1932, no. 2 also dates LL 3910 to 1910.

4 For all these commissions see Furst, *op. cit.*, pp. 53–84.

5 Barbizon House Record, *op. cit.*

## BROCKHURST, Gerald Leslie
(1890–1978)

### *Jeunesse Dorée*

LL 3908 (LP 38)
Board[1]: 76.2 × 63.1 cm
Signed: *Brockhurst*

The model for *Jeunesse Dorée* (and for much of the artist's work in the 1930s) was his close friend Kathleen (or Dorette) Woodward whom the artist met around 1928 at the Royal Academy where she was a model for the students. She eventually married the artist in 1947.[2] Brockhurst painted her frequently in the 1930s under various fanciful titles often combining as here a Renaissance format, Symbolist colours and intensity, an enticing sensuality with – from the title – a hint of upper class decadence more commonly associated with the 1920s than the 1930s.[3] At the 1934 Royal Academy, however, the critics were most impressed by Brockhurst's hard finish and detail[4] but H. Granville Fell[5] observed that 'Mr. Gerald Brockhurst continues to astonish us with his meticulous and sometimes disconcerting analysis of the opposite sex' and described *Jeunesse Dorée* as 'sophisticated and worldly wise'.

REPR: *Royal Academy Illustrated*, 1934, p. 61; *Tatler*, 17 October 1934, p. 125 (in colour); *Studio*, 1934, vol. 108, p. 5.

PROV: Bought from the artist 1934 (£850).[6]

EXH: Royal Academy 1934 (14).

1 Inscribed: *CROSSLAND FLEXIBLE GESSO/ PATENT NO 383755/THE COLLECTOR'S PICTURE RESTORING CO. LTD/STUDIO 3/59 SOUTH EDWARDES SQ./ KENSINGTON/LONDON W8.*

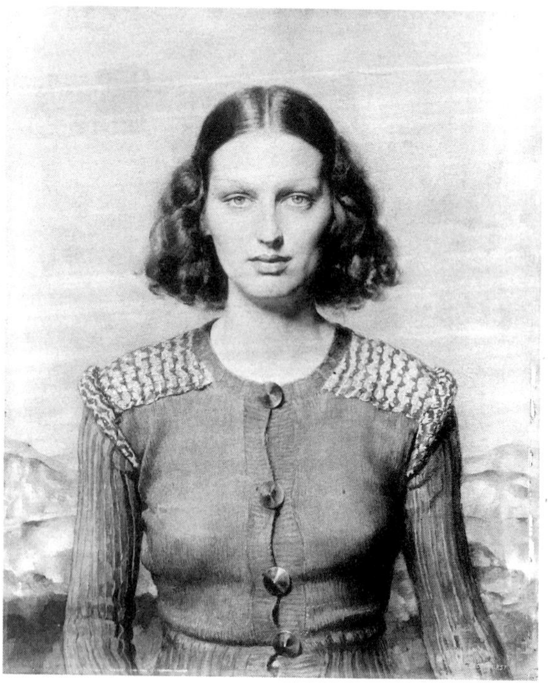

*Jeunesse Dorée* LL 3908

The Provisional Patent specification (accepted on 24 November 1932) explains that gesso grounds can be made flexible by the incorporation into them of layers of muslin or cotton fabric. This is presumably the process used for the ground of LL 3908 and accounts for its sharp, hard 'early Renaissance' technique.

2 Graves Art Gallery, Sheffield, *Brockhurst*, 1986, pp. 8, 16, 18. Her role and career were much discussed in the popular press of the period; see for example the *Daily Mail*, 8 May 1934, *Sunday Express*, 7 June 1936 and 21 November 1937, *News Review*, 25 November 1937 and *Daily Express*, 18 November 1937.

3 For another analysis of these paintings see Graves Art Gallery, *op. cit.*, p. 18.

4 Herbert Furst, 'Royal Academy Paintings', *Apollo*, 1934, vol. 19, p. 296; 'Pictures of the Month', *Artist*, July 1934, vol. 7, p. 152.

5 'At the Royal Academy', *Connoisseur*, 1934, vol. 93, p. 396. Douglas Goldring, 'The Royal Academy', *Studio*, 1934, vol. 108, p. 2 merely described LL 3908 as 'good of its kind'.

6 The second Lord Leverhulme seems to have tried to buy Brockhurst's *Dorette* (now Harris Museum and Art Gallery, Preston) for the Lady Lever Art Gallery from the 1933 Royal Academy (Graves Art Gallery, *op. cit.*, p. 31).

## BROWN, John Alfred Arnesby
(1866–1955)

### *In June*

LL 3907 (WHL 4748, LP 10)
Canvas[1]: 131.8 × 152.5 cm
Signed: *Arnesby Brown*

This painting was well received by the critics at the 1917 Royal Academy but the artist was criticized for repeating a well-established formula – a group of cattle in the foreground with an open distant landscape and a dramatic sky above. The *Times* critic[2] wrote:

*Though Mr. Arnesby Brown's cattle piece,* In June, *is a success we feel that we have seen the same picture before. He has painted these fine bulls in the foreground with a rolling sky above them so often that it*

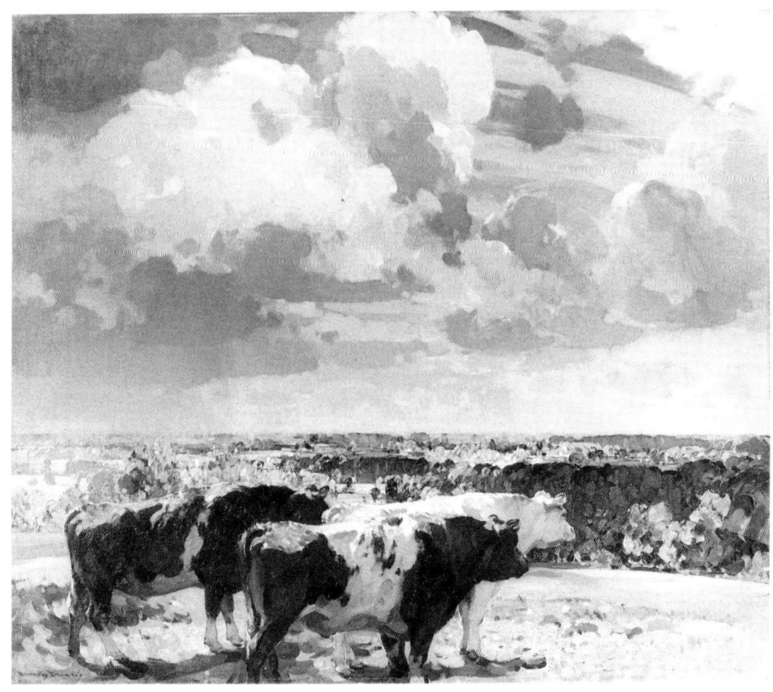

*In June* LL 3907

*is ceasing to be an adventure for him, and for us. And now we feel there is a touch of the cattle show about his cattle; they are so obviously prize animals that we begin to be aware of the connoisseur rather than the artist. It is all very well done but we wish he would do something else.*

The critic of the *Connoisseur*[3] was more enthusiastic but had the same reservations:

*Of landscapes in the gallery, the most important is Mr. Arnesby Brown's* In June, *a group of cattle set in a wooded champaign under a cloudy summer's sky. It is only a slight variant of numerous themes which the painter has given us in previous years, and of which he has two smaller examples in an adjoining room. This, perhaps, is the finest of the series. The picture, though rather blue in tone, is a fine example of aerial perspective, so successfully realised that even the objects in the immediate foreground appear enveloped in atmosphere.*

There is some uncertainty about the date of this painting. The Captain Harvey sale catalogue[4] states that it was exhibited in Glasgow in 1914 and in Oldham in 1915. Neither statement seems to be correct and it would have been very unusual for an artist of Arnesby Brown's eminence to have exhibited a major work in the provinces before showing it at the Royal Academy. Furthermore, Harold Sawkins dates it to 1917.[5] By 1917 the artist's principal sketching ground was Norfolk, where he is likely to have made the studies[6] for *In June*.

REPR: *Royal Academy Illustrated*, 1917, p. 56.

PROV: Captain John Audley Harvey sale, Christie's 2 May 1924, lot 125, bought Gooden and Fox (£441) for Lever (£452.0*s*.6*d*.).

EXH: Royal Academy 1917 (15).

1 Canvas stamp: *C. ROBERSON AND CO LTD/ 99 LONG ACRE, LONDON*; frame maker's label: *C.M. MAY AND SON. Gilders and Picture Frame Manufacturers, 134 Wardour Street, Soho.*

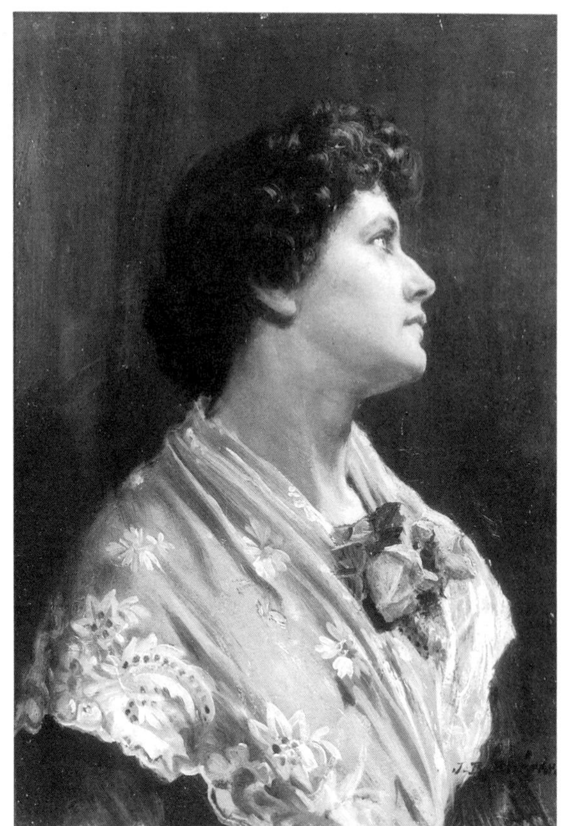

*Head of a Woman* LL 3713

2 *The Times*, 10 May 1917.

3 *Connoisseur*, 1917, vol. 48, p. 110. There is a further brief comment in the *Studio*, 1917, vol. 71, p. 16 and on the occasion of the Captain Harvey sale A.L. Baldry contributed a long analysis of LL 3907 to the *Studio*, 'Captain J. Audley Harvey's Collection', 1921, vol. 82, pp. 87–8.

4 See provenance. This statement seems to be based on Oldham 1915 and Glasgow 1914 labels on the frame; probably the artist originally used the frame of LL 3907 for another painting.

5 Harold Sawkins, 'J.A. Arnesby Brown', *Artist*, 1933, vol. 5, p. 187.

6 His working methods are described in Sawkins, *op. cit.*; he lived near Norwich.

## **BURGESS, John Bagnold** (1829–1897)

### ***Head of a Woman***

LL 3713 (WHL 1483, TM 64)
Panel[1]: 28 × 21 cm
Signed: *J.B. Burgess/J.B. Burgess 1885*

PROV: The artist's sale, Christie's 26 March 1898, lot 237, bought Agnew (£19.19*s*.), for Lever (£20.18*s*.11*d*.).

1 There is a Lechertier Barbe and Co. label on the back (now only partially visible).

## **BURNE-JONES, Edward Coley** (1833–1898)

### ***The Beguiling of Merlin***

LL 3121 (WHL 3509)
Canvas[1]: 186 × 111 cm
Signed: *E. BURNE JONES MDCCCLXXIV*

*The Beguiling of Merlin* was commissioned by Frederick Leyland around 1870 and begun in about 1872;[2] it ultimately became an important feature of Leyland's new 'aesthetic' interior at 49 Prince's Gate, London, the house which he acquired in 1874; it hung in the drawing room together with a large number of paintings by Rossetti.[3] In 1873, however, the paint on the first version proved insecure and the artist began a new version (the Lady Lever Art Gallery painting) which, although dated 1874, was not completed until 1877.[4]

The subject had interested the artist as early as 1857 when he painted it as part of the Oxford Union Murals; but the 1857 version and the gouache of 1861 (Victoria & Albert Museum inv. 257–1896 – entitled *Merlin and Nimue*) are entirely different in composition from the 1870–7 painting; they both simply have two standing figures and the stone or pit under, or into, which Nimue is enticing Merlin. Merlin had fallen in love with Nimue (or Nimiane, or Viviane, or Vivien). She profited from his infatuation by learning his skills in enchantment. Here in the Lady Lever Art Gallery painting she is using this skill to send Merlin into a deep sleep. The intensity and close relationship between the two figures may be due to the meaning which the painting had for Burne-Jones's private life. Mary Zambaco was a member of the Ionides family who were important patrons of contemporary art in 19th-century London; she fell in love with Burne-Jones in the 1860s and they remained very close even in the early 1870s; in 1893 he wrote to Helen Mary Gaskell about Mary Zambaco:[5]

> *The head of Nimuë in the picture called* The Enchanting of Merlin *was painted from the same poor traitor and was very like – all the action is like – the name of her was Mary. Now isn't that very funny as she was born at the foot of Olympus and looked and was primaeval and that's the head and the way of standing and turning . . . and I was being turned into a hawthorn bush in the forest of Broceliande – every year when the hawthorn buds it is the soul of Merlin trying to live again in the world and speak – for he left so much unsaid.*

The model for Merlin's head was the American journalist W.J. Stillman.

Another reason for the differences between the Lady Lever Art Gallery version and Burne-Jones's earlier renderings of the subject relates to the exact source he used on this occasion for the background and setting. This was not Malory or Tennyson but (probably) a 15th-century English translation of one of the French romances first published in 1865–6 by the Early English Text Society:[6]

> *Than he be-gan to devise the crafte vnto hir, and she it wrote all that he seide; and whan hadde alle devised, the damesell hadde grete ioye in herte, and he hir loved more and more, and she shewed hym feirer chere than be-forn; and so thei soiourned to-geder longe tyme, till it fill on a day that thei wente thourgh the foreste hande in hande, devisinge and disportinge, and this was in the foreste of brochelonde, and fonde a bussh that was feire and high of white hawthorne full of floures, and ther thei satte in the shadowe; and*

*Merlin leide his heed in the damesels lappe, and she be-gan to taste softly till he fill on slepe; and whan she felt that he was on slepe she a-roos softly, and made a cerne with hir wymple all a-boute the bussh and all a-boute Merlin, and be-gan hir enchauntementz soche as Merlin hadde hir taught, and made the cerne ix tymes, and ix tymes hir enchauntementes; and after that she wente and satte down by hym and leide his heed in hir lappe, and hilde hym ther till he dide a-wake.*

A sketchbook at the Fitzwilliam Museum Cambridge (inv. 962) contains studies of Nimue for the Lady Lever Art Gallery painting, and there are also drapery and other studies for the figures of Merlin and of Nimue in the Fitzwilliam Museum (inv. 1993, dated 1872, inv. 1997, inv. 2022A, inv. 2002–2005, etc.). A pencil and chalk study of heads and hands is in the Rodney Todd-White Collection. A study for the figure of Nimue – or a copy after it – was sold at Christie's London, 3 February 1976, lot 161 (black chalk and oil on canvas). A pencil study for the head of Nimue, signed and dated 1870, was sold at Christie's London, 24 March 1981, lot 50, and a gouache study for the same head is in the Delaware Art Museum, Wilmington (see note 5). A replica of the painting was exhibited in the artist's studio after his death (catalogue no. 27).[7] Two drawings at the Tate Gallery (inv. A00065 and A00066) are now regarded as containing studies for the painting – the former for the head of Merlin. Many more studies are recorded in the artist's two studio sales and in the various exhibition catalogues of 1896–9, all listed on p. 13 below (under LL 3634).

At the 1877 Grosvenor Gallery exhibition Burne-Jones's eight pictures occupied the whole south wall of the west gallery and were seen against red silk. The critics were deeply impressed; Ruskin, writing of all eight, stated: 'His work, first, is simply the only art work at present produced in England which will be received by the future as classic in its kind – the best that has been or could be'; the *Portfolio* referred to 'the grace of gesture now studied with assured knowledge of form and the witchery of a certain passionately sad type of beauty' and to 'the accomplished technique dealing with fresh subtleties of pigment and cunning mediums with the use of metal grounds and rare hues'.[8] The *Academy* critic, W.M. Rossetti,[9] liked 'the grand figure of Nimue dark and lovely with a loveliness that looks ominous and subtle without being exactly sinister and the exquisite painting of the lavish white hawthorn blossom'. Henry James[10] in *Galaxy* defended the pictures from the popular complaint that they were 'literature, erudition, edification, a superior education, a reminiscence of Oxford, a luxury of culture'; he found the *Beguiling of Merlin* 'a brilliant piece of simple rendering', demanding 'a vast deal of looking on the painter's part'. Sidney Colvin[11] also defended the painting from popular derision and particularly commended its expressive power: 'The countenances are passion incarnate, the profile of Nimiane especially never to be forgotten; and in like manner every line of the figure and drapery, every tone of the ashen and white and steely purple colouring combine to give a perfect imaginative expression to the passion and tragedy of the scene.' The *Athenaeum*[12] disliked the figure of Merlin which had caused the artist so much trouble:

*Nimue's face in its snaky intensity of malice is marvellous, not so the weak and womanish visage of Merlin; her attitude is unquestionably fine; his correspondingly weak and ill-expressed. Her draperies of dark purple are finely painted but the tumultuous folds on her thighs are not accounted for; most lovely is the painting of the blooming hawthorn; there is no shadow rather a shimmering light of witchery about the picture.*

*The Times*[13] found Burne-Jones too close to Italian late 15th-century painting: 'it can never be invention and imagination of the healthiest and highest order that stands thus detached from the forms and life of its own time and can only find a voice through long silent lips'. Graham Robertson[14] recalled that the *Beguiling of Merlin* 'wrought the most potent spell . . . It was mercilessly ridiculed.

The lovely and intricate patternings of the blossoming may-trees, the sinuous pose of the malign sorceress passed unnoticed while the critics proclaimed that the head of Vivien was too small for her body.' Perhaps the most perceptive critic was Oscar Wilde[15] who wrote:

*Were this Mr. Burne-Jones's only work it would be enough of itself to make him rank as a great painter. The picture is full of magic; and the colour is truly a spirit dwelling on things and making them expressive to the spirit, for the delicate tones of grey, and green, and violet seem to convey to us the idea of languid sleep, and even the hawthorn-blossoms have lost their wonted brightness, and are more like the pale moonlight to which Shelley compared them, than the sheet of summer snow we see now in our English fields.*

After its London success the *Beguiling of Merlin* was sent to the 1878 Paris *Exposition Universelle* where according to D.G. Ros-

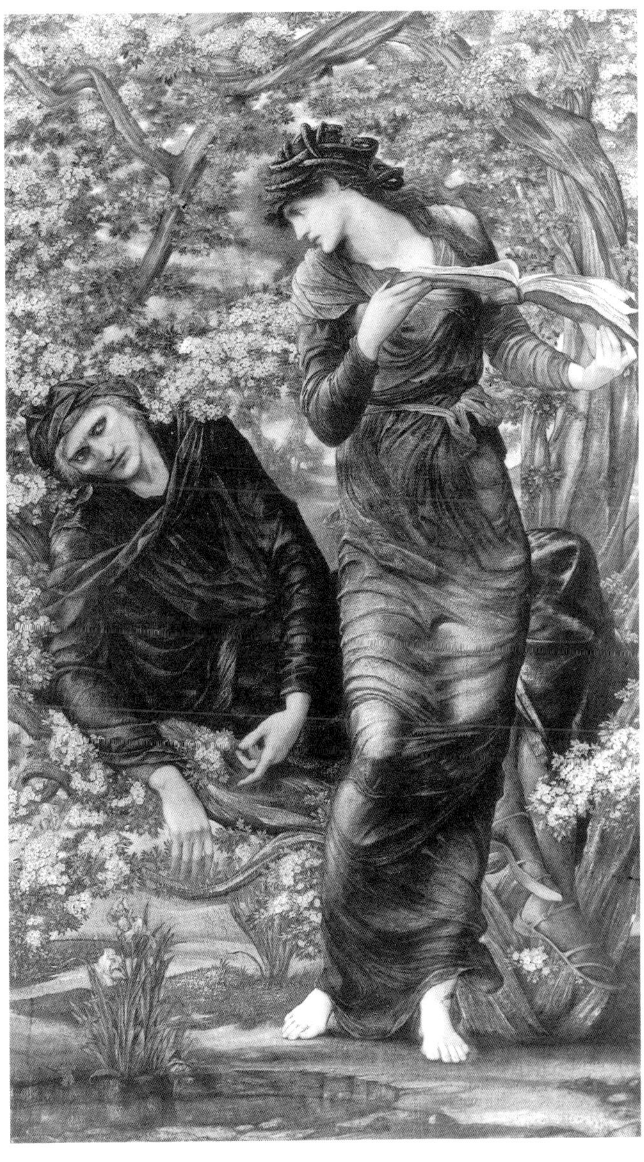

*The Beguiling of Merlin*
LL 3121 (colour plate 1)

setti it was expected to carry off all the major prizes; in fact in Paris only the critics admired it,[16] although an etching after it was published there by *L'Art*; Burne-Jones's popular success in Paris occurred only in the 1880s.[17] Charles Blanc,[18] however, wrote in 1878: 'a mon sens la plus étonnante peinture qui nous soit venue de Londres est celle de Burne-Jones: *Merlin et Viviane*. Il y a là une quintessence d'idéal, une poésie sublimée qui m'appréhende au coeur.' Similarly Duranty[19] in the *Gazette des Beaux Arts* confirmed that 'le type maigre aux grands yeux caves que M. Burne-Jones a donné à la Vivianne du Moyen-Age est encore un type anglais, le type des âmes poétiques par excellence' – indeed Duranty isolated in his review those expressive twisting linear rhythms throughout the picture which constitute its greatness.

REPR: Lalauze (etching) published in *L'Art*, 1877, vol. 3, p. 80. Henry Blackburn, *Catalogue Illustré, Exposition Universelle*, Paris, 1878, no. 121, p. 33.

PROV: Commissioned by Frederick Leyland about 1870; his sale, Christie's 28 May 1892, lot 41, bought Agnew's (£3,780); Lilian Duchess of Marlborough sale, Christie's 10 May 1918, lot 94, bought Gooden and Fox (£2,730) for Lever (£2,798.5*s*.).

EXH: Grosvenor Gallery 1877 (59); Exposition Universelle, Paris 1878 (121); Birmingham Museum and Art Gallery, *G.F. Watts and Edward Burne-Jones*, 1885 (101); New Gallery, *Edward Burne-Jones*, 1892–3 (65); New Gallery, *Sir Edward Burne-Jones*, 1898–9 (68); Arts Council, *Burne-Jones*, 1975 (129); Royal Academy, *Lord Leverhulme*, 1980 (5).

1 Canvas stamp: Prepared by Charles Roberson 99 Long Acre, London.

2 Georgiana Burne-Jones, *Memorials of Edward Burne-Jones*, 1904, vol. 2, pp. 11, 38–9, 67, 77, 85. Malcolm Bell, *Sir Edward Burne-Jones*, 1901, pp. 48–52. Edward Burne-Jones, 'List of my designs, drawings and pictures' (MSS Fitzwilliam Museum, Cambridge).

3 See M. Susan Duval, 'F.R. Leyland, A Maecenas from Liverpool', *Apollo*, 1986, vol. 124, pp. 110 ff. The Bedford Lemere photograph, no. 11529 of 1892 (now National Monuments Record) shows LL 3121 hanging in the drawing room.

4 He wrote to George Howard about the insecure paint: 'I don't know if it was my fault or Roberson's – let us call it Roberson's' (Penelope Fitzgerald, *Edward Burne-Jones*, 1975, p. 151). Bell, *op. cit.* and E. Burne-Jones, *op. cit.*, record a substantial amount of work done on LL 3121 during 1875.

5 Fitzgerald, *op. cit.*, p. 150. There is a long account of Burne-Jones's infatuation with Mary Zambaco in Jan Marsh, *The Pre-Raphaelite Sisterhood*, 1985, pp. 269 ff. A gouache study of Mary Zambaco for the head of Nimue in LL 3121 is now in the Samuel and Mary R. Bancroft Collection, Delaware Art Museum, Wilmington. The subject is analysed by Martin Harrison and Bill Waters in *Burne-Jones*, 1973, pp. 110–11 as 'the eternal struggle between the sexes'. Debra Mancoff in *The Arthurian Revival in Victorian Art*, 1990, pp. 218 ff. argues that Burne-Jones's 1857 and 1861 versions have a largely virtuous Nimue acting in self-defence against a predatory Merlin (as in Malory's *Morte D'Arthur*), while LL 3121 portrays Nimue as a relentless and irresistible *femme fatale* (as in Tennyson's *Idylls of the King* of 1859); Burne-Jones had earlier denounced Tennyson's new interpretation of Nimue's character and Tennyson used one of her other names (Vivien) to signal the new characterization (Georgiana Burne-Jones, *op. cit.*, vol. 1, p. 182).

6 *Merlin or the Early History of King Arthur*, ed. Wheatley, Early English Text Society, Original Series, 1865–6, vols. 10 and 21, reprinted 1899 as *Merlin*, vol. 2, p. 681. The artist quoted from this source (using a modernized text) in the 1877 Grosvenor Gallery Catalogue. The hawthorn tree in flower was often associated with love in medieval romance – and, more specifically, with

fairy trysting places – in Celtic mythology (see M. Whitaker, *The Legends of King Arthur in Art*, 1990, p. 245); similarly the iris could mean passion.

7 E. Burne-Jones, *op. cit.*, records a large number of studies for LL 3121 then in his sketchbooks. For the drawings at the Fitzwilliam Museum, see particularly Nantes, Musée des Beaux Arts, *Burne-Jones*, 1992, p. 110. For the replica of LL 3121, see P. Burne-Jones, 'Notes on Some Unfinished Works of Sir Edward Burne-Jones', *Magazine of Art*, 1900, pp. 159–60.

8 J. Ruskin in *Fors Clavigera*, letter 79 of 18 June 1877 reprinted in *Works*, ed. Cook and Wedderburn, 1907, vol. 29, p. 159; *Portfolio*, 1877, p. 99.

9 *Academy*, 1877, vol. 11, p. 467. Kate Greenaway also particularly admired the tree in LL 3121 – she identified it as a may tree – see M.H. Spielmann and G.S. Layard, *The Life and Work of Kate Greenaway*, 1905, p. 230. John Christian thought that the branches of the tree had the knotty quality of the olive trees which the artist saw on his Italian trips of 1871 and 1873 – see Nantes, *op. cit.*, p. 51.

10 Henry James in *Galaxy*, August 1877, reprinted in *The Painter's Eye*, ed. Sweeney, 1956, p. 145.

11 Sidney Colvin, 'The Grosvenor Gallery', *Fortnightly Review*, June 1877, vol. 27, pp 827–8.

12 *Athenaeum*, 5 May 1877, p. 584. The *Saturday Review*, 12 May 1877, p. 580 admired Nimue's and Merlin's faces but disliked all other aspects of the two figures.

13 *The Times*, 1 May 1877.

14 Graham Robertson, *Time Was*, 1931, p. 47.

15 *Dublin University Magazine*, July 1877, reprinted in *Complete Works: Miscellanies*, ed. Ross, 1908, vol. 15, pp. 13–14. For the critical reaction to the entire 1877 Grosvenor Gallery exhibition see Barrie Bullen, 'The Palace of Art: Sir Coutts Lindsay and the Grosvenor Gallery', *Apollo*, 1975, vol. 102, pp. 352–7.

16 Fitzgerald, *op. cit.*, p. 172 quoting an apparently unpublished letter from Rossetti to Howell, now in the University of Texas at Austin; see also Arts Council, *Burne-Jones*, 1975, no. 129, p. 51 for the Paris exhibition and Georgiana Burne-Jones, *op. cit.*, p. 85.

17 See Jacques Lethève, 'La connaissance des Préraphaelites anglais en France', *Gazette des Beaux Arts*, 1959, pp. 318–19 for the whole problem.

18 Charles Blanc, *Les Beaux Arts à L'Exposition Universelle de 1878*, 1878, p. 335. C. Tardieu in 'La Peinture à l'Exposition Universelle de 1878, Ecole Anglaise', *L'Art*, 1879, vol. 1, pp. 95–6 also saw LL 3121 as one of the most interesting British paintings at the 1878 Exposition Universelle and he praised the artist's combination of Arthurian subject matter and inspiration with an Italian early Renaissance style.

19 E. Duranty, 'Les écoles étrangères de peinture', *Gazette des Beaux Arts*, 1878, vol. 1, pp. 299, 306, 309–10. The composition and expressive power of LL 3121 are also analysed in depth by R. de la Sizeranne, *Peinture anglaise*, 1895, pp. 195–7 by Harrison and Waters, *op. cit.*, and by John Christian in Arts Council, *Burne-Jones*, 1975, p. 51. The links between LL 3121 and the Symbolist movement of the end of the century are, however, most clearly demonstrated by Fernand Khnopff in his description of the picture ('L'Enchantement de Merlin', *Académie Royale de Belgique, Bulletins de la Classe des Beaux Arts*, 1919, vol. 1, pp. 13 ff.: 'Merlin, réduit à l'impuissance, est languissamment couché dans les basses branches. Ses mains pendent inertes; dans ses yeux vitreux passe une derrière lueur de haine et de désespoir; son pâle et triste sourire semble exprimer un lointain retour de pensée vers sa force perdue, et l'intense émotion de ce drame silencieux paraît enchassée dans le scintillement fleuri de l'arbuste en fête.') Khnopff wrote a sonnet on the enchantment legend but it seems not to have been inspired by LL 3121.

## *The Annunciation*

LL 3634 (WHL 4685)
Canvas[1]: 250 × 104.5 cm
Signed: *18EBJ79*

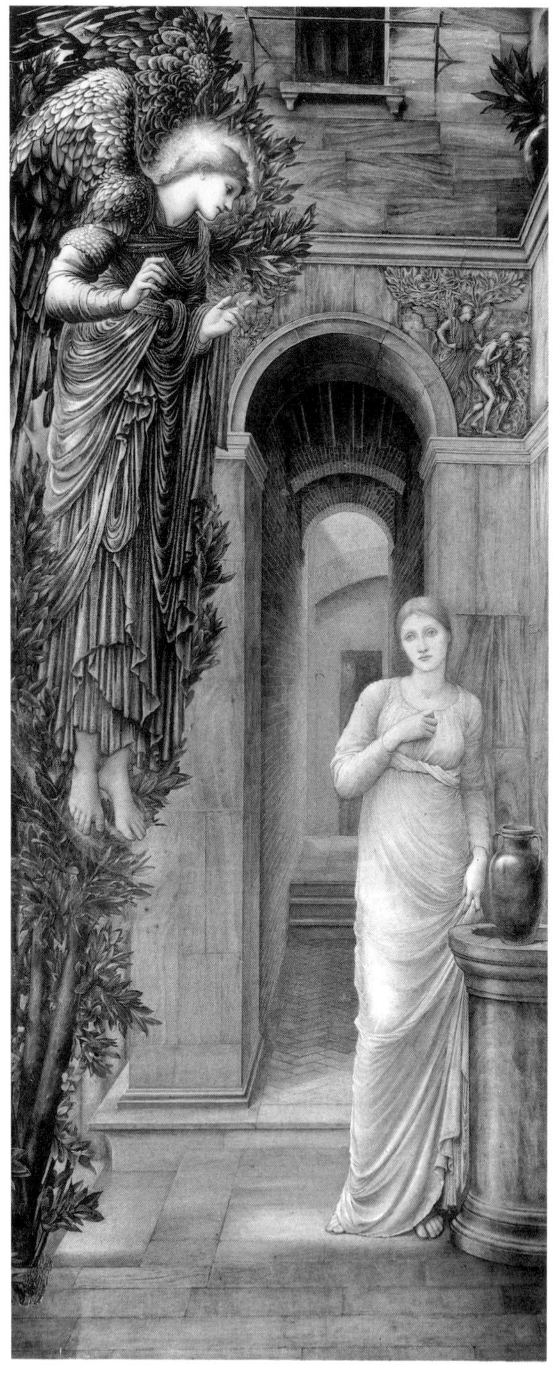

*The Annunciation* LL 3634 (colour plate 2)

This subject was frequently painted by Burne-Jones; there were: (1) a gouache of about 1857–61 (Birmingham City Museum and Art Gallery);[2] (2) two triptychs of 1861 (Tate Gallery and St. Paul's Church, Brighton);[3] (3) a tile design of 1862 (Birmingham City Museum and Art Gallery);[4] (4) two gouaches of 1863, one in the form of a triptych (private collections);[5] (5) a copy of 1869 after one of the gouaches of 1863 (with Agnew's in 1968);[6] (6) a design in gold on vellum of 1874;[7] (7) The Lady Lever Art Gallery painting of 1876–9;[8] (8) the preparatory cartoon for no. 7 reworked as a watercolour in 1886 (Castle Museum, Norwich);[9] (9) design for the mosaics of the American Protestant Episcopal Church in Rome of about 1892.[10] None of these many examples of the artist's treatment of this subject (except of course no. 8 above), however, approaches the Lady Lever Art Gallery version in classical austerity and in monumental severity.[11]

Many of the critics at the 1879 Grosvenor Gallery were more concerned to detect the artist's Italian prototypes; thus Oscar Wilde[12] wrote:

*the Virgin Mary, a passionless, pale woman, with that mysterious sorrow whose meaning she was so soon to learn mirrored in her wan face, is standing, in grey drapery, by a marble fountain, in what seems the open courtyard of an empty and silent house, while through the branches of a tall olive tree, unseen by the Virgin's tear-dimmed eyes, is descending the angel Gabriel with his joyful and terrible message, not painted as Angelico loved to do, in the varied splendour of peacock-like wings and garments of gold and crimson, but somewhat sombre in colour, set with all the fine grace of nobly-fashioned drapery and exquisitely ordered design. In presence of what may be called the mediaeval spirit may be discerned both the idea and the technique of the work.*

The critic of the *Athenaeum*[13] was more precise:

*'The Annunciation', a large upright design in which two tall figures appear in the garden of the house of*

*the Virgin, who stands by a well to which she has come for water. The background is architectural, and there is a glimpse by an open doorway through the house, emblematic sculptures are over the door. A lofty bay tree is on our left, and affords the darkest if not the richest piece of colour in the picture. The brown-bronze foliage, sculpturesque leaves, and rigid lines assort with the long curves of the draperies of the angel who, speaking to the Virgin, floats high above the earth, with downward pointed feet and upraised hands. The robes of the angel are of a rich purplish brown, and, in their long, nebular, multiform, and gracefully adapted folds form drapery like that we find throughout the School of Mantegna, the antetype of Jones's art, its ancient illustrious example, which our own artist has not in any way copied. The action and expression of the messenger indicate at once the dignity of his nature and the noble respect he feels for the object of his ministration. There is in this figure a dash of greater beauty than Mantegna affected; a mood similar to that of Piero della Francesca pervades its high refinement and pure grace; we recognise something which is to the Mantuan's art what Greek art was to Roman. The beautiful face of the Virgin indicates her condition; the eyes express more than that astonishment or simple reverence which most of the old masters imparted to their versions of the Annunciation; there is wonderful beauty and less self-abnegation than its prototypes. This is by far the most complete picture our artist has produced; the execution is more searching, the finish more thorough, the design has been more effectually carried out than in any former work of his.*

The architectural background with its new simplicity and grandeur is derived from the artist's Italian travels of 1871 and 1873.[14] Over the arch are reliefs of (?) *The Fall of Man* on the left and the *Expulsion from Eden* on the right;[15] behind the relief on the right is inscribed *MA/LEDICTA/TERRA/IN OPERE/TUO* (perhaps from Genesis 3: 17). The model for the Virgin is generally said to have been Mrs. Leslie Stephen.[16]

Many drawings survive: (1) *Head of the Angel*, Sotheby's (New York), 28 February 1990, lot 165, pencil signed and dated 1879; (2) *Figure study for the Angel* (Rodney Todd-White collection); (3) *Hands of the Angel* (unannotated Witt Library photograph); (4) Sketchbook with studies of Mrs. Leslie Stephen (Fitzwilliam Museum, Cambridge, inv. 962); (5) Two sketchbooks made in Italy in 1871 and 1873 (Mary Chamot Collection and Fitzwilliam Museum, Cambridge, inv. 1070.5); (6) A sketchbook of 1876 and other drawings of 1878 (Fitzwilliam Museum, Cambridge);[17] (7) The preparatory cartoon later reworked in watercolour in 1886 (Castle Museum, Norwich); (8) *Head of a Girl*, Christie's 11 October 1983, lot 183; (9) Studies recorded in the Fine Art Society, *Exhibition Catalogue of Studies and Drawings by Sir Edward Burne-Jones*, 1896; (10) Studies recorded in the artist's studio sales, Christie's 16 July 1898 and 5 June 1919; (11) Studies recorded in the New Gallery 1898–9 *Exhibition of the Works of Sir Edward Burne-Jones*, and in the Burlington Fine Arts Club, 1899, *Exhibition of Drawings and Studies by Sir Edward Burne-Jones*.

A small version in watercolour ($18\frac{1}{2} \times 7\frac{1}{2}$ in.) was sold from Clouds, the home of the Wyndhams, in 1933; it was probably commissioned by Percy Wyndham who knew the artist; it was no. 2 at the Burlington Fine Arts Club, 1899, *Exhibition of Drawings and Studies by Sir Edward Burne-Jones*.[18]

REPR: H. Blackburn, *Grosvenor Notes*, 1879, p. 47; Felix Jasinski (engraving) for Arthur Tooth and Sons 1897.

PROV: George Howard, ninth Earl of Carlisle;[19] executors of Rosalind Countess of Carlisle, Sotheby's 10 June 1922, lot 97, bought Berisly (£980); bought by Lever from D. Croal Thomson (Barbizon House) 15 June 1923 (£850).[20]

EXH: Grosvenor Gallery 1879 (166); New Gallery, *Edward Burne-Jones*, 1892–3 (32); New Gallery, *Sir Edward Burne-Jones*, 1898–9 (86).

1 LL 3634 is painted on to a double canvas. On the backing canvas appears the stamp of Charles Roberson, 99 Long Acre. On the frame there is a

framer's label: Paul Vacani, 22 Dean St., High Holborn.

2 Arts Council, *Burne-Jones*, 1975, no. 26.

3 Arts Council, *op. cit.*, nos. 66 and 67.

4 Arts Council, *op. cit.*, no. 73.

5 Arts Council, *op. cit.*, nos. 43 and 44. No. 43 at this exhibition, *The Flower of God*, was at Christie's 12 June 1992, lot 97.

6 See Arts Council, *op. cit.*, no. 43 and Malcolm Bell, *Sir Edward Burne-Jones*, 1901, p. 40.

7 Bell, *op. cit.*, p. 51.

8 Georgiana Burne-Jones, *Memorials of Edward Burne-Jones*, 1904, vol. 2, p. 68 gives 1876 as the year in which LL 3634 was begun. Edward Burne-Jones, 'List of my designs, drawings and pictures' (MSS Fitzwilliam Museum, Cambridge) states that LL 3634 was designed and begun in 1876; more work was done on it in 1878 and it was finished by May of 1879.

9 Bell, *op. cit.*, p. 64.

10 Bell, *op. cit.*, p. 68. This list excludes stained glass designs but the *Annunciation* designed for Topcliffe church in Yorkshire in 1860 should be mentioned; in this design the Virgin clasps the dove – the symbol of the Holy Spirit – to her bosom; William Butterfield, the architect, objected to this as too sensual for the subject and Burne-Jones lost the commission; see M. Harrison and B. Waters, *Burne-Jones*, 1973, p. 31 and A.C. Sewter, *The Stained Glass of William Morris and his Circle*, 1975 vol. 1, p. 13, vol. 2, pp. 1–3.

11 For an analysis of the stylistic differences between LL 3634 and earlier representations of this subject see Harrison and Waters, *op. cit.*, pp. 145–6: 'An Italianate elegance has replaced the Gothic intimacy'; elsewhere, however, Harrison and Waters see some link between LL 3634 and the *Annunciation* of 1863 (see p. 130).

12 Oscar Wilde, *Complete Works: Miscellanies*, ed. Ross, 1908, vol. 15, p. 25.

13 *Athenaeum*, 3 May 1879, p. 575. Other reviews appeared in *The Times*, 2 May 1879 – which criticized the over-melancholy Virgin and the stiff draperies; in the *Art Journal*, 1879, p. 135; in the *Portfolio*, 1879, p. 127: 'Still the picture is delightful, and carries us back to the old Pre-Raphaelite times'; in the *Saturday Review*, 3 May 1879, p. 556 and in the *Builder*, 3 May 1879, p. 481 (very critical); see also Henry James, *The Painter's Eye*, ed. Sweeney, 1956, p. 182 and Bell, *op. cit.*, pp. 98–9.

14 See Arts Council, *op. cit.*, nos. 136, 345 and 346, Nantes, Musée des Beaux Arts, *Burne-Jones*, 1992, p. 51 and Hilary Fraser, *The Victorians and Renaissance Italy*, 1992, pp. 125–32 for the impact of Italian classicism on Burne-Jones.

15 According to Harrison and Waters, *op. cit.*, p. 130, the *Expulsion* relief is based on a stained glass design of 1877 for Lamerton in Devon. Burne-Jones is using the traditional iconography according to which the Virgin is fulfilling the promise of the fallen Eve.

16 Arts Council, *op. cit.*, no. 136, Penelope Fitzgerald, *Edward Burne-Jones*, 1975, p. 179 suggests that she sat at the suggestion of G.F. Watts; the artist had met her first at Little Holland House, the home of her uncle Thoby Prinsep; she married first Herbert Duckworth and then (on 26 March 1878) Leslie Stephen; her daughter Vanessa (later the artist Vanessa Bell) was born on 13 May 1879. The cartoon for LL 3634 (now Castle Museum, Norwich) seems to have a different model for the Virgin. According to Fitzgerald, *op. cit.*, Mrs. Stephen appears in LL 3634 'in all the grave beauty of early pregnancy'.

17 See Harrison and Waters, *op. cit.*, fig. 186 and Nantes, *op. cit.*, p. 114. A large number of studies for LL 3634 then in the artist's sketch books are recorded in E. Burne-Jones, *op. cit.*

18 Clouds sale, Knight, Frank and Rutley 21 June 1933, lot 336. A photograph of this version

hanging at Clouds is reproduced in C. Dakers, *Clouds*, 1993, p. 258, plate 135. The compiler is grateful to Caroline Dakers for these details.

19 Virginia Surtees, *The Artist and the Autocrat*, 1988, p. 120, states that he bought LL 3634 at the 1879 Grosvenor Gallery Exhibition varnishing day; it hung in the boudoir (an extension of the drawing room) at his London home, 1 Palace Green, where it provoked considerable controversy between the artist, William Morris, and Rosalind Howard (George Howard's wife) about appropriate wall coverings behind it.

20 Barbizon House, *An Illustrated Record*, 1923, no. 32.

## *The Tree of Forgiveness*

LL 3635 (WHL 3616)
Canvas[1]: 196 × 106.8 cm
Signed: *E.B.J. 1882*

On his return from the conquest of Troy, Demophoon, son of Theseus, stayed at the Thracian court where Phyllis, the king's daughter, fell in love with him and he agreed to marry her; however, he had first to return to Attica to settle his affairs; he delayed his return to Thrace for so long that Phyllis, believing that he had deserted her, killed herself; the gods took pity on her and transformed her into an almond tree; on his eventual return the remorseful Demophoon embraced the tree, which immediately blossomed, and at the same time Phyllis reappeared to her lover.[2] Here she leans out from the tree to forgive him.

This is Burne-Jones's second version of this subject and it differs considerably from the first – a watercolour of 1869–70 (now Birmingham City Museum and Art Gallery entitled *Phyllis and Demophoon*) which the artist withdrew from the 1870 Old Water-Colour Society exhibition after protests at the nudity of Demophoon;[3] in particular the 1869–70 Phyllis was partially draped but here she is entirely nude.[4] The earlier watercolour was probably inspired by the artist's violent infatuation with Mary Zambaco[5] (see p. 7 above); certainly the aggressiveness of Phyllis in that watercolour, and in this oil painting, is in sharp contrast with, for example, the more understanding and passive approach of the same figure in J.W. Waterhouse's *Phyllis and Demophoon* of 1907 which portrays exactly the same scene.[6] It is, however, unclear why the artist should have done a second version of this composition in 1881–2[7] when he had apparently lost his early enthusiasm for Mary Zambaco – and this may indicate that the original subject had more meaning for him than his feelings for Mary Zambaco.[8]

The critics at the 1882 Grosvenor Gallery generally disapproved of the anatomy in the *Tree of Forgiveness* – the *Art Journal* being predictably hostile over this – and *The Times*[9] also disliked the artist's flesh painting. The expressive power of the painting was widely admired as was the rendering of the tree and other background details. The review in *The Times* was the most characteristic:

*As the Grosvenor has always chiefly depended upon the Pre-Raphaelite element, we may first speak of Mr. Burne-Jones's paintings. There are many of these, but the three most important ones are 'The Tree of Forgiveness' . . . Of these, the first is a new rendering of an old subject, one that many of our readers will remember at the Gallery of Painters in Water Colours at the same time that Mr. Jones belonged to that society . . . 'The Tree of Forgiveness' is the 'almond', and the picture is an illustration of the story of Phyllis and Demophoon, and shows how Phyllis bursts forth from one tree and clasps Demophoon in her arms. The picture is a strange one, its effect repellant in the extreme. Unlike Mr. Burne-Jones's usual way of treating the human figure, the anatomy is not only shown, but insisted on – flung violently in the spectator's face, so that for some time nothing can be seen but muscles of every description, all of them twisting and straining, and like Carlyle's pitcher of tamed vipers, 'each struggling to get its head uppermost'. Then, again, the flesh-painting is very peculiar, and can hardly be accepted as giving any fair*

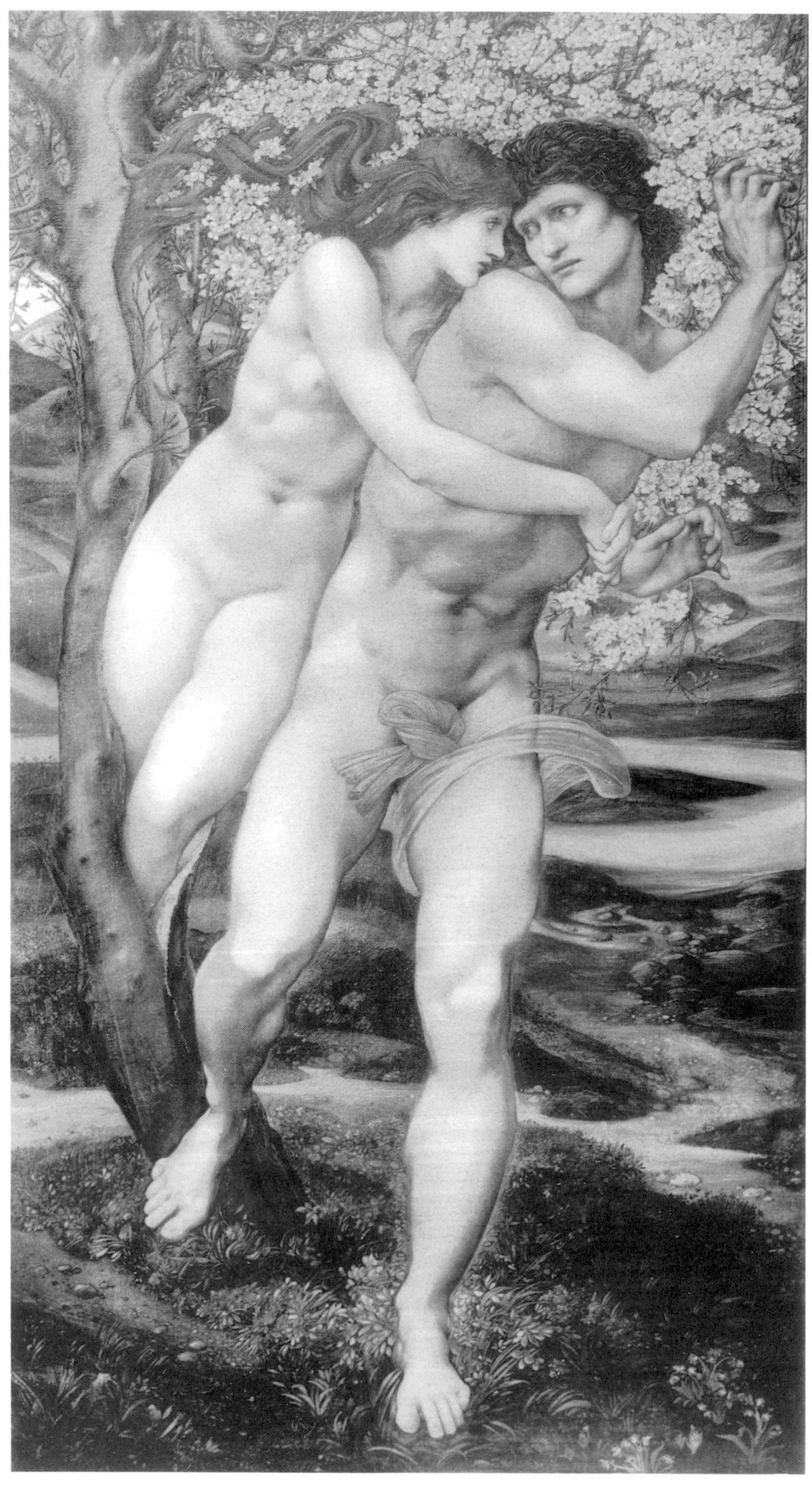

*The Tree of Forgiveness*
LL 3635

*representation of human flesh. It is strange in colour and texture, of a consistency between that of marble and leather, and apparently admitting of a smooth polish. The bodies of the lovers, which are nude, are in such attitudes as could not have been maintained for more than a moment and this gives to the composition an air of strained and unnatural action, which greatly mars its effect. So much must be conceded to truth and those who do not care for Pre-Raphaelite work, but with all these faults the picture has, nevertheless, passages of great beauty. The grass, flowers and landscape, beneath and behind Demophoon, and the white almond blossom are drawn and painted with a thoroughness, with a depth of colour and a minuteness of detail, which can hardly be over-praised, and from one end of the picture to the other there is literally not a spot of careless or hurried work. There is great beauty, too, though of a somewhat painful kind, in the expression of the lovers. Altogether the work is one which will rank as a painting as high as any of this artist's performances, though it has not the glowing colour of the 'Chant d'Amour', nor the tender feeling of the 'Annunciation'.*

The *Athenaeum*[10] was, however, more sympathetic and better informed:

*'The Tree of Forgiveness', a smaller version of which, differing in some respects, has already been exhibited. The picture illustrates, with new passion and fresh adjuncts, the nude figure of Phyllis half issuing from the trunk of the almond tree in which the gods, pitying her sorrow for the false Demophoon, had enclosed her. Considerable alterations have been made since we described this work in December last. The draperies have been entirely altered, and the lower limbs of Phyllis are displayed in all their lovely yet wan morbidezza. Her long dark hair trails about her head and sets it off finely as to colour and to line. Her wistful eyes have gained in fascination, and the action of her lithe body and slender limbs has become more expressive. The linking of her hands so as to clasp the waist of Demophoon is one of the beauties of a picture which is remarkable for its earnest and profound pathos as well as for the wonderful loveliness of its colour. The modelling and drawing of Phyllis's figure are eminently beautiful; the torso is faultless if not a little too long. The legs of the startled lover have been studied with extreme care, but at present their contours are a little 'bumpy', and their shadows and lights lack fusion.*

The most searching explanation of the scene may be that provided by Mary Gladstone after she visited the artist and saw the painting in April 1882:[11] 'She flings herself upon him out of the almond tree, and he is represented in wild flight, yet turning upon her a face in which terror and love are fiercely contending.'

D.G. Rossetti[12] noted that Burne-Jones may have borrowed the figures of Phyllis and Demophoon from the two very similar figures at the far right of Botticelli's *Primavera* (Uffizi, Florence).

The various sketches and drawings for this composition – for example, the cartoon for the whole group in the National Museum of Wales, Cardiff, the pencil study for the two figures in the William Morris Gallery, Walthamstow, and the pencil studies for Demophoon, one sold at Christie's 12 June 1992, lot 75, and another formerly exhibited at the Piccadilly Gallery (Hartnoll and Eyre) 1971, no. 13 – presumably relate to the Birmingham gouache of 1870 not to the Lady Lever Art Gallery painting. A pencil drawing for Phyllis now in the Art Gallery of South Australia, Adelaide (acc. no. 557D9),[13] a drawing in the Tate Gallery (inv. 04113) and further pencil studies for the same figure sold most recently at Christie's 13 November 1992, lot 104, may, however, relate more specifically to the latter.

PROV: Bought from the artist by Thomas Agnew and Sons 1 May 1882; sold to William Imrie 16 December 1882 (£2,100);[14] his sales, Christie's 28 June 1907, lot 114, bought in (£1,105), Christie's 10 July 1908, lot 124, bought in (£609), Christie's 15 July 1910, lot 136, bought David (£472.10*s*.); Lord St. Davids' sale, Christie's 14 July 1918, lot 137, bought Gooden and Fox (£1,575) for Lever (£1,614.7*s*.6*d*.).

EXH: Grosvenor Gallery 1882 (144); New Gallery, *Sir Edward Burne-Jones*, 1898–9 (116).

1 There is a Roberson label on the stretcher.

2 This label is stuck on to the back of LL 3635:

*T[H]E TREE OF FORGIVENESS/
PHILLIS AMIDST HER MOURNING/
BECAUSE DEMOPHOON HAD
FORSAKEN/
HER WAS TURNED BY THE KIND/
GODS INTO AN ALMOND TREE/
AND AFTER AS HE PASSED BY/
CONSUMED WITH SORROW FOR/
HER SHE BECAME ONCE MORE/
VISIBLE TO HIM NO LESS LOVING/
TH[AN] OF OLD TIME: AND THIS WAS/
THE FIRST BLOSSOMING OF T[HE]/
ALM[O]ND TREE.*

The same lines are quoted against LL 3635 in the Grosvenor Gallery 1882 Catalogue (no. 144). The story can be found in Ovid's *Heroides* (part 2) and in Chaucer's *Legend of Good Women* but neither of these versions of the story include the blossoming of the almond tree or the reappearance of Phyllis. Burne-Jones certainly knew these two sources as he used the *Legend of Good Women* for embroidery designs at Winnington in 1863 and he quoted line 27 of the *Heroides* part 2 in the New Gallery 1892–3 exhibition catalogue (*Edward Burne-Jones*) against the Birmingham gouache: 'Dic mihi, quid feci, nisi non sapienter amavi [Tell me what I have done, unless it was to love unwisely]'. For other versions of the story see particularly R.W. Frank, *Chaucer and The Legend of the Good Women*, 1972, pp. 146 ff. and J.M. Fyler *Chaucer and Ovid*, 1979, pp. 109–10. There are various classical and later sources for the blossoming of the almond tree but no source, ancient or modern, is known to the compiler for the physical reappearance of Phyllis in LL 3635.

3 In LL 3635 Burne-Jones was careful to conceal Demophoon's genitals behind the fragment of drapery; Gay Daly in *Pre-Raphaelites in Love*, 1989, p. 296 argues that this more prudish approach reflected the artist's sexual suppression in the 1880s; it seems more likely to have been intended to forestall the moral objections of 1870.

4 Phyllis was to have been partially draped in LL 3635 as well. The *Athenaeum* reported on 24 December 1881, p. 859:

*MR. E. BURNE-JONES has lately finished a picture of Phyllis and Demophoon, which comprises a woodland scene where two life-size figures appear. She is half enclosed by the rind of the serpent-like almond tree, and one of her feet is caught within its cleft trunk. She twines her arms and clasps her hands about Demophoon, while he, astonished and yet enchanted, turns, but not as if to escape, and looks away from her pity-seeking face, which earnestly approaches his lips. Her draperies are of dark sea-green, and kirtle-like, fall from her waist. Her scarf, the design of which illustrates the mode of that school to which the art of Mr. Jones frequently refers, partakes of its mistress's emotion, and, wind-driven, twines around the limbs of Demophoon. The picture is a delightful exercise in fine tints, subtly harmonized tones and lines.*

Having decided at the last moment to have a nude Phyllis, the artist left the fragment of drapery around Demophoon (originally part of Phyllis's garment) without any physical support or justification.

5 In his letter to Helen Mary Gaskell of 1893 in which he outlines the autobiographical elements in LL 3121 (see p. 7 above) he went on to say: 'the head of the Phyllis in the Demophoon picture is from the same [that is, Mary Zambaco] – and would have been very arch for a portrait' (quoted in Penelope Fitzgerald, *Edward Burne-Jones*, 1975, p. 127 and in J.A. Kestner, *Mythology and Misogyny*, 1989, p. 85); the alleged suicide pact between the artist and Mary Zambaco may be reflected in the suicide of Phyllis – see J.A. Kestner, 'Edward Burne-Jones and the Nineteenth Century Fear of Women', *Biography*, 1984, vol. 7, p. 102. Fitzgerald, *op. cit.*, pp. 119–20 draws a less exact parallel between the composition and the artist's relationship with Mary Zambaco.

6 Reproduced in A. Hobson, *The Art and Life of J.W. Waterhouse*, 1980, plate 124, p. 126.

7 Edward Burne-Jones, 'List of my designs, drawings and pictures' (MSS Fitzwilliam Museum, Cambridge) records that he began LL

3635 in 1881 and worked on it extensively in that year; he finished it in 1882; I am indebted to John Christian for this reference. The face of Phyllis had not been finished on 8 April 1882 (Mary Gladstone, *Diaries and Letters*, ed. Masterman, 1930, p. 245).

8 Fitzgerald, *op. cit.*, p. 127, argues that LL 3635 has less feeling and movement than the watercolour of 1869–70 and that the face of Phyllis is no longer a likeness of Mary Zambaco – both elements reflecting the artist's break with Mary Zambaco. Alison Carroll, however, in 'A Study by Sir Edward Burne-Jones for the Story of Phyllis and Demophoon', *Bulletin of the Art Gallery of South Australia*, 1978, vol. 36, p. 46 believes that in LL 3635 Demophoon turns away more vigorously and Phyllis clasps more intently than in the earlier watercolour but she agrees with Fitzgerald about the reduced resemblance to Mary Zambaco in LL 3635. Both authors speculate extensively about the psychological implications for the artist's sexual history. Alison Carroll also suggests that the changed title for LL 3635 – the *Tree of Forgiveness* rather than just *Phyllis and Demophoon* – may link it to the Christian iconographic tradition in which Christ as the descendant of Adam forgives Adam and Eve with the Tree of Forgiveness referring back to the Tree of Knowledge.

9 *Art Journal*, 1882, p. 189; *The Times*, 8 May 1882.

10 *Athenaeum*, 6 May 1882, p. 575. Other reviews appeared in *Magazine of Art*, 1882, p. 352 and the *Portfolio*, 1882, p. 114. Some reviews of the 1869–70 watercolour are quoted in Carroll, *op. cit.*, p. 48.

11 Mary Gladstone, *op. cit.*; she may have had this interpretation directly from the artist.

12 *Dante Gabriel Rossetti and Jane Morris, their Correspondence*, ed. Bryson, 1976, p. 110. Burne-Jones had made sketches from this painting in 1859 – see Arts Council, *Burne-Jones*, 1975, no. 117, p. 47. In 1867 Henry Holiday reminded him of the painting which he had by then apparently forgotten (see Henry Holiday, *Reminiscences of my Life*, 1914, p. 140).

13 Carroll, *op. cit.*, p. 48.

14 The Mappin Art Gallery, Sheffield, *Burne-Jones* Catalogue of 1971, no. 161 states that William Morris was the first owner of LL 3635. This must be wrong. Imrie was a partner in Ismay, Imrie and Co. (the White Star Line) and a friend of the artist. A photograph of LL 3635 hanging in Imrie's Liverpool home, Holmstead, Mossley Hill, is now in the Royal Commission on the Historical Monuments of England, Fortress House (neg. no. BB91/2063); the photograph dates from 1901.

## BURNE-JONES, Edward Coley (1833–1898), after

### *Ananias*[1]

LL 3636 (WHL 4005B)

### *Azarias*[2]

LL 3637 (WHL 4005)

Canvas[3]: 155 × 50 cm
Inscribed: *Ananias* (LL 3636) and *Azarias* (LL 3637)

These appear to be nude studies for two of the main figures in the west window of All Saints Church, Middleton Cheney, Northamptonshire.[4] However, John Christian notes that large canvas studies for stained glass were very rarely done by Burne-Jones and he feels that LL 3636–3637 are possibly versions made after the windows were completed.[5] The window dates from 1870 and also has the figure of Misael[6] with – in the tracery – Adam and Eve, crouched angels with harps and the six days of creation.

Burne-Jones's source was *The Song of the Three Holy Children*, an apocryphal addition to Daniel, chapter 3.

PROV: The artist's sale, Christie's 5 June 1919, part of lot 175, bought Gooden and Fox (£178.10*s.*) for Lever (£182.19*s.3d.*).

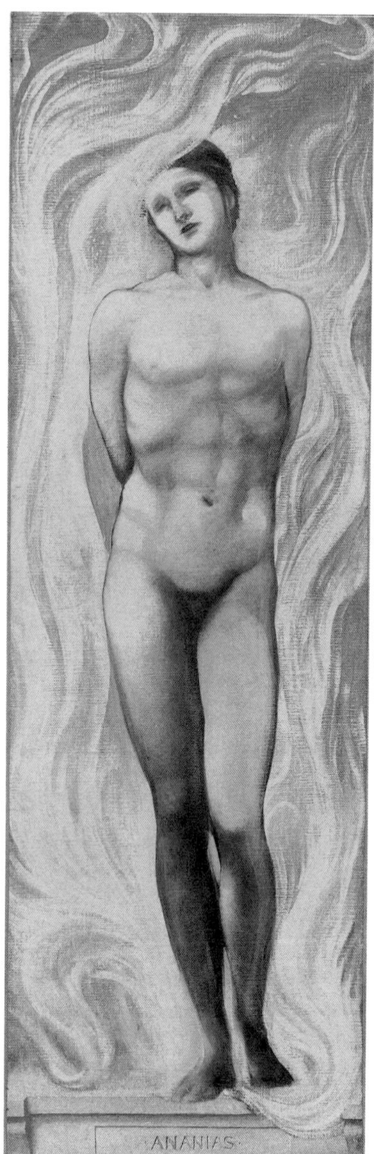


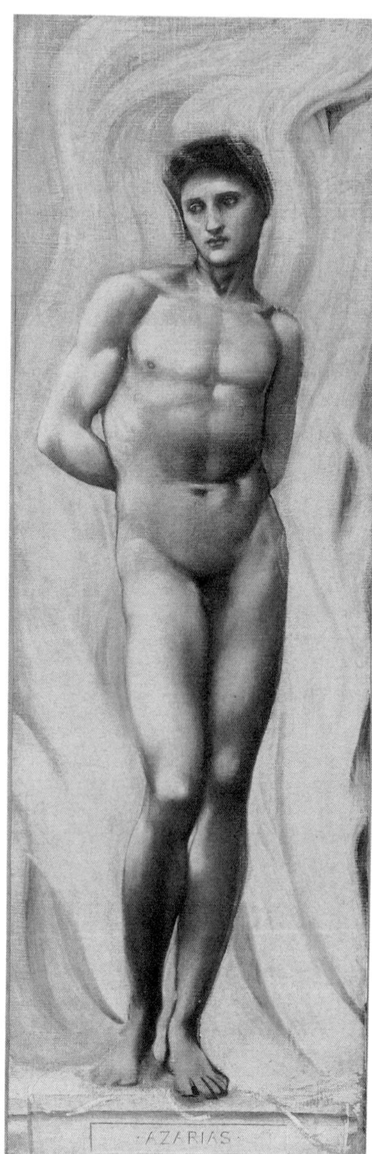


Left
*Ananias* LL 3636

Right
*Azarias* LL 3637

1 Better known as Shadrach.

2 Better known as Abednego.

3 LL 3637 has a Charles Roberson stamp on the stretcher.

4 For further details see A.C. Sewter, *The Stained Glass of William Morris and his Circle*, 1975, vol. 1, p. 134; the window is reproduced in vol. 2, p. 322. Burne-Jones seems to have been working on the designs for this window in July 1870; his account book has an entry apparently datable to that month: 'By 6 little figures, 6 Days of Creation . . . £30. 2 more little figures, Adam and Eve £15. Holy Children £45. 2 tracery spaces £5. £95.' The stained glass window in the south aisle of Farnworth Church (near Widnes) has the same subject as LL 3636–3637 and is also by Morris and Co.; it dates from 1875.

5 Letter to the compiler, 27 August 1990.

6 Better known as Meshach. The canvas nude study related to this figure was bought by Lever at the artist's sale of 5 June 1919, together with LL 3636 and LL 3637 and was inventoried by him as WHL 4005 A; however, it was in his executors' sale, Knight, Frank and Rutley 15 June 1926, lot 19, bought in (£16.16*s*.) and was then presented by the second Viscount Leverhulme to the King's Weigh-House Church. It appeared at Sotheby's 8 June 1993, lot 47 as *Misael*.

## **CAMERON, David Young** (1865–1945)
### ***Clunie***

LL 3857 (LP 37)
Canvas: 62.5 × 110.5 cm.
Signed: *D. Y. Cameron*

Clunie (or Cluanie) gives its name to a glen and loch on the borders of Ross and Cromarty and Inverness-shire. The artist[1] wrote from Dun Eaglais to Lockett Thomson of Barbizon House in 1933: 'The picture you write about was done some years ago as the result of many visits to the district. Glen Cluanie is the great glen running across Inverness-shire to Loch Duich in Kintail – a great Jacobite country. It falls to Loch Duich and Loch Alsh. I always thought that one of my good pictures – I mean by that above the average of my productions, and that was the opinion held by many visitors here. I think it would represent the maturer phase of my work well in any collection.' In a further letter to Lockett Thomson of about the same date the artist stated that he had worked on the painting both in 1929 and in 1930 and that its execution was prolonged due to the size of the canvas.

In 1929 Cameron exhibited *Cluanie – wash* at the Royal Academy (1034), this may have been related to LL 3857.[2]

REPR: *Barbizon House Record*, 1934 (15).

PROV: Fine Art Society. Bought from Barbizon House 1933 (£600).

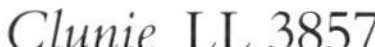
*Clunie* LL 3857

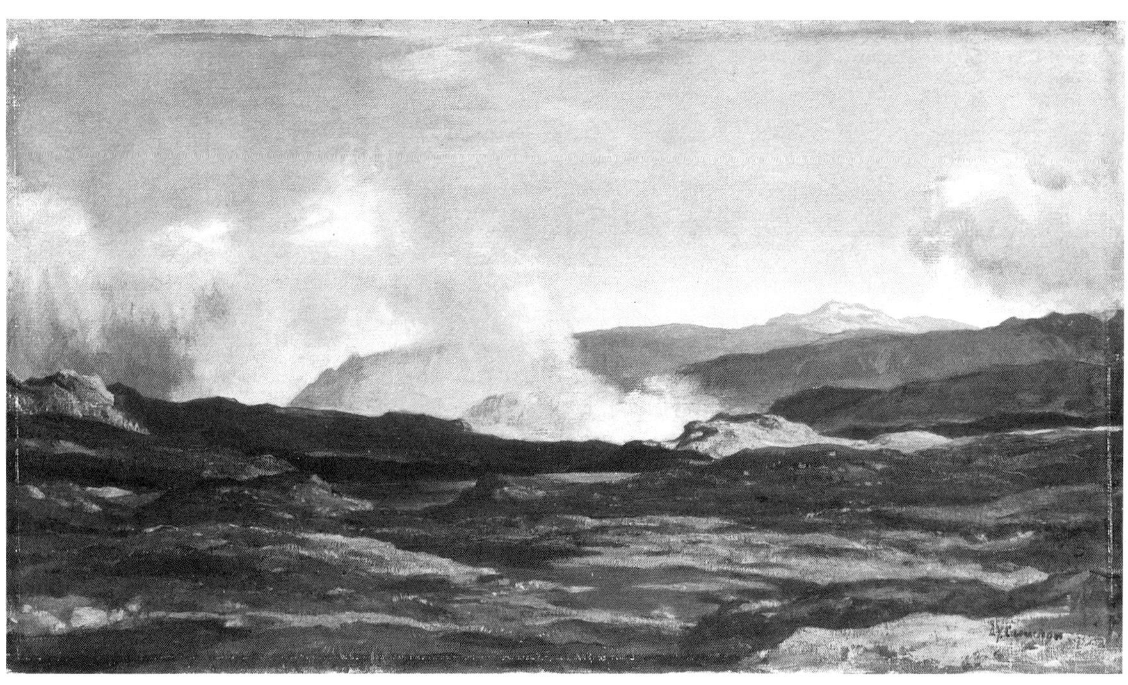

EXH: Barbizon House 1934 (15).

1 All this correspondence survives in the form of typescripts copied from the original letters.

2 It may also relate to the wash drawings which Cameron did as illustrations to *Highways and Byways in the West Highlands* by Seton Gordon first published in 1935.

## **COLLIER, Hon. John** (1850–1934)

### ***A Water Baby***

LL 3412 (WHL 2909)
Canvas: 127 × 81 cm
Signed: *John Collier 1890*

This painting was used as a soap advertisement by A. and F. Pears,[1] and was presumably bought by them for that purpose. It appears in the list of Collier's work compiled by W.H. Pollock in 1914.[2]

REPR: H. Blackburn, *Grosvenor Notes*, 1890, p. 70; Pall Mall Gazette, *Pictures of 1890*, p. 112.

PROV: Bought by A. and F. Pears from the artist August 1890 (£150);[3] bought by Lever August 1916;[4] transferred by him to the Port Sunlight Lever Brothers Works and Offices 1922; presented by Lever Brothers 1983.

EXH: Grosvenor Gallery, 1890 (288).

1 An advertisement reproducing LL 3412 and inscribed: *Pears Soap*, is in the John Johnson Collection, Bodleian Library, Oxford. For the use of paintings to advertise soap in the advertisements of A. and F. Pears see p. xiv. The Pears advertisement incorporating LL 3412 is reproduced in Edward Morris, 'Advertising and the Acquisition of Contemporary Art', *Journal of the History of Collections*, 1992, vol. 4, p. 198 where the problems encountered by A. and F. Pears and by their manager T.J. Barratt, with nudity in their advertisements, is discussed.

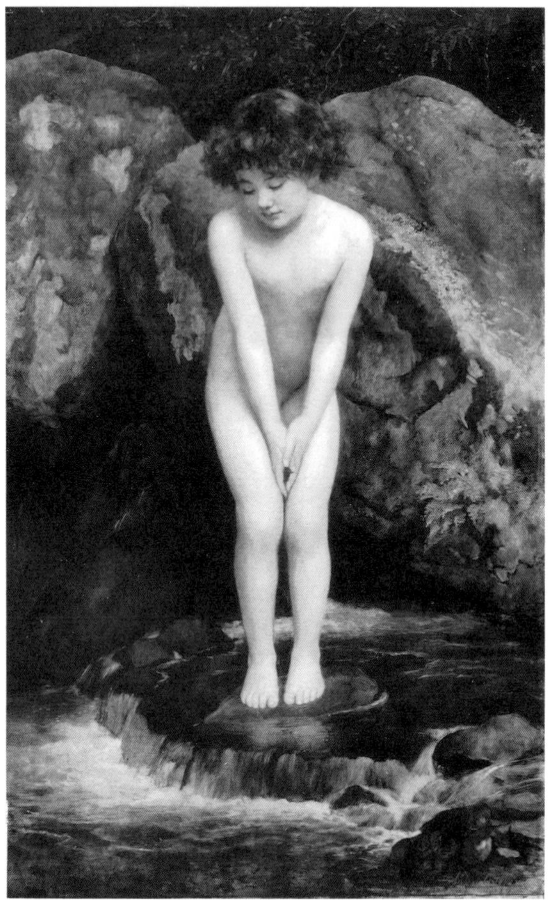

*A Water Baby* LL 3412

2 W.H. Pollock, 'The Art of John Collier', *Art Annual*, 1914, p. 26.

3 A. and F. Pears, *Inventory of Works of Art*, no. 106, p. 7, MSS Unilever Historical Archives, Port Sunlight.

4 There is in the Lady Lever Art Gallery a typescript list of a large number of paintings bought by W.H. Lever or by Lever Brothers from A. and F. Pears; it is dated August 1916 and in it LL 3412 is valued at £50. Lever Brothers acquired a substantial interest in A. and F. Pears in 1915.

**DAWSON, Henry** (1811–1878)

## *H.M.S. Victory*

LL 3430
Canvas: 61 × 91 cm

This painting can be identified with reasonable certainty as Dawson's *H.M.S. Victory*, although it was listed in 1910 and sold in 1926 simply as *The Flagship, Sunset*. The principal ship in it is certainly a first rate of the right period and corresponds with H.M.S. *Victory* except that the galleries protruding underneath the boat hanging from the stern were removed in 1803 from H.M.S. *Victory* and thus the artist could not have seen them when he visited Portsmouth in 1854 and 1856; at that time H.M.S. *Victory* was afloat in Portsmouth Harbour as the flagship of the Admiral Superintendent.[1] Probably Dawson was in fact copying from an early print or was deliberately portraying the ship as built rather than as modified in 1803. The painting is certainly not an exact record as H.M.S *Victory* never moved from Portsmouth Harbour after 1820[2] and here she is shown in the open sea. This is rather an imaginary evocation of Britain's maritime supremacy on the same lines as the artist's *Wooden Walls of England* of 1853 or his *British Bulwarks* of 1855.[3]

Style indicates a date in the 1850s for the painting and the uniforms of the sailors in the foreground boat confirm this dating.[4]

PROV: James Orrock[5] sale, Christie's 4–6 June 1904, lot 256, bought in (£44.2*s*.) as *The Victory*; bought by Lever from Orrock 1910 (£40);[6] his executors sale, Knight, Frank and Rutley 15 June 1926, lot 182, bought in for display at Hulme Hall, Port Sunlight; transferred to the Lady Lever Art Gallery probably in 1950.[7]

*H.M.S. Victory* LL 3430

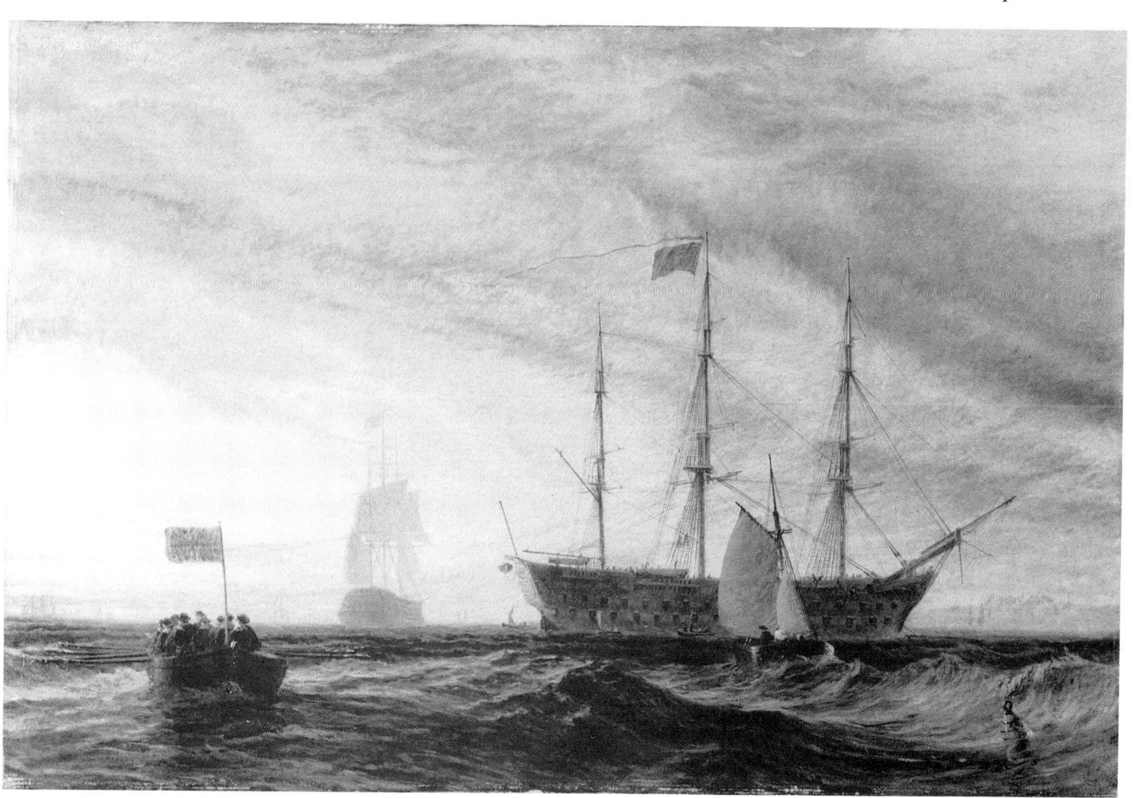

EXH: Glasgow International Exhibition 1888 (127), as *The Victory* lent by James Orrock.[8]

1 Colin White, letter to the compiler, 5 August 1991.

2 White, *op. cit.*

3 For these two paintings, see Nottingham University Art Gallery, *Henry Dawson*, 1978, pp. 31, 52. The *Wooden Walls of England* was also effectively a painting of H.M.S. *Victory*; its symbolic significance is explained in Byron Webber, *James Orrock R.I.*, 1903, vol. 1, p. 40.

4 White, *op. cit.*

5 Orrock was an important patron of Dawson at least from 1856; see Alfred Dawson, *The Life of Henry Dawson*, 1891, p. 102.

6 LL 3430 is listed on page 40 of the 1910 typescript inventory of works of art acquired by Lever from Orrock.

7 Old label on the back of LL 3430.

8 An old label reading *1655 / Glasgow* is on the back of LL 3430.

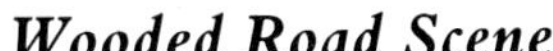

### *Wooded Road Scene*

LL 3701 (WHL 2015, HH 67)
Canvas[1]: 30.5 × 41.5 cm.
Signed: *HD* [monogram] *55*

PROV: Bought by Lever from James Orrock[2] 1910 (£30).

EXH: Possibly at the Edinburgh International Exhibition 1886 (1467) lent by James Orrock.

1 Canvas stamp: *2 John Street* (the rest is illegible); this was the address of John Reeves from 1853 to about 1868.

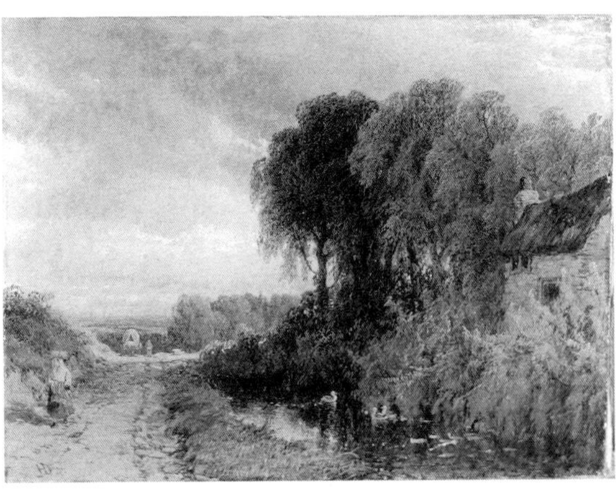

*Wooded Road Scene* LL 3701

2 Orrock was an important patron of Dawson; they seem to have first met in 1856, a year after LL 3701 was painted – see Alfred Dawson, *The Life of Henry Dawson*, 1891, p. 102. LL 3701 is listed on p. 37 of the 1910 typescript inventory of works of art acquired by Lever from Orrock.

## **DAWSON, Henry** (1811–1878), **follower of**

### *Landscape with Cottage in Distance and Pool in Foreground*

LL 3705 (WHL 2295, HH 63)
Panel: 23.8 × 31.1 cm.

Although Orrock was a major patron of Dawson and seems to have attributed this painting to Dawson in his 1910 typescript inventory, quality alone would indicate that it must be by a follower or imitator.[1]

PROV: Bought by Lever from James Orrock 1910 (£10).

1 LL 3705 is listed on p. 36 of the 1910 typescript inventory of works of art acquired by Lever from Orrock. A barely legible Christie's stencil on the back of LL 3705 indicates that the painting was at Orrock's Christie's sale of 4–6 June 1904, but it cannot be identified in the catalogue.

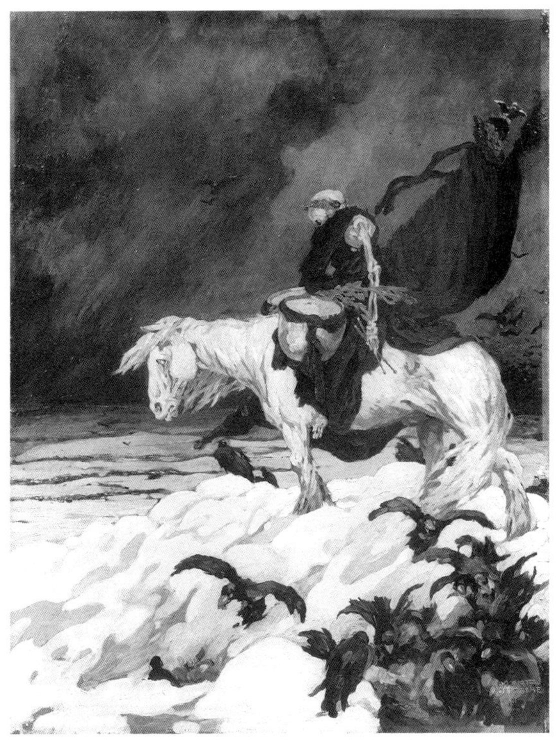

*'1812' LL 3749*

## DE LA BERE, Stephen Baghot

(active 1904–1915)

### *'1812'*

LL 3749 (WHL 686)
Canvas: 91.5 × 71.1 cm
Signed: *Baghot de la Bere 1911*

Death is seated on his pale horse and looks across the Russian snows, the scene of Napoleon's ill-fated invasion of 1812.[1]

The artist exhibited *Illustration to 1812: Tchaikovsky* at the 1912 Fine Art Society *Exhibition of Watercolours and Drawings by Stephen Baghot de la Bere* (42).

REPR: *Bibby's Annual*, 1918, p. 3 (in colour).

PROV: Bought by Lever[2] from Gooden and Fox 14 August 1913 (£26.5*s*.).

EXH: Royal Academy 1913 (853).

1 There is a long description of LL 3749 in *Bibby's Annual*, 1918, p. 3, but the author admitted that he had been unable to contact the artist to verify his interpretation. He saw the figure in LL 3749 as partly Death on the pale horse (Revelation 6: 8) and partly 'General Winter' of Napoleon's 1812 Russian Campaign. He added: 'What sinister apocalyptic figure must be brooding today over Flanders and the northern plains of France.'

2 The painting originally hung in the Napoleon Room in the Lady Lever Art Gallery and was presumably intended by Lever to represent the cost in human suffering of Napoleon's conquests.

*Landscape with Cottage in Distance and Pool in Foreground* LL 3705

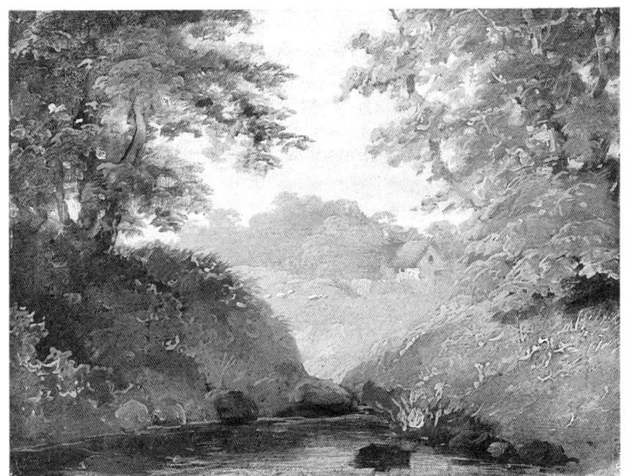

## DICKSEE, Francis Bernard (Frank)

(1853–1928)

### *The Magic Crystal*

LL 3622 (WHL 25)
Canvas: 168.5 × 102 cm
Signed: *Frank Dicksee 1894*

The *Magic Crystal* was described by Dibdin[1] as representing 'a medieval clairvoyante of voluptuous type seated on a very ornate carved chair or throne apparently fixed in the panelling of a wall of a chamber more or less Byzantine in character'. Many critics[2] praised the artist's technical skill but were less enthusiastic about his imaginative power; the *Athenaeum*,[3] however, was entirely hostile:

*Mr. F. Dicksee is far from fortunate in the selection of his subjects. Had he been wise he would have avoided a theme like that of* The Magic Crystal . . . *His life-size damsel in gorgeous array is seated upon a sumptuous couch, the whole being so magnificent that the pathos of the incident is destroyed, while attention is drawn from the romance of an inquiry into the future by means of an oracular sphere. She does not look as if she saw anything in the crystal or even tried to do so, but only cared to look as if she was looking. The artifice is more transparent than the sphere itself and an offence to art. There is great want of research and study, but much of the affectation of both, in the draperies of this large painting.*

Dicksee's *Magic Crystal* may have had some

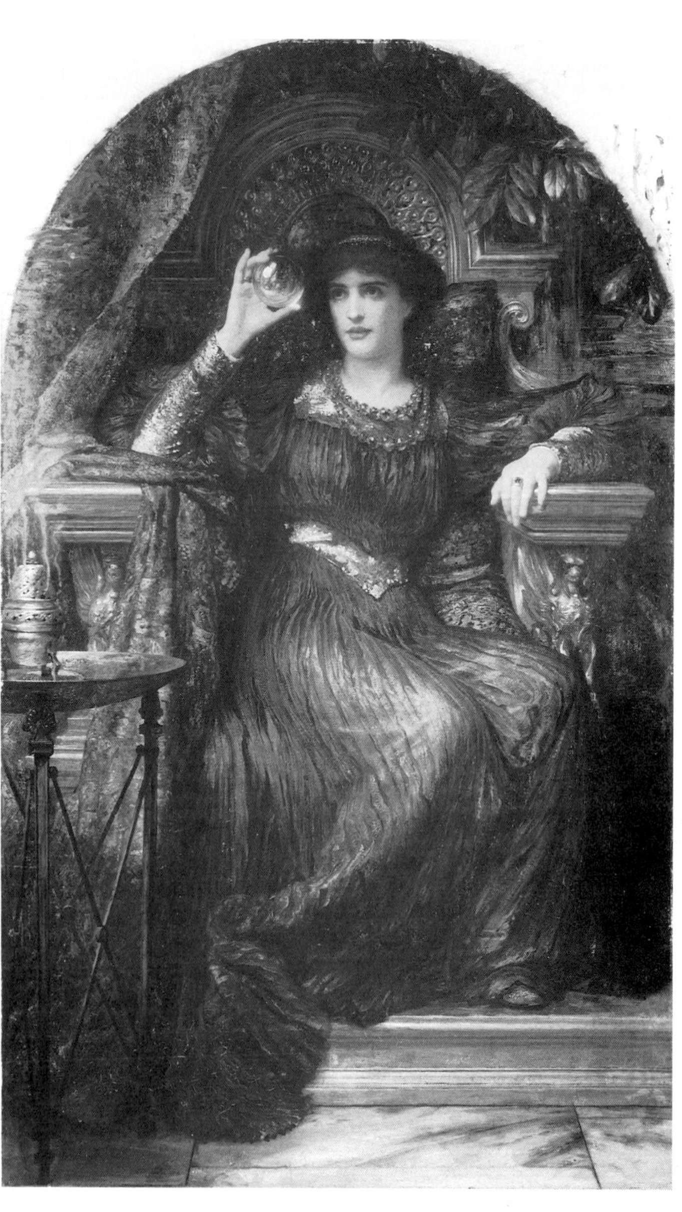

*The Magic Crystal* LL 3622

influence on J.W. Waterhouse's *Crystal Ball* of 1902.[4]

Lever also owned a watercolour by Dicksee with this subject (inv. WHL 3303, his executors' sale, Anderson Galleries (New York) 3 March 1926, lot 151).

REPR: *Handbook to the Royal Academy*, published by Black and White, 1894, p. 4; *Royal Academy Pictures*, 1894, p. 135; H. Blackburn, *Academy Notes*, 1894, p. 69; H. Blackburn, *Academy Sketches*, 1894, p. 10; Pall Mall Gazette, *Pictures of the Year*, 1894, p. 2; (photogravure) *Art Journal*, 1906.

PROV: Sir Walter Palmer.[5] Anon. sale, Christie's 29 April 1911, lot 55, bought Gooden and Fox (£546) for Lever (£567.17*s*.).

EXH: Royal Academy 1894 (218).

1 E.R. Dibdin, 'Frank Dicksee', *Art Annual*, 1905, p. 12.

2 M.H. Spielmann in *Magazine of Art*, 1894, p. 272; Claude Phillips in the *Academy*, 12 May 1894, p. 400; *The Times*, 16 May 1894. Claude Phillips, for example, wrote:

> *A capacity for taking infinite pains is the chief attribute of Mr. Frank Dicksee. In 'The Magic Crystal' the strenuous endeavour to attain to ideality of conception, with the aid of well-ordered design and beautiful colours, is very apparent. The magnificently attired damsel, who seeks to read futurity in the transparent globe which she holds in her hand, sits on a throne of burnished copper and brass, wearing a robe of peach-blossom hue, over which falls a semi-diaphanous material as splendid in hue as the wing of an exotic beetle. A necklace of deep-hued amber completes the carefully thought-out arrangement, which is brilliant enough in effect, and would be still more so, were the artist capable of painting flesh so as to support the juxtaposition with these accumulated splendours. It is the vivifying spark that is wanting here, the power to infuse some personal charm and distinctiveness into the glittering hollow shell so faultlessly fashioned.*

3 *Athenaeum*, 19 May 1894, p. 552. Similarly the *Saturday Review*, 12 May 1894, p. 494, commented: 'Mr. Frank Dicksee is sumptuous and slightly artificial in a large beryl-coloured composition, called "The Magic Crystal".'

4 Anthony Hobson, *J.W. Waterhouse*, 1980, pp. 118 ff., plate 109.

5 M.H. Dixon, 'A Painter of Modern Life', *Lady's Realm*, 1904–5, vol. 17, p. 572.

## **DRAPER, Herbert James** (1864–1920)

### ***The Lament for Icarus***

LL 3911 (WHL 18)
Panel[1]: 48.4 × 41.6 cm
Signed: *HJD*

This is a 'completed study'[2] for Draper's *Lament for Icarus* of 1898 now in the Tate Gallery. Three other studies for the painting, apparently drawings, are reproduced by A.L. Baldry[3] who also describes the Tate Gallery painting in some detail. A study for the nymph at the bottom right is reproduced in an unidentified photograph in the Witt Library.

PROV: George McCulloch sale, Christie's 23–30 May 1913, lot 130, bought Gooden and Fox (£94.10*s*.) for Lever (£96.17*s*.).

EXH: Society of Oil Painters 1898–9 (273), priced at £115; Royal Academy, *Winter Exhibition*, 1909 (251).

1 Panel stamp: *REEVES AND SONS / PREPARED PANEL / LONDON*; frame maker's label: *H.W. TAYLOR AND CO, 61 Queen's Road, Bayswater, London (late GETHING AND TAYLOR)*.

2 This is how the artist described LL 3911 in the Society of Oil Painters 1898–9 catalogue. LL 3911 corresponds more or less exactly with the Tate Gallery painting.

3 A.L. Baldry, 'Our Rising Artists: Mr. Herbert J. Draper', *Magazine of Art*, 1899, pp. 49 ff.

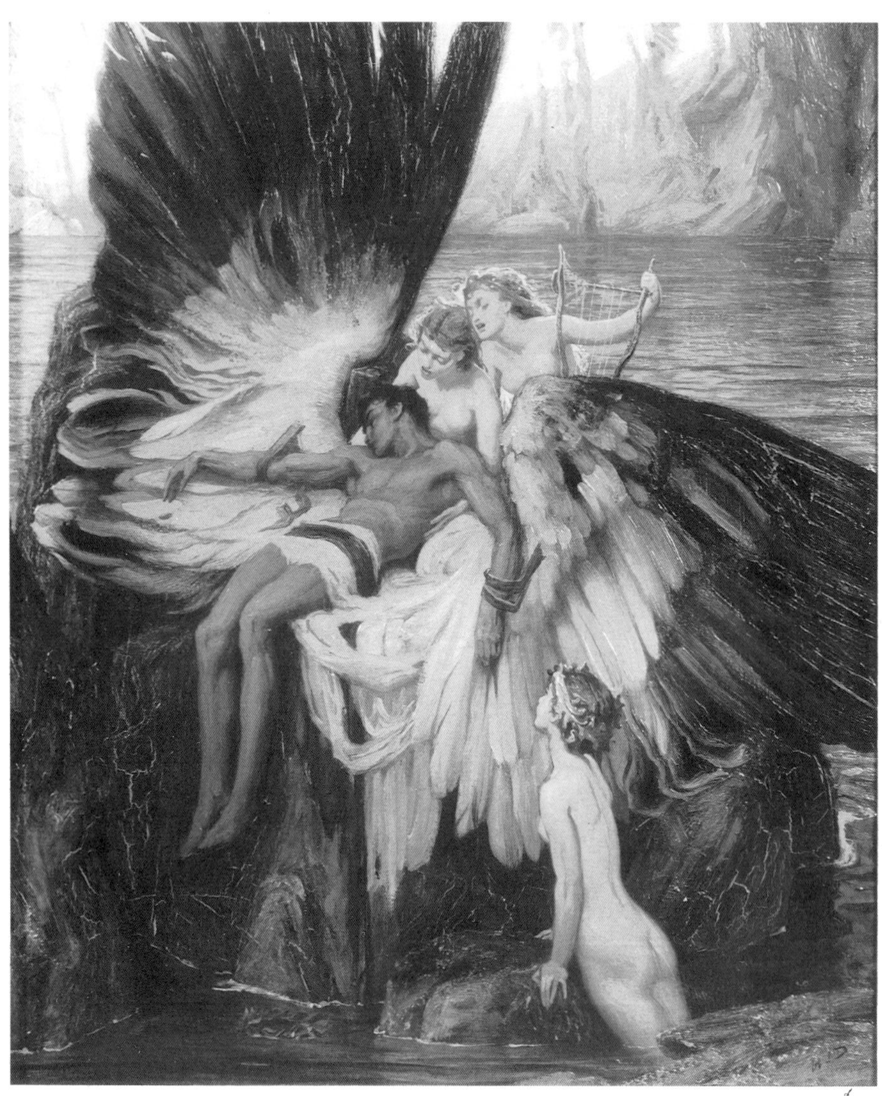

*The Lament for Icarus* LL 3911

### *The Kelpie*

LL 3619 (WHL 1179)
Canvas[1]: 135 × 193 cm
Signed: *Herbert Draper*

Kelpies were reputed to haunt rivers and lakes and to delight in causing the drowning of travellers and others. T. Millie Dow contributed his painting *The Kelpie* to the Royal Glasgow Institute of the Fine Arts in 1895[2] and John Byam Shaw exhibited *A Kelpie* at the Royal Institute of Oil Painters in 1901; Reid Dick's bronze statuette *The Kelpie* was at the 1914 Royal Academy exhibition (no. 2127)[3] while Draper's *Water Nixie*[4] of 1908 was another female nude seated on (rather than near) a river.

A drawing by Draper[5] inscribed *Study for a Bather* seems to have been used for *The Kelpie*; it was sold at Sotheby's London 12

December 1972, lot 31. The critics at the 1913 Royal Academy seem not to have been interested in Draper's painting.[6]

REPR: *Royal Academy Pictures*, 1913, p. 114.

PROV: Bought by Lever from the artist 1913 (£400).

EXH: Royal Academy 1913 (490); Liverpool Autumn Exhibition 1913 (887).

1 Canvas stamp: *REEVES AND SONS/ LONDON/PREPARED CANVAS.*

2 See David Martin, 'The Kelpie: A Painting by T. Millie Dow', *Studio*, 1895, vol. 5, pp. 21–3; Kelpie was a word of Scottish origin and Millie Dow's version seems to have been the first one to be painted; the subject suited his move towards symbolism and Martin described this kelpie as 'a small frightened female spirit of the woodland pool, sad-eyed and with wistful expression of countenance whose beautiful form, so sleek and lithe, would fascinate and then disappear from the rocky perch into the still deep waters of her home'; Dow seems to have been unaware of the kelpie's more sinister reputation and this seems also to have been true of later artists (including Draper).

3 See Alfred Yockney, 'Modern British Sculptors', *Studio*, 1916, vol. 67, p. 29 (rep).

4 Reproduced in *Royal Academy Pictures*, 1908, p. 75.

5 Reproduced in 'Figure Studies by Herbert Draper', *Studio*, 1916, vol. 68, p. 107.

6 See for example the review in the *Studio*, 1913, vol. 59, pp. 21 ff.

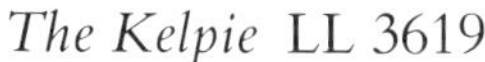

*The Kelpie* LL 3619

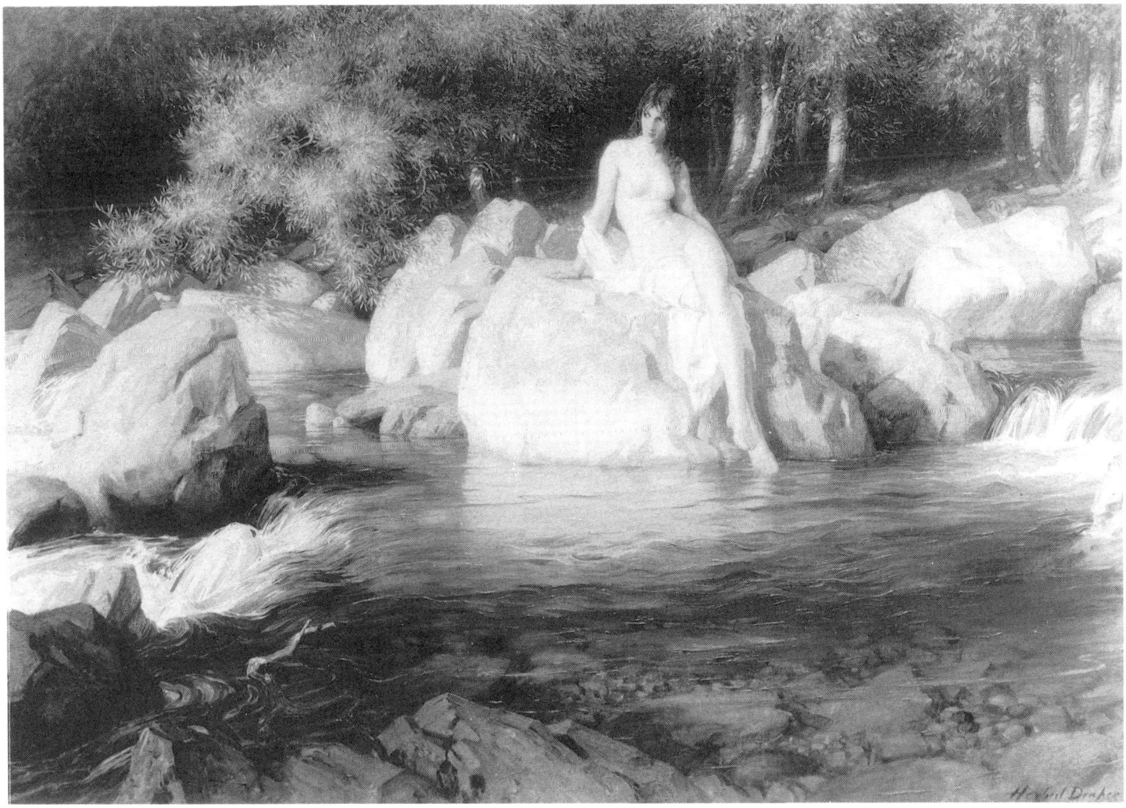

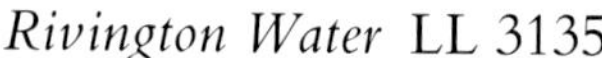


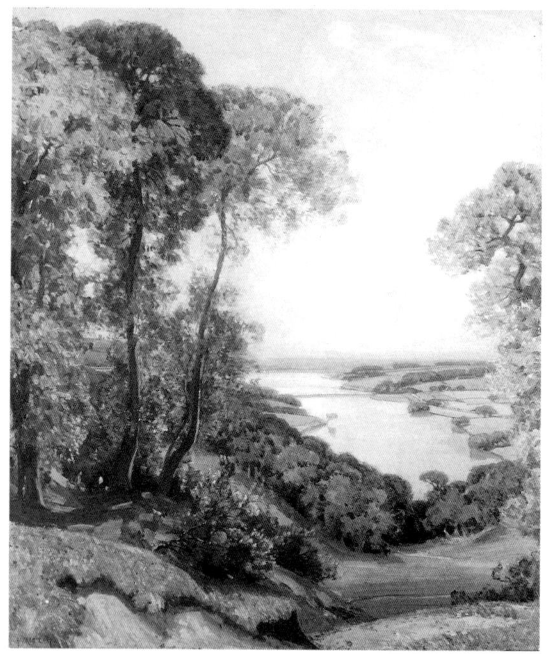

**EAST, Alfred** (1849–1913)
***Rivington Water***
LL 3135 (WHL 22, TM 35)
Canvas: 183 × 158 cm
Signed: *Alfred East*

The artist was a friend of Lever[1] and often visited Lever's Rivington home, The Bungalow,[2] which can just be seen through the trees on the hillside at the left of this painting. In the distance are the Rivington Reservoirs and to the left of the Reservoirs is Lever Park[3] (seen here through the trees). The view has been taken from Anglezarke looking south-south-east over the reservoirs.

East's contributions to the 1911 Royal Academy were generally praised; *The Times*,[4] however, observed of this painting that his pictures 'have a foreign look even when he paints England because of their lack of character and accent . . . his pleasures in the beauties of the earth are too purely artistic and empty of human associations.'

A large painting now at Bolton School and entitled *Rivington Water* or *Lever Park, Bolton*, is closely related.[5] A smaller version of the Lady Lever Art Gallery painting, differing slightly from it, is now in a private collection in Oxfordshire; another version, stated to be identical to the Oxfordshire picture, was recorded in 1974 in a private collection in Euxton, near Chorley.[6]

REPR: *Art Journal*, 1911, p. 168; *Royal Academy Pictures*, 1911, p. 28; Pall Mall Magazine, *Pictures of 1911*, p. 13.

PROV: Bought by Lever from the artist 1910 (£200).[7]

EXH: Royal Academy 1911 (248); Royal Academy, *Lord Leverhulme*, 1980 (7).

1 Viscount Leverhulme, *Viscount Leverhulme*, 1927, p. 281. It is not clear when the two men first met, but Lever owned East's *Haru-no-Yuki (Snow in Spring)* of 1906 (Viscount Leverhulme sale, Anderson Galleries (New York) 17 February 1926, lot 72) and East contributed Rivington views to the 1910, 1911, 1912 and 1913 Royal Academy and Royal Society of British Artists' Exhibitions. There are now paintings, drawings and watercolours of Rivington by East in the Bolton Museum and Art Gallery, at Bolton School and in Kettering Art Gallery; in addition a large number are recorded: (1) *Paintings and Drawings by Sir Alfred East*, Leicester Galleries 1912 (60) *Lever Park*; (2) *Memorial Exhibition of the Work of the late Sir Alfred East*, Leicester Galleries 1914 (4 and 53) *In Lever Park*; (3) Trustees of the Lady Lever Art Gallery sale, Christie's 6 June 1958, lot 115, bought Hazlitt (£12.12*s*.), *Rivington Water* (27 × 35 in.) (stated to be a smaller and slightly different version of LL 3135); (4) Roy Miles, *Sir Alfred East: Exhibition of Landscapes*, 1978 (8) *Lever Park Bolton*; (5) Sotheby's (Belgravia) 13 February 1979, lot 147, *Rivington Pike from the Bungalow*; (6) Christie's 5 March 1982, lot 216, *Lever Park*.

2 The Bungalow was built for Lever in 1900–1 and was burnt down by suffragettes in 1913.

3 Lever Park was landscaped by T.H. Mawson and others at Lever's expense as a country park open to the public; work began in 1902 and was unfinished on Lever's death in 1925; there were formal openings on 18 May 1904 and on 10 October 1911; for further details see T.H. Mawson, *Civic Art*, 1911, pp. 342–8, M.D. Smith, *Leverhulme's Rivington*, 1984, pp. 67 ff. and Michael Shippobottom, 'Unmatched for Drama', *Country Life*, 13 September 1984, pp. 678 ff. East was also a friend of Mawson (T.H. Mawson, *The Life and Work of an English Landscape Architect*, 1927, p. 226). East's landscapes show the Park and the grounds of The Bungalow as they were gradually being planted and improved.

4 *The Times*, 8 May 1911.

5 A drawing nearly identical with the Bolton School painting is reproduced in T.H. Mawson, *Civic Art*, 1911, fig. 272.

*Besieged* LL 3417

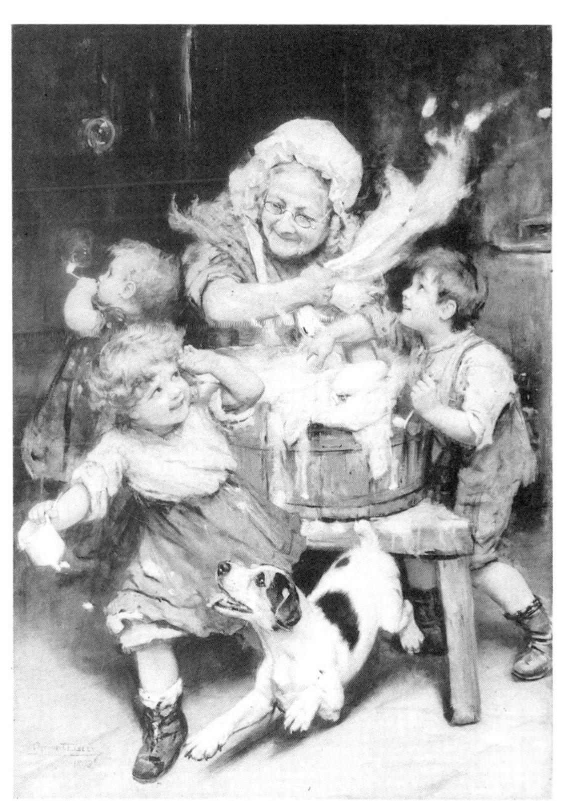

6 Either of these two versions might have been the small version of LL 3135 sold by the Trustees of the Lady Lever Art Gallery in 1958 (see note 1) but both came from the Rivington area whereas the version sold in 1958 was bought by a London dealer; moreover, the Oxfordshire picture is stated to measure 30 × 26 in., whereas the picture sold by the Trustees measured 27 × 35 in.

7 Lever owned a considerable number of East's Rivington landscapes; in particular, the three watercolours and two oils now in the Bolton Museum and Art Gallery and the *Rivington Water* sold by the Trustees of the Lady Lever Art Gallery in 1958. The compiler is indebted to Michael Shippobottom for help with this entry.

## **ELSLEY, Arthur John** (born 1861)

### ***Besieged***

LL 3417
Canvas: 92.5 × 66.5 cm
Signed: *Arthur J. Elsley 1893*

This painting was presumably bought by Lever for advertising purposes.[1]

PROV: Presented by Lever Brothers 1983.

1 Two different undated advertistments for Sunlight Soap reproducing LL 3417 and giving it the title *Besieged* are in the Port Sunlight Heritage Centre. A bar of Sunlight Soap has been added to the picture in the advertisements. For further details about paintings bought by Lever for advertising purposes see p. xiii.

## **FARQUHARSON, Joseph** (1846–1935)

### ***The Shortening Winter's Day is near a Close***[1]

LL 3152 (WHL 26)
Canvas: 117 × 171 cm
Signed: *J. Farquharson*

The artist became well known for his paintings of sheep in the snow after the purchase of his *The Joyless Winter Day* from the Chantrey Fund in 1883 (now Tate Gallery).

The *Magazine of Art*[2] described the Lady Lever Art Gallery painting as 'lighted with prismatic colours by the sun', while the *Academy*[3] observed:

*It has not the impulse of the pictures of the La Thangue school: it is, if I may say so, a constructed landscape, but for ingenuity of painting, and for the power to convey the illusion of sunlight on snow, darkened by the shadows and the leafless trees behind which the winter sun is setting, this landscape is a* tour de force. *Mr. Farquharson's vision of nature is always interesting, and he is one of the few members of the Academy who resist the shackles of conventionalism.*

A small replica of LL 3152 (with slight variations) was owned by Richard Green in 1972.[4]

REPR: *Royal Academy Pictures*, 1903, p. 116; H. Blackburn, *Academy Notes*, 1903, p. 58; H. Sedcole (colour engraving) for Frost and Reed 1905.

PROV: Bought from the artist by Thomas Agnew and Son 25 March 1903; sold to Lever 30 March 1903 (£850).

EXH: Royal Academy 1903 (174); Liverpool Autumn Exhibition 1904 (8); Royal Glasgow Institute of Fine Arts 1905 (349); Franco-British Exhibition 1908 (291).

1 Like many of Farquharson's titles this does not seem to be a quotation. A photograph of LL 3152 with this title and dated 1903 is included in the artist's four-volume record of his pictures; see Aberdeen Art Gallery, *Joseph Farquharson of Finzean*, 1985, no. 89. He gave the same title to a quite different composition of 1897 depicting a fox in the snow – it was no. 69 in the 1897 Royal Academy and was reproduced in the *Art Journal*, 1897, p. 163, and in W.M. Sinclair, 'Joseph Farquharson', *Art Journal*, 1912, p. 17; this was presumably the picture in the Christie's sale of 25 March 1938, lot 142 (114 × 89 cm). Yet another composition was entitled by the artist: *The Sun*

*The Shortening Winter's Day is near a Close* LL 3152

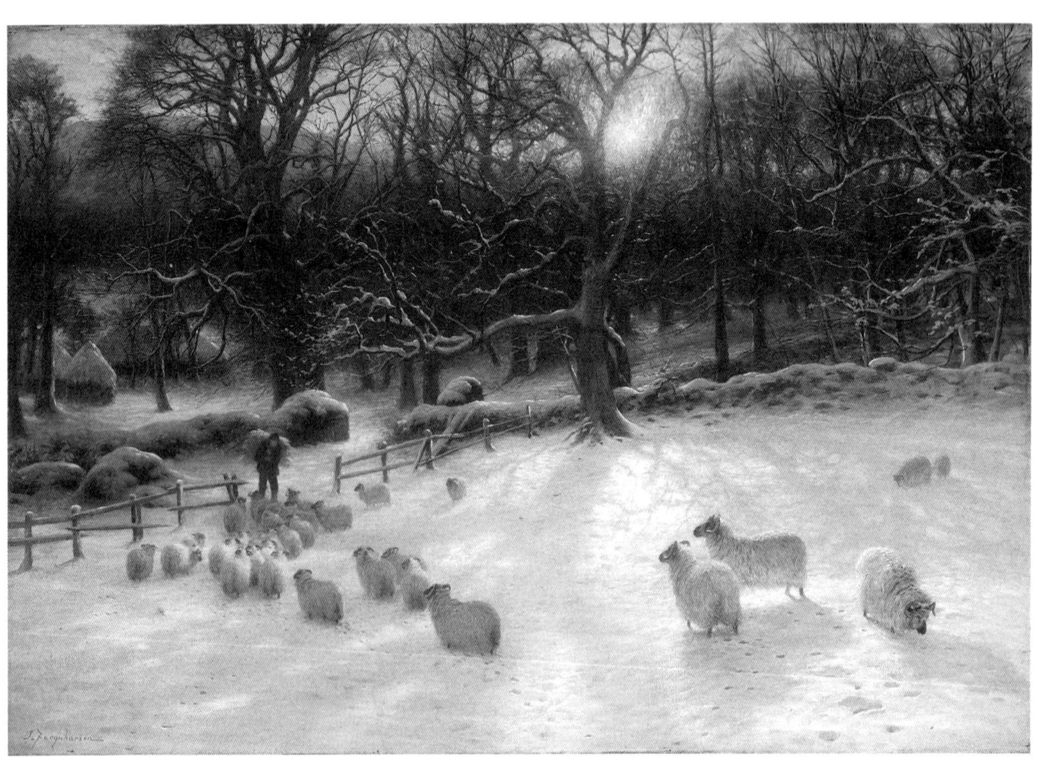

*had Closed the Winter's Day*; see Aberdeen Art Gallery, *op. cit.*, nos. 54–55.

2 *Magazine of Art*, 1903, p. 426 (M.H. Spielmann).

3 *Academy*, 9 May 1903, p. 467. Further reviews are mentioned in Arts Council, *Great Victorian Pictures*, 1978, no. 12, with a discussion of the artist's career; see also Royal Academy, *Lord Leverhulme*, 1980, no. 8, pp. 46–7.

4 *Country Life*, 1 June 1972 (51 × 76 cm).

## **FILDES, Samuel Luke** (1843–1927)

### *An Al-fresco Toilette*

LL 3621 (WHL 16)
Canvas: 173 × 108 cm
Signed: *Luke Fildes 1889*

This painting, originally entitled *The Morning of the Fiesta*,[1] was begun in Venice in 1887 with the background painted first; the background was, however, repainted in 1888; the central figure was painted from the artist's wife and the small child at the table facing the spectator from the artist's son, Luke V. Fildes;[2] the building in the background was the studio of Henry Woods, Fildes's close friend and brother-in-law.[3]

*An Al-fresco Toilette* was Fildes's last major Venetian painting before he devoted himself to portraiture.[4] Its completion between his return to London from Venice in late October 1888 and the opening of the Royal Academy exhibition in April–May 1889 caused him much trouble and anxiety; he wrote to Henry Woods[5] on 6 February 1889 noting that he had done nothing except work on it since his return from Venice and adding: 'I begin to think I have stuck and will never do anything more. Certainly this is the worst thing I have ever done and with an agony of labour. Nothing done but what is taken out the next day.' Woods replied: 'This Venetian picture has bothered you more than any I can remember. It certainly went well here a week or two before you left.' Fildes wrote back on 8 March about both this painting and the portrait, also destined for the 1889 Royal Academy: 'It's a great pity I am so short of time for otherwise I could make good things of them both'; in the same letter he asked Woods for 'a study of a piece of ground [foreground]' for his picture and remarked that 'Holland' had given him a commission for another Venetian picture similar to it. Fildes's difficulties may have encouraged him to turn to portraiture.

The *Athenaeum*[6] described this painting as representing:

> *The courtyard of an ancient Venetian palazzo, long ago let out in tenements to humble folk, some of whom are assembled in the soft sunlight near a pergola which casts its shadow upon the dark portal and its lofty side-columns on our right . . . The animated expressions and differing characters and degrees of emotion evinced are as acceptable as the bright, soft, and pleasing coloration and chiaroscuro of the picture, which is one of the most carefully thought out of Mr. Fildes's studies of those Venetian subjects which he continues to affect, although, we believe, with less good fortune than attends his more serious and dramatic themes.*

A little later the same periodical[7] observed:

> *The Venetian girls who are preparing for a* festa *are exceptionally well painted, and altogether the picture is marked by little or no striving for effect, and none of the coquetry which is common in the works of Heer van Haanen, to whom the world owes the whole tribe of Venetian pictures of this kind. Its softness and agreeable colour, the animation of the design and expressions, and the just effect are worthy of Mr. Fildes at his best. At the same time even his tact and facility cannot prevent us from being heartily tired of the buxom wenches who have so often appeared in his pictures as well as those of Heer van Haanen and Mr. Henry Woods.*

Other reviews similarly praised Fildes's painting in particular, but were less enthusiastic about the Neo-Venetian school in general. In the *Academy*[8] Claude Phillips praised the colour and delicacy of *An Al-fresco Toilette* but noted that 'there is a deadness

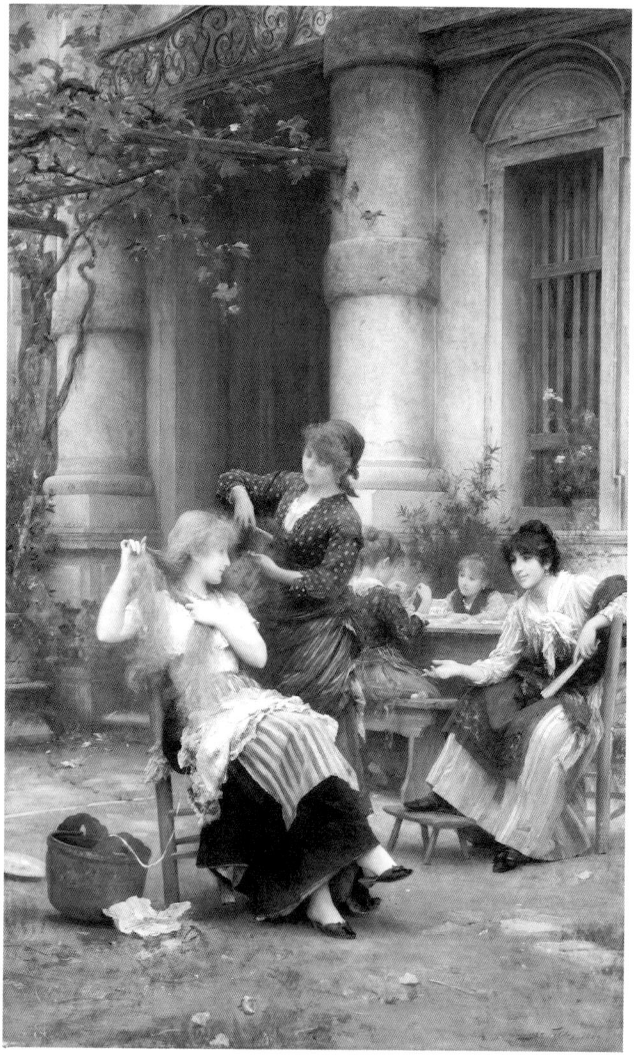

*An Al-fresco Toilette* LL 3621 (colour plate 3)

about the whole, a want of the reality of life which renders the work depressing in general effect. It is as if it were rather a composition carefully wrought out and pieced together than a real page of life'; he went on to argue that Fildes should return to British subject matter, and so did the critic of *The Times*[9] while praising the painting for being 'less smooth, pretty and composed' than most Neo-Venetian works. The *Portfolio*[10] noted that 'the so-called Venetian School is not so strong as was expected. Mr. Fildes however shows one of those gay groups of girls performing an Al-fresco Toilette which he paints with much aplomb.' These critics may have played some part in Fildes's abrupt change of subject matter in 1889 to portraiture, although perhaps the popularity of the artists of the Newlyn School, with their very different and much more realistic attitude to peasant subject matter, may have been more significant in Fildes's decision to abandon Venetian subjects. None of these critics seems, however, to have observed that Fildes has contrasted the solidity and gravity of Venetian 16th–17th-century architecture with the frivolity of its current tenants in an almost 18th-century manner.

J.W. Waterhouse's *The Toilet* of 1889–90 has a very similar subject and may have been inspired by Fildes's painting; Waterhouse's *Toilet* was, however, performed at Capri, not at Venice.[11] Lever bought the Waterhouse in 1896 (it was sold in 1926[12]) – presumably both pictures were suitable for advertising soap. One of Fildes's early major Venetian paintings, *The Venetians* of 1885 (now Manchester City Art Galleries) portrayed Venetian women doing their washing on steps leading down to a canal, but this was never owned by Lever. Similarly, Fildes's *Venetian Life* of 1884[13] is very close to *An Al-fresco Toilette* in subject matter, composition and feeling.

A pencil sketch for the seated girl at the left combing her hair is reproduced by D.C. Thomson.[14] There were apparently two sketches for the painting in the artist's sale (Christie's 24 June 1927): lot 7, *The Toilet, a young girl plaiting her hair*, 28½ × 22 in. bought Hancock £48.6*s*., and lot 8, *The Toilet, a girl holding a plait of her hair*, 28½ × 22 in. bought Hancock £33.12*s*.).

REPR: Goupilgravure for Boussod, Valadon and Co. 1890 – there is an impression in the Lady Lever Art Gallery (LP 14).

PROV: Commissioned[15] by Arthur Anderson; his sale, Christie's 19 May 1894, lot 32, bought Tooth (£1,365); George McCulloch sale, Christie's 29 May 1913, lot 135, bought Gooden and Fox (£1,575) for Lever (£1,614).

EXH: Royal Academy 1889 (307); Guildhall, London 1892 (33); Royal Academy, *Winter Exhibition*, 1909 (32); Liverpool Autumn Exhibition 1922 (501); Royal Academy, *Winter Exhibition*, 1928 (282).

1 *Athenaeum*, 6 April 1889, pp. 446–7.

2 L.V. Fildes, *Luke Fildes*, 1968, p. 113; Mrs. Luke Fildes was noted for her 'mass of Titian-red hair' (Fildes, *op. cit.*, p. 28). The information about the identity of the model for the small boy probably came from Luke V. Fildes himself – he was for many years a Trustee of the Lady Lever Art Gallery.

3 *Art Journal*, 1889, p. 217. This studio is described at length in the *Art Journal*, 1886, pp. 98–9, where a drawing of one side of it is reproduced, and in James Greig, 'The Art of Henry Woods', *Art Annual*, 1915, pp. 16–17.

4 Fildes, *op. cit.*; D.C. Thomson, 'Luke Fildes', *Art Annual*, 1895, pp. 17–18; see Arts Council, *Great Victorian Pictures*, 1978, p. 35, for a brief account of the Neo-Venetian school. Fildes first visited Venice in 1874 but the key picture for the group was probably Eugen von Blaas's *A Festa Day* exhibited at the 1875 Royal Academy and described in the *Art Journal*, 1875, p. 251. Thomson's remark that the event in LL 3621 was witnessed by the artist and then painted on the spot seems scarcely accurate.

5 The letters exchanged between Woods and Fildes are now in the Victoria & Albert Museum Library 86, PP 3.

6 *Athenaeum*, *op. cit.*

7 *Athenaeum*, 18 May 1889, p. 636.

8 *Academy*, 1889, vol. 35, p. 365.

9 *The Times*, 22 May 1889. Similarly, the *Spectator*, 25 May 1889, p. 712, argued that Fildes, 'one of our cleverest painters' should 'leave the Van Haanen business alone and seek pastures new'. Van Haanen was a leading member of the Neo-Venetian school.

10 *Portfolio*, 1889, p. 118. There is a similar analysis of the reviews of LL 3621 in Arts Council, 1978, *op. cit.*

11 A. Hobson, *J.W. Waterhouse*, 1980, p. 183, plate 38.

12 Anderson Galleries (New York) 17 February 1926, lot 281.

13 Christie's 25 November 1988, lot 161, but apparently withdrawn from the sale.

14 Thomson, *op. cit.*, p. 17.

15 According to the McCulloch sale catalogue – see provenance. The artist in his letters to Henry Woods (see note 5) refers to Anderson in discussing LL 3621 before its completion. A photograph of 1893 now in the Royal Commission on the Historical Monuments of England (negative no. BL 12165) shows LL 3621 hanging in Anderson's drawing room at 43 Wimpole Street, London.

## *William Hesketh Lever*, later first Viscount Leverhulme LL 3114

## *Mrs. William Hesketh Lever*, later first Lady Lever LL 3115

Canvas: each 119 × 84.3 cm

Lever commissioned the portrait of his wife apparently on the advice of Thomas Agnew and Sons in 1896 and its success encouraged him to commission the portrait of himself in March 1897.[1] At first, however, Fildes was distinctly cautious about this commission; he wrote to Henry Woods on 30 June 1896: 'I am doing several things here – one of Mrs. Lever of "Sunlight" fame which will be an awful job.' Lockett Agnew wrote to Fildes on 16 March 1897 with similar apprehension: 'a client of mine . . . wanted his portrait painted, and you had been so consistently nice, so warmly appreciative of his wife's character, and so painstaking that he really must offer you the commission. Now when I tell you that this client whom you have charmed is the Lever of soap fame, you will clearly understand the rocks ahead.'[2] But Lever soon became a friend of the artist and Fildes opened his *Art Exhibition to celebrate the Coronation of King Edward VII* at Hulme Hall, Port Sunlight, on 21 June 1902; Fildes's speech there pleading for the elevating role of public art galleries in an industrial community may have influenced the founding of the Lady Lever Art Gallery; the artist's son, L. V. Fildes, eventually became Secretary of Lever Brothers.[3]

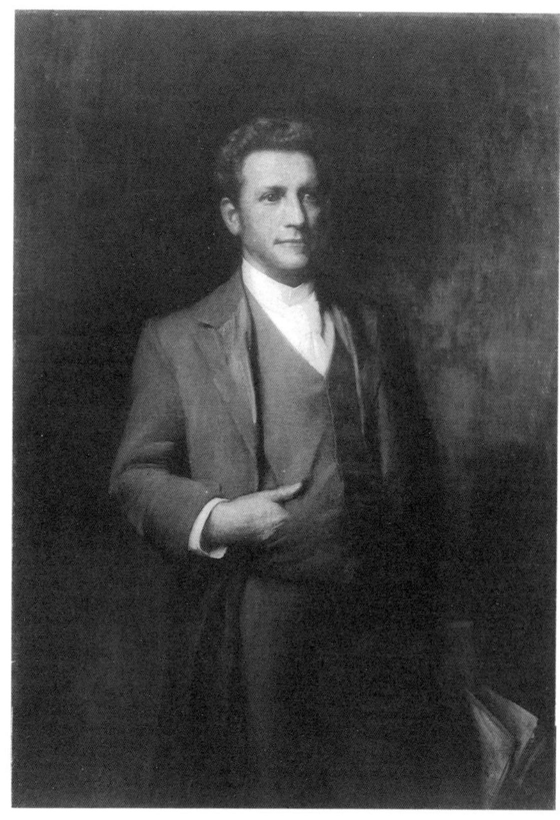

*William Hesketh Lever, later first Viscount Leverhulme* LL 3114

REPR: Photogravures after LL 3114–3115 are in the collection (LP 25–6).

PROV: Commissioned by Lever 1896–7;[3] by descent to P.W.B. Lever, third Viscount Leverhulme, who presented them to the Gallery 1980.

EXH: Royal Academy 1897 (444) – LL 3115 only; Hulme Hall, Port Sunlight, *Art Exhibition to celebrate the Coronation*, 1902 (144 and 152) and *Autumn Exhibition*, 1902 (164 and 172); Royal Academy, *Winter Exhibition*, 1928 (283) – LL 3115 only; Royal Academy, *Lord Leverhulme*, 1980 (10 and 11).

1 L.V. Fildes, *Luke Fildes, R.A.*, 1968, p. 144.

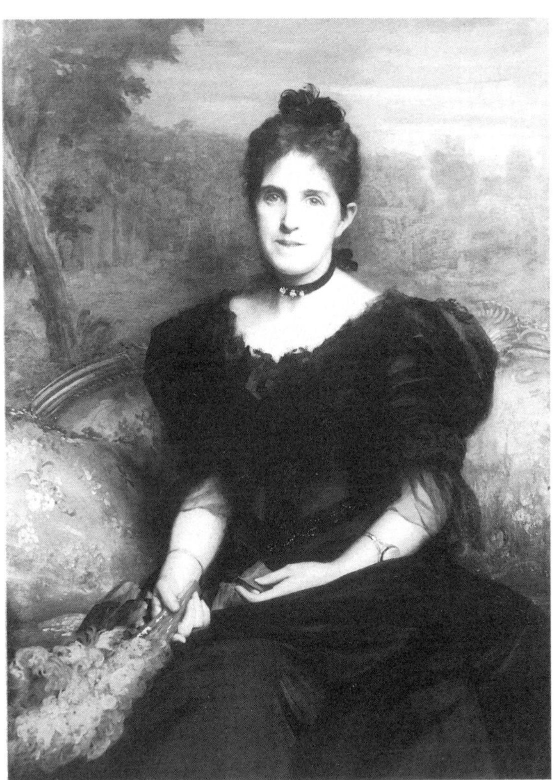

*Mrs. William Hesketh Lever, later first Lady Lever* LL 3115

2 MSS Victoria & Albert Museum Library 86, PP 4 and PP 10. The completion of LL 3114 and other portraits prevented Fildes from going to Venice in the autumn of 1897 (letter from the artist to Henry Woods of 5 November 1897, MSS Victoria & Albert Museum Library 86, PP 4).

3 Artist and sitter were, however, already friendly by July 1897 when Lever got Fildes a balcony from which he could watch the Jubilee Day processions (letter from Fildes to Henry Woods of 15 July 1897, MSS Victoria & Albert Museum Library 86, PP 4); see also Lever Brothers, *Progress*, 1902, vol. 3, pp. 230 ff.; Fildes, *op. cit.*, pp. 164–5; Royal Academy, *Lord Leverhulme*, 1980, p. 49. Both portraits were collected from the artist's studio by Thomas Agnew and Sons on 12–14 April 1898; Lever paid Agnew's £735 for LL 3114 on 22 April 1898.

## FORTESCUE-BRICKDALE, Eleanor
(1872–1945)

### *The Forerunner*

LL 3652 (WHL 4282)
Canvas: 59.6 × 122 cm
Signed: *E. F-BRICKDALE*

Leonardo da Vinci is showing a model of his flying machine to his patrons, Ludovico Sforza and Beatrice d'Este, Duke and Duchess of Milan. The Duke stands to the right of Leonardo; the Duchess is seated; one of the Duke's sons stands just to the left of Leonardo. Savonarola is the figure in black further to the left.[1] There is a famous description of the court of Ludovico Sforza in Jacob Burckhardt's *The Civilization of the Renaissance in Italy* of 1867[2] but the artist's source was more probably the evocative account of the erudite and brilliant Milanese court in Julia Cartwright's *Beatrice d'Este*, which went through many editions between 1899 and 1920.[3]

The model seems to be largely based on a drawing in the so-called Codex or MSS B in the Institut de France[4] which is now thought to date from the late 1480s. Leonardo was in Milan between 1482 and 1499; he returned later but by then Milan was under French rule; Ludovico Sforza was the Duke of Milan between 1494 and 1499. There was considerable interest in Leonardo's work on flight during the early 1920s prompted no doubt by the rapid development of aviation at that time.[5]

*The Forerunner* does not seem to have attracted much attention at the 1920 Royal Academy;[6] elaborate historical reconstructions were no longer fashionable although it was presumably the sale of this painting to Lever that encouraged the artist to paint *Botticelli's studio: the first visit of Simonetta presented by Giulano and Lorenzo de Medici* for the 1922 Royal Academy.

REPR: *Royal Academy Illustrated*, 1920, p. 93.

PROV: Bought from the artist by Lever 1920 (£315).

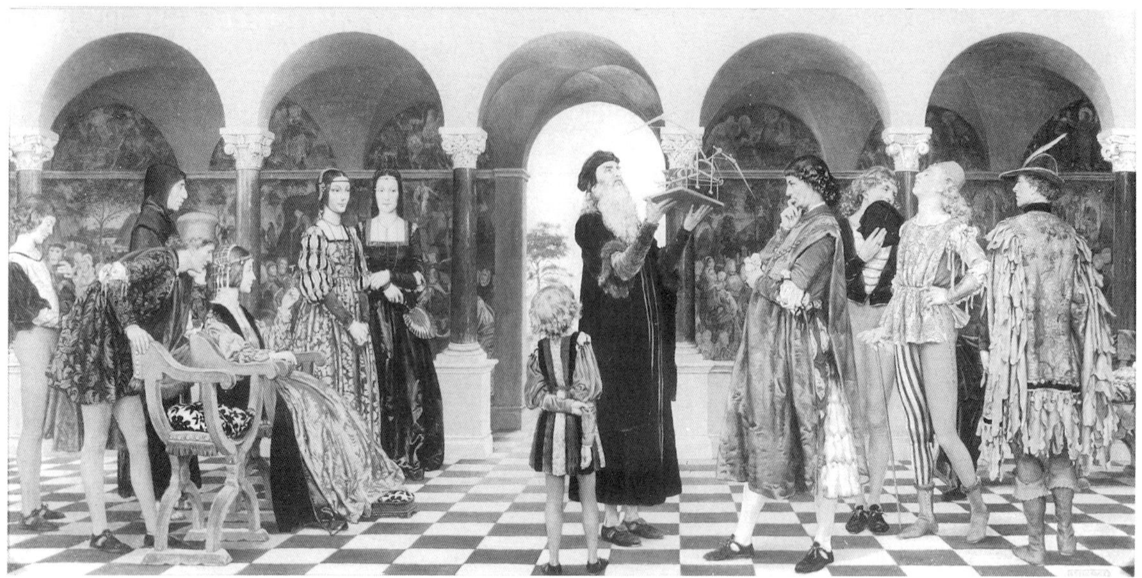

*The Forerunner* LL 3652

EXH: Royal Academy 1920 (532); Liverpool Autumn Exhibition 1920 (833); Ashmolean Museum, Oxford, *Eleanor Fortescue-Brickdale*, 1972 (39).[7]

1 These identifications are based on Gallery records and seem plausible. The presence of Savonarola at Leonardo's presentation must be regarded as extremely implausible.

2 Ed. Goldscheider, 1944, pp. 26–7.

3 1899 edition, pp. 133–40.

4 See Reale Commissione Vinciana, *I Manoscritti e i Disegni di Leonardo da Vinci*, 1941, vol. 5, p. 147. Eleanor Fortescue-Brickdale's reconstruction differs very substantially from the most recent model made from Leonardo's drawings; this model is reproduced in the South Bank Centre catalogue, *Leonardo da Vinci*, 1989, p. 237; this catalogue also reproduces and discusses other flying machine drawings by Leonardo; see also C.H. Gibbs-Smith, *Leonardo da Vinci's Aeronautics*, 1967, pp. 7–13 and 37–8 which contains a brief account of the influence of Leonardo da Vinci on the early history of aviation.

5 For example, I.B. Hart's article, 'Leonardo da Vinci as a Pioneer of Aviation', was published in the *Journal of the Royal Aeronautical Society*, 1923, vol. 27, pp. 244–69. This article (p. 244) conveniently lists the publications of Leonardo's aviation drawings before the 1920s, any of which Eleanor Fortescue-Brickdale might have used.

6 The reviews in the *Connoisseur*, 1920, vol. 57, pp. 115–16 and in the *Studio*, 1920, vol. 79, pp. 123 ff. do not mention LL 3652.

7 This catalogue invites a comparison between LL 3652 and the predella of the artist's *Guardian Angel* of 1916.

**FRITH, William Powell** (1819–1909)

***The New Frock***

LL 3419
Canvas: 92 × 72 cm
Signed: *W.P. Frith 1889*

At the 1889 Royal Academy exhibition the artist gave this painting the sub-title: 'Vanitas vanitatum; omnia vanitas' evidently intending to parody 16th–17th-century *Van-*

*itas*-type still life paintings; the *Art Journal*[1] critic observed that Frith's painting 'introduces us to a winsome little lady in red to whom the motto "Vanitas vanitatum, omnia vanitas" can hardly yet be said to be applicable'; the *Athenaeum*[2] found 'pretty and apt sentiment, expression and colour but the attitude and design are awkward. The opaque yellowness and dinginess of the complexion mar a face, which, though of an inherent commonness of type, is true to nature and animated.'

Lever bought the painting at the 1889 Royal Academy Exhibition and immediately reproduced it on Sunlight Soap advertisements adding the captions *Sunlight Soap* and *So Clean*; Frith protested against this treatment of his painting, arguing that his art had been degraded by the connection with advertising but, no agreement having been made about copyright when Lever bought the picture, the right to reproduce it was unrestricted by law; Lever contended, moreover, that the wide distribution of Frith's work in advertisements enhanced the artist's reputation and generally spread an interest in art of high quality.[3]

A small version, 21.5 × 17 cm, was sold at Sotheby's 15 October 1952, lot 146, bought Agnew (£18); it is now in a British private collection.

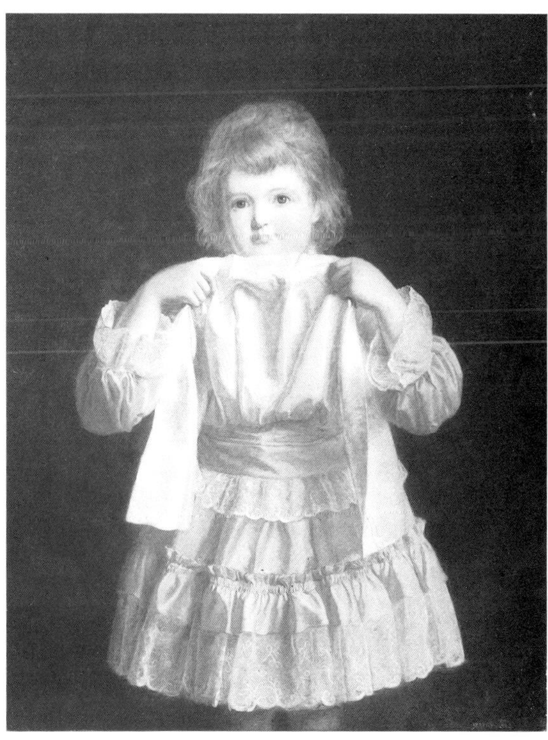

*The New Frock* LL 3419

REPR: Pall Mall Gazette, *Pictures of the Year*, 1889, p. 15; *Royal Academy Pictures*, 1889, p. 31; H. Blackburn, *Academy Notes*, 1889, p. 27.

PROV: Bought by Lever 1889 (£157.10*s*.); presented by Lever Brothers 1983.

EXH: Royal Academy 1889 (272); Royal Academy, *Lord Leverhulme*, 1980 (16).

1 *Art Journal*, 1889, p. 217.

2 *Athenaeum*, 1 June 1889, p. 701.

3 *Pall Mall Gazette*, 9, 11, 13, 17, 19 July 1889; W.P. Frith and the Editor, 'Artistic Advertising', *Magazine of Art*, 1889, pp. 421 ff.; *Art Journal*, 1890, p. 95; Viscount Leverhulme, *Viscount Leverhulme*, 1927, pp. 43–4; Charles Wilson, *The History of Unilever*, 1954, vol. 1, pp. 41–2; Royal Academy, *Lord Leverhulme*, 1980, pp. 14, 53; J.P. Navailles, 'L'art et la publicité à fin de l'époque Victorienne', *Gazette des Beaux Arts*, 1985, pp. 197–204; Lever's controversy with Frith largely repeated T.J. Barratt's dispute with Millais over the use of Millais's *Bubbles* for advertisement in 1888 – see J.G. Millais, *The Life and Letters of Sir John Everett Millais*, 1899, vol. 2, pp. 189–90; it is at least arguable that Frith's and Millais's anger at the use of their later works for advertising reflected their awareness that their art had by the 1880s, to a large extent, descended to the level of popular advertisements. Frith contended, however, that his objection to this practice reflected the low quality of reproduction in the advertisements and Lever's failure to secure his consent. There was general agreement that advertisers should be encouraged to commission work from established artists but that the unauthorized use of paintings produced as works of art could be objectionable. For further details over Lever's use of paintings for advertising see p. xiii.

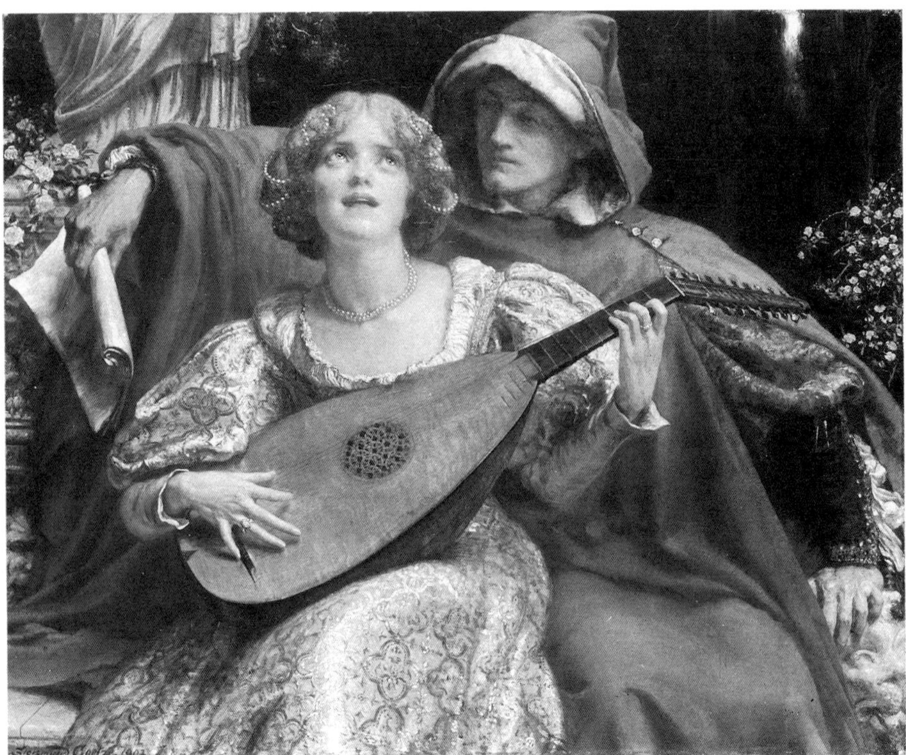

*'Thy Voice is like to Music heard ere Birth / Some Spirit-Lute touched on a Spirit Sea'*
LL 3912

**GOETZE, Sigismund Christian Hubert** (1866–1939)

***'Thy Voice is like to Music heard ere Birth / Some Spirit-Lute touched on a Spirit Sea'***

LL 3912 (WHL 3318)
Canvas: 43.5 × 53.8 cm
Signed: *Sigismund Goetze 1902*

The painting is probably closely related to Goetze's *The Echo of a Voice* of 1901.[1] The two figures and the lute appear in both paintings but in the earlier painting the lute is being played by the male figure and there is a third (male) figure not present in the later picture. The 1901 picture was exhibited at the Royal Academy with this quotation set against it in the catalogue: 'If two lives join, there is oft a scar; / They are one and one, with a shadowy third; / One near one is too far.' This is in fact a quotation from stanza forty-six of Robert Browning's poem, *By the Fire-Side*, first published in his *Men and Women* of 1855. The poem is generally held to be in part an account of Browning's love for his wife and the 'shadowy third' appears also in the love letters exchanged between Browning and his future wife in 1845–6;[2] both in the poem and in the love letters the 'shadowy third' seems to keep the two lovers apart. The 'shadowy third' is therefore possibly the third figure present in the 1901 painting. The quotation which serves as the title for the Lady Lever Art Gallery painting has been identified by Leonee Ormond as lines 143–4 of Stephen Phillips's *Marpessa*, first published in his *Poems* of 1898. There seems however to be no connection between the painting and the subject of the poem – Marpessa choosing between Apollo and a mortal lover Idas.

PROV: James Gresham sale, Christie's 16 July 1917, lot 383, bought Gooden and Fox (£68.5*s.*) for Lever (£69.19*s.*).

1 Reproduced in *Royal Academy Pictures*, 1901, p. 37 and last recorded at Sotheby's (Belgravia) 27 June 1978, lot 52. It measured 106.5 × 169 cm.

2 See R.B. Browning, *Men and Women*, ed. P. Turner, 1972, p. 323. The Browning love letters in question are those of 31 August 1845, 26 February 1846 (two), 27 February 1846 (two). These letters were first published in 1899 by the poet's son (a painter) amidst much publicity. They may have suggested to Goetze the idea for LL 3912 and for the 1901 *Echo of a Voice*.

## **GREGORY, Edward John** (1850–1909)
### ***Boulter's Lock, Sunday Afternoon***

LL 3149 (WHL 33)
Canvas: 215 × 142 cm
Signed: *E J G*

Boulter's Lock, near Maidenhead on the Thames, was built in 1830 with a 6-foot fall and then rebuilt in 1912; the main river goes over an adjacent weir.[1] This part of the Thames – not far from Cliveden – has fine scenery and was particularly popular during

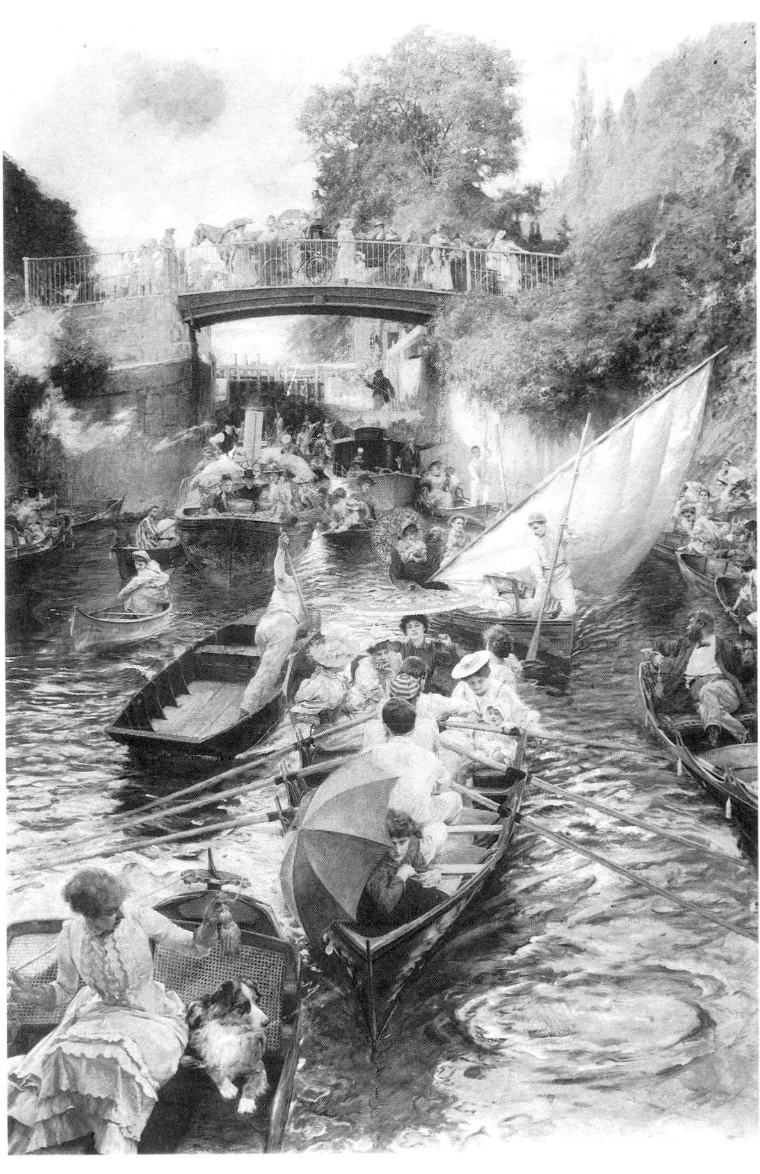

*Boulter's Lock, Sunday Afternoon* LL 3149 (colour plate 4)

*Study for Boulter's Lock*
LL 3578

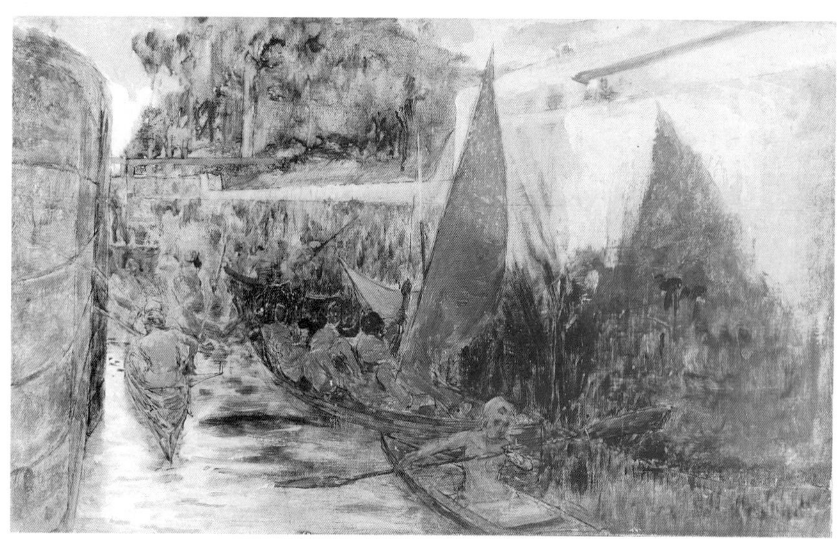

the Thames boating craze which culminated around 1910; on Ascot Sunday in 1888 around 800 boats and some 72 steam launches passed through Boulter's Lock; the Henley Regatta week was the other peak period in the year.[2] The bridge, lock and surroundings are generally painted with great accuracy, although Gregory has moved the Cliveden Reach escarpment on the east bank (the trees in the background to the right) closer to the lock and thus into the picture; moreover, he has omitted the three sluice columns (wooden posts holding a ratchet and pinion) from the top right-hand lock gate; the roof and chimney belong to an old cottage which once formed part of Ray Mill.[3] The boats are painted with similar precision: the sailing boat and the treble rowing boat (three oarsmen) are probably gigs not skiffs; the punt is of the plain working variety or possibly a boat hired out for fishing with a water-filled compartment holding live bait; there is also a Canadian canoe; sails were widely used on gigs, punts and even canoes but their deployment in these crowded conditions would have been hazardous;[4] rowing or sculling would have been difficult with the boats so close to each other so oars are being used as paddles or punt poles;[5] the small boats are all concerned to get out of the way of the steam boats which should have entered the lock first for safety reasons;[6] at the top left is Solomon J. Solomon's private canoe (or 'Koopity') – he travelled in it to Rotterdam with his friend Frank Emanuel.[7] Gregory's only error seems to have been to omit the funnel on the top of the cabin launch. The costume too has been closely observed by the artist and provides evidence that the painting was probably worked on over a long period. The dress of the woman in the foreground and probably that of the woman under the parasol date from about 1885 while the other figures wear costume of about 1895.[8]

Many of the figures are sharply characterized: the foreground woman, with her lap dog, delicately holding the tasselled steering ropes is contrasted with the woman energetically paddling her own canoe; in the treble rowing boat the woman in the bows peers anxiously forward – separated from the five chatting relaxed women in the stern by the three men; on the right the bearded man reclining lazily in the stern of his boat and looking over his shoulder is a self portrait of the artist[9] – he is contrasted with the man in the punt vigorously working his pole.

Gregory was fond of Thames subjects and must have known J.J. Tissot's many similar fashionable boating scenes particularly his *Henley Regatta* of 1877 (Leander Club) and his *On the Thames: A Heron* of 1871–2 (Minneapolis Institute of Arts). Gregory has Tissot's Japanese composition (boats arbitrarily cut by the side of the picture and a rather high view-point) but less obviously than in a similar work by Tissot, while Gregory's social and sexual comment is much less equivocal than Tissot could offer.[10]

The critics were pleased by Gregory's picture which had been begun in about 1882 but was first exhibited in 1897;[11] the *Magazine of Art*[12] saw its even lighting and consistently red tonality as creating a problem successfully overcome by the artist. The *Art Journal*[13] and *The Times*[14] noticed the same absence of strong contrasts of light and dark and the *Art Journal* observed that 'it is the kind of picture which foreign critics recognise as national; it is in fact the three-volume novel in art, the guide book and encyclopaedia of the manners and customs of the English people.' The more intellectual *Academy*[15] and *Athenaeum*[16] were less complimentary; the *Athenaeum* found 'some clever portraits' but complained of 'the coarse and heavy painting of the water and the need of finish and a firmer touch'; the *Academy* was more scathing: 'Mr. Gregory's great lock picture is dull for all its cleverness. He has piled it with all the signs of vivacity, he has laid all his difficulties low and his painting is extraordinary; nevertheless it would be difficult for a less able man to paint a less desirable picture; the bridge itself is enough to make one look another way.' D.S. MacColl in the *Saturday Review*[17] having criticized Monet's colour schemes went on: 'Mr. Gregory has given himself enormous trouble to treat a picture radically conceived as a Frith ("Boulter's Lock") with a dose of realistic light study. The Frith foundation suffers from the new interest, and those yellows and blues cannot be called beautiful.'

A large number of studies in oil, watercolour and pencil for this picture were included in the artist's studio sale at Christie's, 31 January 1910 and some twenty-five pencil sketches were acquired by the Lady Lever Art Gallery in 1928 (LP 21). Forty-six more pencil, chalk and watercolour studies appeared in an exhibition at the Maas Gallery, *Themes and Variations: Boulter's Lock*, 1970. Of these forty-six studies, twenty-six were acquired for the Gallery in 1989 (WAG 10779, 10787–10812). In addition Lever owned at least five oil studies and one watercolour study for Boulter's Lock of which three oil studies (see below) and the watercolour study (inv. WHL 1502) remain in the Lady Lever Art Gallery. There is yet another watercolour sketch in the Ashmolean Museum, Oxford.

This painting is widely regarded as Gregory's masterpiece and probably secured for him election to the Royal Academy in 1897–8.[18]

*Study for Boulter's Lock* LL 3579

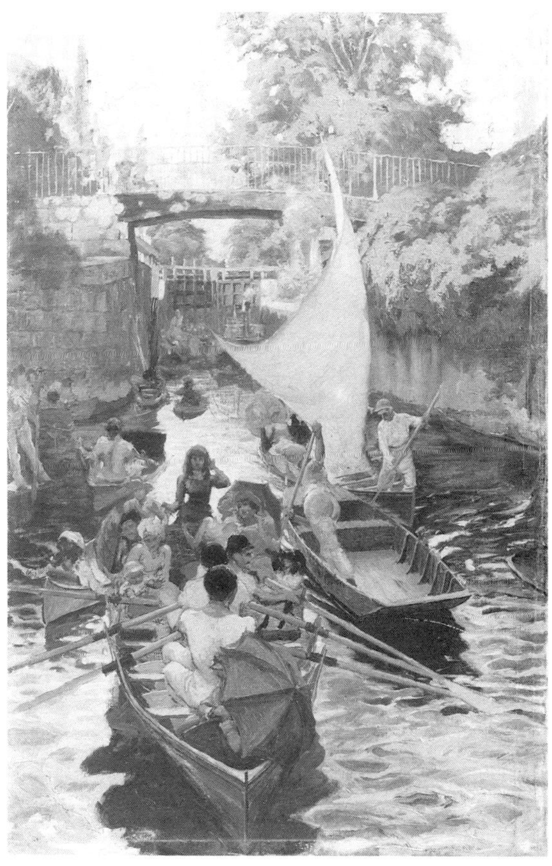

REPR: H. Blackburn, *Academy Notes*, 1897, p. 77; *Royal Academy Pictures*, 1897, frontispiece.

PROV: Charles J. Galloway[19] sale, Christie's 24 June 1905, lot 60, bought Gooden and Fox (£808.10*s*.) for Lever[20] (£848.18*s*.6*d*.).

EXH: Royal Academy 1897 (328); Paris, *Exposition Universelle*, 1900 (107); Glasgow International Exhibition 1901 (624); Franco-British Exhibition 1908 (175).

1 See *Taunt's Shilling Guide to the River Thames*, 1882, p. 26, map 2 and his *Illustrated New Map and Guide of the River Thames*, 1879, p. 48; the lock was originally called Ray Mill Pound Lock and may derive its present name from 'bolting', a milling term; it appears in a painting by E.J. Niemann, *The Thames at Maidenhead* of 1842 now in the Maidenhead Public Library and reproduced in D.G. Wilson, *The Making of the Middle Thames*, 1976, p. 130, see also F.S. Thacker, *Thames Highway*, 1920, vol. 2 (Locks and Weirs), pp. 319–29.

2 R.R. Bolland, *Victorians on the Thames*, 1974, p. 17 and D.G. Wilson, '200 Years of Pleasure Boating', *Waterways World*, July 1979, vol. 8, no. 7, pp. 47–9; Jerome K. Jerome's famous *Three Men in a Boat* was first published in 1889.

3 There are contemporary illustrations of the lock in Bolland, *op. cit.*, and in D.G. Wilson, 1976 and 1979, *op. cit.*, and in D.G. Wilson, *The Thames*, 1987, p. 72. Mr. D.G. Wilson kindly provided further details of the topography in two letters to the compiler of 19 July 1979 and 7 August 1979.

4 D.G. Wilson, letters to the compiler, 19 July 1979 and 7 August 1979.

5 Bolland, *op. cit.*, p. 119.

6 D.G. Wilson, 1979, *op. cit.*, p. 47.

7 O.S. Phillips, *Solomon J. Solomon*, n.d., p. 53.

8 Stella Mary Newton, letter to the compiler, 25 September 1979; notoriously Gregory worked very slowly (A.L. Baldry, 'The Art of Edward John Gregory', *Studio*, 1909–10, vol. 48, pp. 87 ff.). Galloway recorded his ownership of LL 3149 as early as 1892 so it is likely to have been far advanced by then (*Catalogue of Paintings and Drawings collected by C.J. Galloway*, 1892, no. 365).

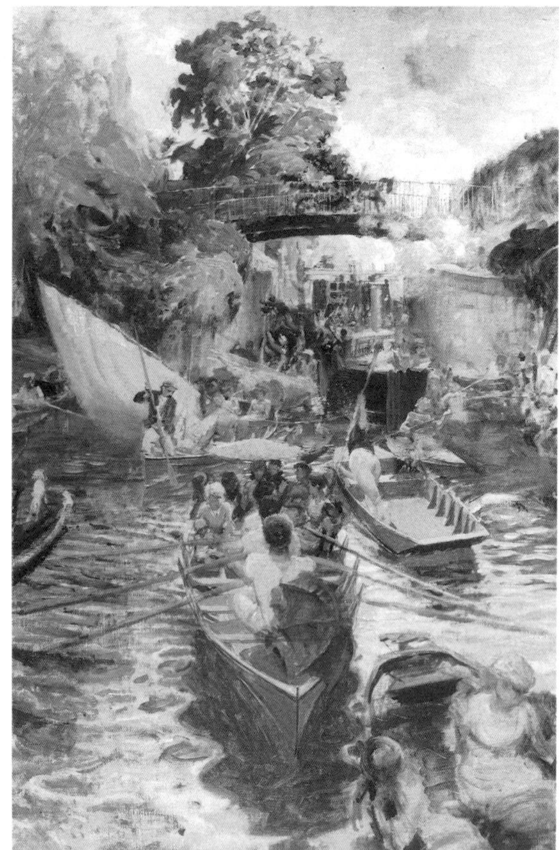

*Study for Boulter's Lock* LL 3600

9 Mr. H.R. Evans, great-nephew of the artist, letter to the compiler, 19 January 1984; compare the self portrait of the artist reproduced in F. Wedmore, 'E.J. Gregory A.R.A.', *Magazine of Art*, 1884, p. 265 and the portrait of the artist by John Parker sold at Sotheby's (Belgravia) 13 May 1980, lot 79. Mr. Evans states that his mother and grandmother, with other relatives of the artist, served as models for the figures in LL 3149.

10 See M.J. Wentworth, 'On the Thames: A Heron', *Minneapolis Institute of Arts Bulletin*, 1975, vol. 62,

pp. 35 ff. and Ian Thompson, 'Tissot and Oxford', *Oxford Art Journal*, April 1979, no. 2, pp. 53 ff.

11 *The Times*, 1 May 1897. D.S. MacColl in the *Dictionary of National Biography* wrote of the 'years of elaboration' devoted by the artist to LL 3149; there seems to be no evidence that it was painted in 1895 as stated by R.R. Tatlock in his Lady Lever Art Gallery Catalogue *English Painting of the 18th–20th Centuries*, 1928, p. 97.

12 *Magazine of Art*, 1897, pp. 59–60.

13 *Art Journal*, 1897, pp. 179–80.

14 *The Times*, *op. cit.*

15 *Academy*, 1897, vol. 51, p. 527.

16 *Athenaeum*, 5 June 1897, p. 751.

17 *Saturday Review*, 22 May 1897, p. 572.

18 MacColl, *op. cit.* (who, however, disliked the painting). J.S. Sargent, on the other hand, seems to have admired LL 3149; see Sotheby's 19 July 1990, lot 412 (the Gregory papers referred to in this catalogue are unseen by the compiler).

19 Galloway was Gregory's most important patron; he bought about one-third of Gregory's paintings and Gregory's portrait of his daughter Mabel was sold at Christie's, 13 November 1992, lot 112; he already owned LL 3149 in 1892 long before its completion but at that date it had not yet reached his house; he also owned an oil sketch for the painting (12 × 20 in.) and a finished watercolour (13 × 16 in.) of Boulter's Lock with a quite different composition which was exhibited at the 1883 Royal Institute of Painters in Water Colours exhibition (Galloway, *op. cit.*, nos. 17 and 267, repr.).

20 Lever sent LL 3149 off for reproduction as soon as he acquired it; he presumably used the resulting colour prints in one of his soap advertising campaigns. See p. xiii for further details of Lever's use of paintings for advertising purposes.

## *Study for Boulter's Lock*

LL 3578 (TM 319, WHL 675)
Canvas stuck down to board: 40.5 × 66 cm

## *Study for Boulter's Lock*

LL 3579 (TM 318, WHL 677)
Canvas: 76.5 × 51 cm

## *Study for Boulter's Lock*

LL 3600 (TM 325, WHL 678)
Canvas: 76 × 51 cm

All these three paintings are studies for *Boulter's Lock, Sunday Afternoon* completed in 1897 (see above).

PROV: The artist's studio sale, Christie's 31 January 1910: LL 3578 (lot 79?), bought Cox (£4.4*s.*) for Lever; LL 3600 (lot 88), bought Cox (£18.18*s.*) for Lever; LL 3579 (lot 93), bought Cox (£31.10*s.*) for Lever; his executors' sale, Knight, Frank, and Rutley 15 June 1926; LL 3578 (lot 77B), bought Lever Brothers; LL 3600 (lot 77C), bought Lever Brothers; LL 3579 (lot 77A), bought Lever Brothers; all three studies were presented by Lever Brothers 1985.[1]

1 Lever also owned two other oil studies for *Boulter's Lock* which are not now in the Lady Lever Art Gallery. They were: (1) TM 76, WHL 1495, 27.3 × 40.6 cm, probably lot 36 in the 1910 sale and probably lot 76 in the 1926 sale. (2) WHL 676, 27.3 × 40.6 cm, probably lot 79 in the 1910 sale and lot 77 in the 1926 sale.

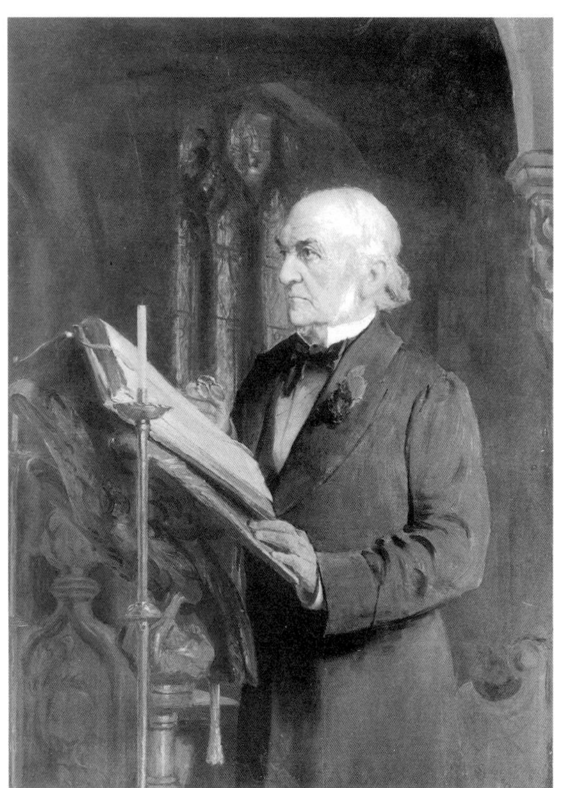

*Gladstone reading the Lesson in Hawarden Church* LL 3746

**HALL, Sydney Prior** (1842–1922)

### *Gladstone reading the Lesson in Hawarden Church*

LL 3746 (WHL 701, TM 266)
Canvas[1]: 65 × 48.3 cm
Signed: *Sydney P. Hall 1892*

The *Graphic* published around 1892 many illustrations after Hall showing Gladstone performing various duties, mainly in Parliament,[2] but this painting does not seem to have been reproduced there although it has a format very similar to Hall's *Graphic* illustrations. There is another version at the National Portrait Gallery;[3] it varies very slightly from the Lady Lever Art Gallery portrait of which there is a copy at St. Deiniols Library, Hawarden where there is also a pen and ink sketch of Gladstone at a lectern by Harry Furniss.

Mr. W.M. Crook[4] described Gladstone reading in church in a letter of 1938:

*I have listened to him when he read the first Lesson on a Sunday morning in Hawarden Church during an Easter holiday more than half a century ago. The lesson was on the story of Korah, Dathan and Abiram. When he thundered out the words, 'You take too much upon you, ye sons of Levi', his articulation and the wonderful modulation of the tones of his voice were an example to all who read the lessons in church, and to all the clergy.*

REPR: Pall Mall Gazette, *Pictures of the Year*, 1893, p. 81; *Handbook to the Royal Academy*, published by Black and White, 1893; H. Blackburn, *New Gallery*, 1893, p. 30; H. Blackburn, *Academy Sketches*, 1893, p. 85.

PROV: J.D. Lever,[5] who lent LL 3746 to the 1893 Liverpool Autumn Exhibition; W.H. Lever.

EXH: New Gallery 1893 (22); Liverpool Autumn Exhibition 1893 (76).

1 Label: *Charles Roberson and Co. / Artist's colour makers / 99 Long Acre London.*

2 See particularly the Graphic, *Parliamentary Pictures and Personalities, Illustrations of Parliament, 1890–1893*, 1893, where many of these illustrations are reproduced.

3 Inv. no. 3641; it is not dated and is said to have been purchased from the 1902 Liverpool Autumn Exhibition (Robin Gibson, letter to the compiler, February 1985) but it does not appear in the catalogue for that exhibition.

4 *The Times*, 1 April 1938. Gladstone attended morning service every day that he was at Hawarden until 1894 (John Morley, *Life of W.E. Gladstone*, 1903, book X, chapter 9). There is an illustration entitled *Mr. Gladstone reading the lessons in Hawarden Church* apparently after W.H. Margetson in T.W. Reid, *Gladstone*, 1898, p. 271; it is very similar in composition to LL 3746.

5 This was Lever's brother. Lever himself acquired

a considerable number of portraits, busts and photographs of Gladstone; he stood unsuccessfully as a prospective Liberal M.P. for Birkenhead in the elections of 1892, 1894 and 1895; Gladstone had visited Port Sunlight in 1891 and made a deep impression on him (Viscount Leverhulme, *Viscount Leverhulme*, 1927, p. 56).

## **HARCOURT, George** (1868–1948)

### *The Birthday*

LL 3913 (LP 72)
Canvas: 180.5 × 267 cm
Signed: *George Harcourt*

The artist's family is celebrating the birthday of his youngest daughter, Anne, in the left foreground. Closest to her is her sister Aletha and next to her is her mother (and wife of the artist), Mary Lascelles Harcourt (née Leesmith), who died in 1948. On the other side of the mother is Mary Edeva, sister of Aletha and Anne, while standing behind the chair is their brother Donath who died while still a boy at Winchester College. All the daughters became portrait painters and their mother was noted for her landscapes, portraits and figure subjects.[1] This painting was plainly influenced by J.S. Sargent who had, by 1910, largely abandoned portraiture.

A.C.R. Carter[2] described *The Birthday* as a 'clever group, gracefully arranged' and the critic of *The Times*[3] also singled it out for praise, remarking that 'there was a question of buying it out of the Chantrey Fund.' The critic of the *Studio*[4] identified it as one of the pictures of the year and saw it as one of the artist's major achievements; it showed how 'a very difficult kind of portrait composition can be made interesting without being too obviously unconventionalized.'

G. Frederic Lees[5] saw in this portrait and in certain related portrait groups a new concern by the artist in the rendering of light and he also observed that these paintings are partly portraits and partly scenes from everyday life and thus have unusual vivacity.

REPR: *Royal Academy Pictures*, 1910, p. 39.

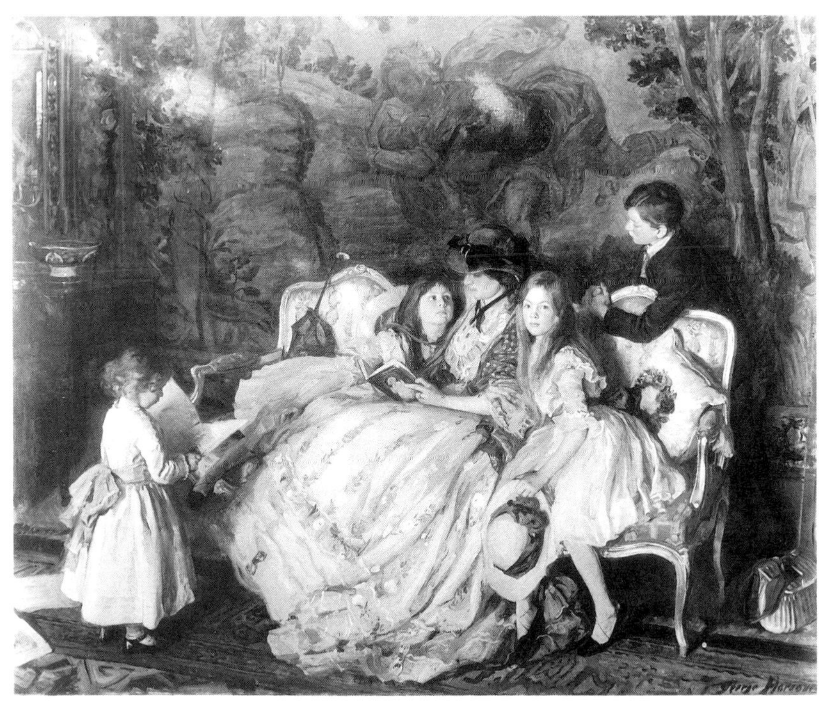

*The Birthday* LL 3913

PROV: Bought from the Art Exhibition Bureau 1950 (£105).

EXH: Royal Academy 1910 (729); Stedelijke Museum, Amsterdam, *Internationale Tentoonstelling van Hedendaagsche Kunst* 1912 (302);[6] Salon, Paris, 1923;[7] Royal Society of Portrait Painters 1939 (198); Royal Institute Galleries, *George Harcourt and Francis Hodge*, 1949 (15).

1 Mrs. Anne Fleming-Williams (née Harcourt), letter to the curator, 5 April 1950.

2 'The Royal Academy', *Art Journal*, 1910, p. 169.

3 *The Times*, 30 April 1910.

4 *Studio*, 1910, vol. 50, pp. 10–11.

5 'The Art of George Harcourt', *Studio*, 1917, vol. 70, pp. 167–8.

6 At this exhibition the painting won a prize of 12,050 florins, one of the largest awarded.

7 See the review of LL 3913 in 'Salon de 1923', *L'Illustration*, 12 May 1923, p. 449, by Jacques Baschet who described the painting as resembling an old master in a museum; he conceded, however, that it was 'belle, grassement peinte, largement, sobre et colorée à la fois, bien construite'. Herbert Furst made much the same point about the picture in his 'Art Notes', *Apollo*, 1939, vol. 30, p. 225: 'one is already able to look back upon these pictures as one looks back upon a Queen Anne Chair or a Tudor Cottage.'

*Storm Clearing Off – Picking up a Lame Duck* LL 3616

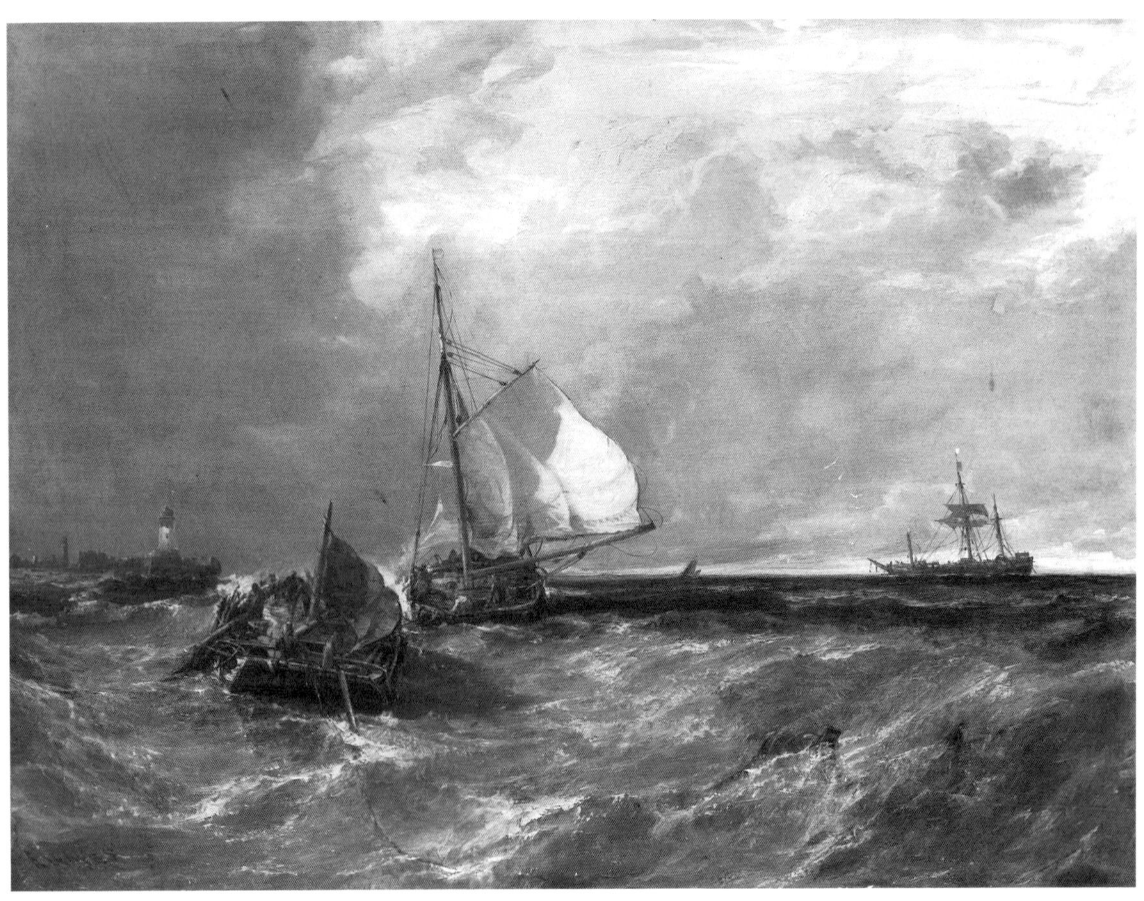

## HAYES, Edwin (1819–1904)

### *Storm Clearing Off – Picking up a Lame Duck*[1]

LL 3616 (WHL 2297, HH 65)
Canvas[2]: 105 × 140.5 cm
Signed: *E. Hayes*

Some long reviews of the first exhibition of the Institute of Painters in Oil Colours were published but this painting, no doubt considered very old-fashioned by 1883, was not mentioned.[3]

PROV: Acquired by James Orrock before 1887; his sale, Christie's 4 June 1904, lot 100, bought in (£65.2*s*.); bought by Lever 1910–11.[4]

EXH: Institute of Painters in Oil Colours 1883–4 (604);[5] Manchester Royal Jubilee Exhibition 1887 (151).

1 This is the title given in the 1883–4 Institute of Painters in Oil Colours exhibition catalogue. LL 3616 has had various titles; in 1887 at the Manchester Royal Jubilee Exhibition it was *Towing a Disabled Boat*; at the 1904 Orrock sale it was *Picking up a Lame Duck after the Storm*; in the 1910 Orrock inventory it was *The Lame Duck: after the Storm*.

2 Canvas stamp: *W. BADGER/EATWELL/ BOUNDARY ROAD/ST. JOHN'S WOOD/ DORSET STREET*. There is also a W. Badger label with the artist's name and address written in ink; the address was Briscoe House, Steel's Road.

3 See *Athenaeum*, 22 December 1883, pp. 821–2 and *Magazine of Art*, 1884, pp. 160–5.

4 1910 Orrock MSS Inventory, p. 37, valued at £75.

5 LL 3616 has not quite the same composition as the drawing reproduced in the Institute of Painters in Oil Colours exhibition catalogue (fig. 12) as an illustration of no. 604 in that catalogue, but the drawing was clearly made by the artist freely from the painting, so an exact correspondence should not be expected.

## HAYLLAR, James (1829–1920)

### *The Centre of Attraction*

LL 3416
Canvas: 102 × 153 cm
Signed: *J. Hayllar/1891*

This is one of many similar cottage scenes which Hayllar painted after moving to Wallingford in 1875; the artist's daughter, Mary, was the model for the woman holding the baby; a contemporary photograph of this painting is in the Hayllar family

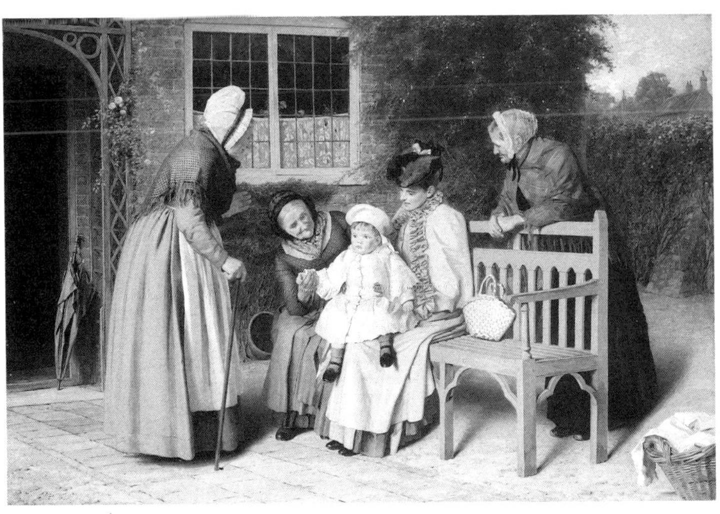

*The Centre of Attraction*
LL 3416

photographic album.[1] A small version of this composition was last sold at Christie's 25 March 1988, lot 70; it was not signed or dated.

PROV: Presented by Lever Brothers 1983.[2]

EXH: Royal Academy 1891 (681).[3]

1 See C. Wood, 'The Artistic Family Hayllar', *Connoisseur*, 1974, vol. 185, pp. 266 ff.; the early photograph of LL 3416 is reproduced as fig. 12.

2 Lever may have bought LL 3416 at the 1891 Royal Academy for use as a soap advertisement. For further details about paintings of this type see p. xiii.

3 Henry Blackburn, *Academy Notes*, 1891, p. 19 describes the Royal Academy picture as 'a baby and three women near some almshouses' but he may have failed to count the women accurately.

## **HERKOMER, Hubert von** (1849–1914)

### ***The Last Muster – Sunday at the Royal Hospital, Chelsea***

LL 3627 (WHL 4705)
Canvas[1]: 214.5 × 159 cm
Signed: *H. Herkomer Mar. 1875*

This famous painting was based on Herkomer's wood engraving in the *Graphic* of 18 February 1871 which, however, shows a smaller section of the congregation and, apart from the two principal figures at the ends of the front two pews, generally different members of it; the description of the wood engraving in the *Graphic* merely gave an account of the Royal Hospital and its inmates; the artist had selected the subject of this wood engraving himself apparently during the winter 1869–70 and received £10 for the drawing although the final engraving was in the artist's opinion of low quality.[2] The patriotic subject matter and attitude to death in Herkomer's engraving and painting are discussed by R. Treble[3] with reference to similar works by David Wilkie, Frank Holl, Lady Butler and Frederick Walker. A watercolour after the drawing for the *Graphic* was commissioned by W.L. Thomas, editor of the magazine, and painted during the winter of 1870–1.[4]

Work on the canvas was begun in January 1875 – the delay having been probably caused by the illness of the artist's wife;[5] no preliminary drawings or studies were made, although a few sketches of the chapel itself were done as the artist was not allowed to take his canvas into the chapel; the figures were sketched in pairs on to the canvas directly from the models; for the two principal figures – those at the ends of the two front pews – the same models were used as for the *Graphic* engraving of 1871. Other models included the artist's father for the white bearded figure in the third row and, for the figures along the back wall, C.E. Fry, the artist's first wife, Anna, Mrs. Fry, the artist himself and the small son of Mr. and Mrs. Fry; a Joseph Winter is stated to have been one of the old soldiers in the front row.[6] The floor tiles were painted in the correct perspective by the use of a board of black and white squares; this board was viewed by the artist from a pin hole with a piece of glass between the board and the pin hole; the artist then drew on to the glass the squares as they appeared to him from the pin hole and this drawing when traced, reversed and enlarged was used for the floor tiles. To obtain the correct recession and diminution of the figures, the artist sketched in the chapel the heads of two models, one seated at the nearest point to the artist, the other at the furthest point from him. Further technical details must be quoted from the artist's account:

*It must be told that there was 'no' oil-colour ground on the canvas; it was a piece of unprepared linen, with nothing but a coating of size. Each figure was sketched on it with zinc-white mixed with paste, using water-colour lampblack and raw sienna for the outlines. This produced that dry, fresco-like appearance, but it was too absorbent, and necessitated the use of much medium to secure the paint on the canvas, as the ground 'drew out' too much of the binding material in the colours. It was not until it had been soaked with medium five or six times, back and front, after it was finished, that the paint ceased to 'chip' in places.*

The artist was at first unhappy with the broader brushwork of this painting on the grounds that it deviated from the work of Frederick Walker which at that time he much admired;[7] furthermore, he noted that 'it was a section of the chapel, with all the figures that came within that section; it had no beginning and no end; in short it was no composition.'[8]

*The Last Muster* was, however, very successful; it was bought by C.E. Fry[9] for £1,200 before it was sent to the Royal Academy; the hanging committee at the Academy clapped when it was brought before them[10] and Frederic Leighton in particular was deeply impressed by it.[11] The artist, too, soon liked the picture and on 2 May 1875 wrote to his uncle and aunt:

*I call it 'The Last Muster'. They are all sitting, some with deep feelings of veneration, others more indifferent. There are about seventy heads to be seen, and all literal portraits. I picked out the most characteristic men and then painted them carefully, keeping their individuality. It is a grand sight to see these venerable old warriors under the influence of divine service. They have been loose (most of their lives), and now coming near their end a certain fear comes over them and they eagerly listen to the Gospel . . . I have not adopted or made use of any rules that are supposed to be necessary in making a picture. I have violated all academic principles. I have painted the scene literally (so to speak), not forgetting the sentiment of course that I wished to impress my spectators with.*

Similarly, in 1882 he wrote: 'The idea was to make every man tell some different story, to be told by his type of face and expression or by some selection of attitude.'[12]

The critics were equally favourable. *The Times*[13] observed: 'The assemblage of various heads, all old and worn with hardship, but differing in every other particular, is presented with a power of painting and a grasp of character as rare as they are admirable. In these respects there is little if anything here exhibited which comes near it.' The *Art Journal*,[14] *Morning Post*[15] and *Graphic*[16] were also complimentary and Ruskin[17] referred to 'the group of grand old soldiers at Chelsea – a most notable, true, pathetic study' – although he had reservations about the artistic value of the painting. The *Athenaeum*[18] offered extended analysis which is worth quoting fully:

*Probably the most original picture here is, putting other qualities aside, Mr. Herkomer's* The Last Muster – Sunday at the Royal Hospital, Chelsea, *a large work reproducing for the most part a sketch which was lately at a watercolour exhibition. It shows a considerable number of old pensioners seated on their parallel benches 'at church', in the chapel which Wren built. An old soldier, placed at the end of one of the benches, has just answered the last call, and ceased to live rather than died, so softly and silently that his neighbour knew it not for a time; but he now turns, and anxiously shakes the lifeless wrist, inquiringly rather than with surprise or pain. It is clear, however, that this man who walked to the bench will have to be carried away. The mortal remains clad in the regimental of the penultimate asylum, sit self-balanced and effortless. The features of the time-worn face have a still dignity and beauty about them which is very touching and fine; the white hair of the old soldier is neatly kept, and he has been trimly shaved; his hat, with the handkerchief in it, was placed at his feet in due order, – acts which marked, while they concluded, a long life of discipline. This group of two soldiers is very pathetic, and finely thought out. Next to the survivor is a tall, long-backed comrade, still staunch and upright, with big, silver-rimmed spectacles on his aquiline nose, sedately and a little laboriously reading the Prayer Book, which he handles with as much stiffness as if it were a musket. His attention has not yet been diverted from the leaf, which he is now sedately turning. Close by is an old man on a bench behind the soldier who has passed away; he has placed his book on his knee and taken off his spectacles, while he listens to the service. In front of the principal group is a big-headed, argumentative-looking trooper, whose long upper lip bespeaks an obstinate disposition, while*

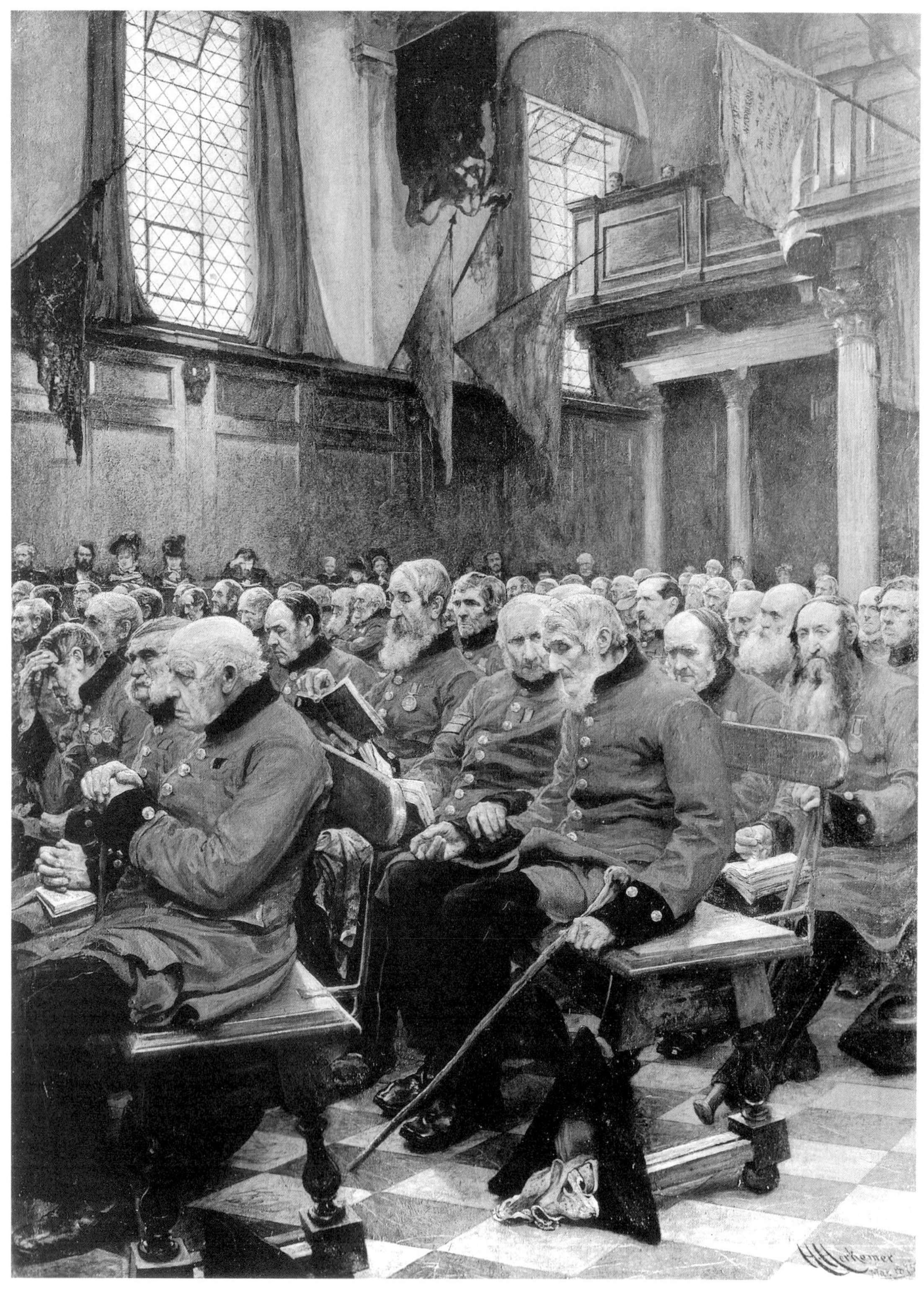

*The Last Muster – Sunday at the Royal Hospital, Chelsea* LL 3627 (colour plate 5)

*his bright eyes show his intelligence. He sits with his hands on the head of a stick, and listens, not without approval, to what is recited before him. Next to him is one who, though white-haired and very old, is still a dandy, with full and cultivated moustaches. These are a few of the numerous figures in this admirably designed picture, a work which is not less remarkable for its fine effect, richness of colour, – the latter being a distinguishing feature, – and breadth of tone, than for its pathetic characterization.*

Writing five years later, Wilfred Meynell[19] emphasized the popularity of the painting and the surprise felt by many critics at seeing such a large, substantial and ambitious work after a series of relatively inconsequential pictures.

In 1878 *The Last Muster* won a gold medal for Herkomer at the Paris Universal Exhibition[20] – the only other British gold medallist in painting being J.E. Millais – while in 1879 Herkomer's first commissioned portrait, the *Lord Stratford de Redcliffe* for King's College, Cambridge, was secured by the artist on the strength of the earlier painting.[21] His *The Old Guards' Cheer* of 1898 was intended as a belated companion picture to *The Last Muster.*[22] Works by other artists relying on Herkomer's painting include *Sons of the Brave* by P.R. Morris of 1880, *Friends in Adversity: Christmas Day at the Dreadnought Hospital, Greenwich* by J.C. Dollman, also of 1880, and R.G. Hutchison's *In Time of Peace* of 1887.[23]

REPR: The artist (wood-engraving) *Graphic*, 15 May 1875, pp. 474–5 (two main figures only); H. Blackburn, *Academy Notes*, 1875, p. 44 (two main figures only); Arthur Turrell (mezzotint) 1878 for Pilgeram and Lefevre; H. Blackburn, *Illustrated Catalogue of the British Fine Art Section, Paris Universal Exhibition*, 1878, no. 107, p. 41 (two main figures only); H. Zimmern, 'Hubert Herkomer', *Die Kunst für Alle*, 1890–1, vol. 6, opp. p. 8; the artist (lithograph) 1909.

PROV: Bought by C.E. Fry in 1875 (£1,200); bought by Sir W. Cuthbert Quilter in 1881;[24] his sale, Christie's 9 July 1909, lot 57, bought in (£3,255); his sale, Christie's 22 June 1923, lot 152, bought Gooden and Fox (£2,940) for Lever (£3,013.10*s*.).

EXH: Royal Academy 1875 (898); Paris, *Exposition Universelle*, 1878 (107); Munich International Exhibition 1883; Whitechapel Fine Art Exhibition 1885 (10); Manchester Royal Jubilee Exhibition 1887 (465); Birmingham, *Paintings by living and deceased artists*, 1887 (166); Chicago, *World's Columbian Exposition*, 1893 (213); Blackburn 1894 (106); Guildhall, London 1894 (7); West Ham, *Third Annual Exhibition*, 1897 (132); Dublin, *International Exhibition*, 1907; London, *Franco-British Exhibition*, 1908 (135); Rome, *International Exhibition*, 1911 (704); Royal Academy, *Winter Exhibition*, 1922 (9).

1 Label: Reginald Dolman and Sons.

2 *Graphic*, 18 February 1871, pp. 151–2; *Autobiography of Hubert Herkomer*, 1890, p. 35; Hubert von Herkomer, *The Herkomers*, 1910, pp. 82–3. The artist in his 'Drawing and Engraving on Wood', *Art Journal*, 1882, p. 166, stated that he got the idea for the subject of the wood engraving from attending a Sunday service in the Chelsea Hospital chapel but he probably never witnessed an actual death there; see L.M. Edwards, *Hubert von Herkomer and the Modern Life Subject*, 1987, p. 154. According to the *Magazine of Art*, 1890, p. 16, LL 3627 was to have been entitled *Sunday at the Royal Hospital, Chelsea* and the incident of the dying man was included as an afterthought at the last moment; the dying man does, however, appear in the 1871 wood engraving. Herkomer must have known David Wilkie's very popular *Chelsea Pensioners receiving the news of Waterloo* of 1822. The original drawing for the wood engraving was destroyed during the engraving process but preliminary studies for it and for LL 3627 are reproduced in L. Pietsch, *Herkomer*, 1901, p. 7, Herkomer, 1910, *op. cit.*, p. 56, and in A.L. Baldry, *Hubert von Herkomer*, 1901, p. 26, while one is now in the Egerton Collection on loan to the Watford Museum; see Watford Museum, *Sir Hubert von Herkomer*, 1982, no. B2, p. 50 repr. and Manchester City Art Gallery, *Hard Times*, 1987, no. 53. A drawing for

the principal figures ($18\frac{1}{2} \times 14$ in.) is recorded in the *Catalogue of Paintings and Drawings collected by C.J. Galloway*, 1892, no. 275. In 1873 the walls of the artist's Chelsea studio were covered with studies of Chelsea pensioners (Edwards, *op. cit.*, p. 155).

3 Watford Museum, *op. cit.*, pp. 38–9. See also Edwards, *op. cit.*, pp. 165 ff., for a discussion of the treatment of old age and death themes by Herkomer, Walker and Pinwell, and other artists in the early 1870s. Quite independently of Herkomer the young George Clausen made a study of a Chelsea Pensioner in 1874; see Cartwright Hall, Bradford, *Sir George Clausen*, 1980, no. 1, p. 18. G.R. Gleigh in *Chelsea Hospital and its Traditions*, 1839, p. 334, had recommended the Chelsea Pensioners at prayer as a subject for artists, and the Hospital became a tourist attraction in the 19th century – although by the 1870s its authoritarian regime made it unpopular with its inmates and closure was threatened; see J.W.M. Hichberger, *Images of the Army*, 1988, pp. 142 ff.

4 Herkomer, 1890, *op. cit.*, p. 36; it was exhibited at the Royal Institute of Painters in Water Colours, *Winter Exhibition*, 1871 (10) as *Chelsea Pensioners in Church* (not for sale) (Baldry, *op. cit.*, p. 115) but is now unlocated.

5 And also possibly by the opposition of W.L. Thomas and other friends; see Herkomer, 1890, *op. cit.*, p. 43. LL 3627 was, however, originally intended for the 1874 Royal Academy and some preliminary work was probably done in 1873–4 – see J. Saxon Mills, *Life and Letters of Sir Hubert Herkomer*, 1923, p. 86. The artist wrote two detailed descriptions of the paintings of LL 3627 – in Herkomer, 1890, *op. cit.*, pp. 42 ff., and in Herkomer, 1910, *op. cit.*, pp. 107 ff.; these two descriptions are broadly similar but differ in detail; the material in the artist's *My School and my Gospel*, 1908, pp. 22 ff., merely repeats the statements in these two sources.

6 Watford Museum, *op. cit.*, p. 37, and Miss K.P. McIntosh, letter to the compiler, 7 October 1960; the figure at the extreme left of the back wall is unidentified; J.D. Winter, letter to the compiler, 21 January 1981.

7 The artist was compelled to paint broadly to get the picture finished in time for the 1875 Royal Academy. R. Treble in Watford Museum, *op. cit.*, p. 25, states that the technique in LL 3627 is indebted to Walker's 'heavily worked watercolour method'. Mills, *op. cit.*, p. 82, noted that LL 3627 also diverged from Walker's work in its absence of sentiment and in its strict realism while the artist himself wrote that LL 3627 'emancipated me from Walker' (Herkomer, 1890, *op. cit.*, p. 45). The relationship between LL 3627 and Walker's work is described in Watford Museum, *op. cit.*, pp. 23 ff. Robert de la Sizeranne, *La peinture anglaise contemporaine*, 1895, pp. 168 ff., noted the similarities in subject and sentiment between LL 3627 and Walker's 1872 *Harbour of Refuge* (Tate Gallery).

8 John Ruskin repeated this criticism, describing LL 3627 as 'scarcely artistic enough to be reckoned as of much more value than a good illustrative wood-cut' (see footnote 17); Martin Meisel, on the other hand, in *Realizations*, 1983, p. 397, sees Herkomer, in moving from black and white illustration to painting, as progressing from the reportorial and specific to the poetic and universal (relatively speaking). L.M. Edwards similarly notes various ways in which the artist made LL 3627 more pictorial and more 'composed' than the 1871 wood engraving (Edwards, *op. cit.*, pp. 156–8).

9 Fry was among the artist's first patrons.

10 According to the artist's friend George Richmond who was there (Herkomer, 1910, *op. cit.*, p. 111).

11 Leighton's letter is quoted in Mills, *op. cit.*, p. 83: 'The refined and close observation of character, the simplicity of the attitudes, the humour without a hint of buffoonery and the subtlety of the modelling go to make your work one of the most striking I have seen for some time.' Leighton's letter made Herkomer shed 'tears of joy', see Mrs. Russell Barrington, *Frederic Leighton*, 1906, vol. 2, p. 226. Holman Hunt also

praised LL 3627; see W. Holman Hunt, *Pre-Raphaelites and the Pre-Raphaelite Brotherhood*, 1905, vol. 2, p. 362.

12 Mills, *op. cit.*, pp. 87–8; Herkomer, 1882, *op. cit.*, p. 166.

13 *The Times*, 1 May 1875.

14 *Art Journal*, 1875, p. 252.

15 Quoted in Mills, *op. cit.*, p. 86.

16 Quoted in Mills, *op. cit.*, p. 85; the *Graphic*, 15 May 1875, reproduced a detail from LL 3627 – the dying man and the man next to him. Vincent van Gogh and Joseph Israels admired the *Graphic* wood engravings related to LL 3627 not the painting itself; see Arts Council, *English Influences on Vincent Van Gogh*, 1974–5, pp. 37, 43 and Barbican Art Gallery, *Van Gogh in England*, 1992, pp. 42, 139, 141. Max Liebermann's *Garten am Altmannerhaus in Amsterdam* of 1880 (Schweinfurt, Sammlung Georg Schafer) and his other asylum subjects of the 1880s, together with Angelo Morbelli's paintings of the Pio Albergo Trivulzio in Milan of 1883 and 1892 (Milan, Civica Galleria d'Arte Moderna and Paris, Musée d'Orsay), may also have been inspired by LL 3627 or by prints after it.

17 John Ruskin, *Academy Notes*, 1875, in *Works*, ed. Cook and Wedderburn, 1904, vol. 14, p. 291.

18 *Athenaeum*, 5 June 1875, p. 755. For further reviews and other critical reaction, see Arts Council, *Great Victorian Pictures*, 1978, no. 20. W.M. Rossetti in the *Academy*, 22 May 1875, p. 538, thought that the principal figure had fallen asleep but he, too, noted the 'resolute unswerving realism' applied to 'a subject of actual life (common in itself, yet far from common in its pictorial externals)'. The *Pall Mall Gazette*, 5 May 1875, also carried a long and interesting review noting that Herkomer had abandoned the idyllic subjects favoured by Frederick Walker for naturalistic portraiture without drama, pathos or any obvious compositional devices; the *Saturday Review*, 29 May 1875, p. 689, detected the influence of Legros in LL 3627; Hichberger, *op. cit.*, p. 146, discusses the relationship between LL 3627, with its heroic treatment of the poor, and French Realism.

19 *Magazine of Art*, 1880, pp. 262–3.

20 J.K. Huysmans (in *L'Art Moderne*, 1969, p. 47) reported that Herkomer's success in Paris in 1878 made him famous there; E. Chesneau, *La Peinture anglaise*, 1882, pp. 294–5, confirms the success of LL 3627 in Paris in 1878 and explains that the painting was 'd'une excellente facture, largement peinte, chose rare chez nos voisins'. Lady Dilke in the *Academy*, 6 July 1878, p. 21, similarly noted that LL 3627 was the most popular British picture at the exhibition. Van Gogh also wrote of the success of LL 3627 in Paris (Barbican Art Gallery, *op. cit.*, p. 141). Charles Tardieu wrote an extended review of LL 3627 at the 1878 Paris *Exposition Universelle* ('La Peinture à l'Exposition Universelle de 1878', *L'Art*, 1879, vol. 16, p. 162):

*mais la grand toile,* la Dernière Assemblée, *qui a été, on peut le dire, une des plus légitimes sensations de l'Exposition universelle, est franchement anglaise, non pas seulement par le sujet, mais par le caractère de l'interpretation. Peindre ce qu'on voit, cela paraît très-simple* [sic]*; mais rien que pour voir, à plus forte raison pour peindre, encore faut-il comprendre. M. Herkomer a peint ce qu'l a vu, mais s'il a compris, s'il a magistralement rendu la scène qu'il avait sous les yeux, s'il en a fidèlement exprimé le sentiment, c'est qu'il est devenu plus anglais qu'allemand. Un peintre-touriste n'eut pas pénétré aussi profondément les types, pour ne pas dire les âmes, parce qu'il n'aurait pas eu le temps de se laisser pénétrer lui-même par les innombrables fluides physiologiques et psychologiques qui se dégagent d'une civilisation nationale et se trahissent dans ses moindres manifestations.*

M. Vachon in *Les peintres étrangers a l'Exposition Universelle de 1878*, 1878, p. 9, found LL 3627 the most remarkable picture of the British section, close to Bonnat in style with figures 'merveilleusement exécutées' and with 'une varieté d'expressions vraiment étonnante' in the faces. An engraving showing crowds of spectators admiring LL 3627 at the 1878 Paris exhibition was published in the *Graphic*, 29 June 1878 (see Barbican Art Gallery, *op. cit.*, p. 141).

21 Herkomer, 1890, *op. cit.*, p. 52.

22 Mills, *op. cit.*, p. 273; so in a different sense was Herkomer's *Eventide* (Walker Art Gallery, Liverpool).

23 See H.D. Rodee, *Scenes of Rural and Urban Poverty in Victorian Painting, 1850–1900*, 1975, p. 218. For Hutchison's painting, which is very close in concept to LL 3627, see Gabriel Setoun, 'R. Gemmell Hutchison', *Art Journal*, 1900, p. 324 (repr) and Fine Art Society, Edinburgh, *Robert Gemmell Hutchison*, 1975, no. 45 (repr).

24 *Sir Cuthbert Quilter's Pictures*, n.d., p. 32, see also F.G. Stephens, 'The Collection of Mr. W. Cuthbert Quilter', I, *Magazine of Art*, 1897, p. 127 with an analysis of LL 3627.

**JACOMB-HOOD, George Percy** (1857–1927)

### *Two Boys in a Boat*

LL 3408 (TM 329, WHL 674)
Canvas: 62.5 × 88 cm
Signed: *P. JACOMB-HOOD '87* (?)
Inscribed: (on boat) *ELIZA*

This painting is probably to be identified with Jacomb-Hood's *Off Boscombe, two boys in a boat, sandy shore in the distance*, 24 × 34 in.[1] and the coast line visible in it does resemble the area around Bournemouth;[2] the subject matter in particular is similar to that used by the artist's close friend, Henry Scott Tuke.

PROV: Possibly Lever sale, Knight, Frank and Rutley 15–18 June 1926, lot 187, retained at Hulme Hall, Port Sunlight;[3] sold to Lever Brothers 1926; presented by Lever Brothers 1983.

1 Lot 187 in the Lever sale of 15–18 June 1926; see provenance.

**HOLLINGSWORTH, Ruth (Mrs. R.S. Hellaby)** (active 1906–1934)

### *The Wood, Thornton Manor*

LL 3651 (WHL 2628)
Canvas: 38.2 × 36 cm
Signed: *R. Hollingsworth*

The gardens at Thornton Manor were laid out from 1905 onwards by Thomas H. Mawson and by Lever himself, the owner.[1] The lake is about a quarter of a mile west of the house.

PROV: Bought by Lever from the artist 1915 (£30).

1 N. Pevsner and E. Hubbard, *The Buildings of England, Cheshire*, 1971, p. 360; Clive Aslet, 'Thornton Manor, Cheshire', II, *Country Life*, 8 July 1982, pp. 110–13.

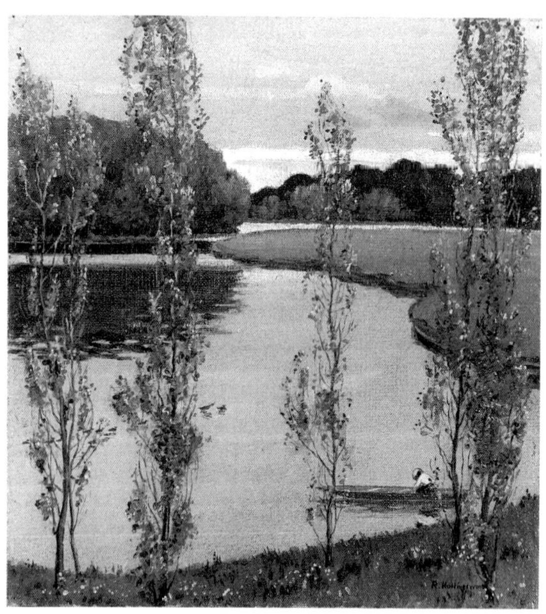

*The Wood, Thornton Manor* LL 3651

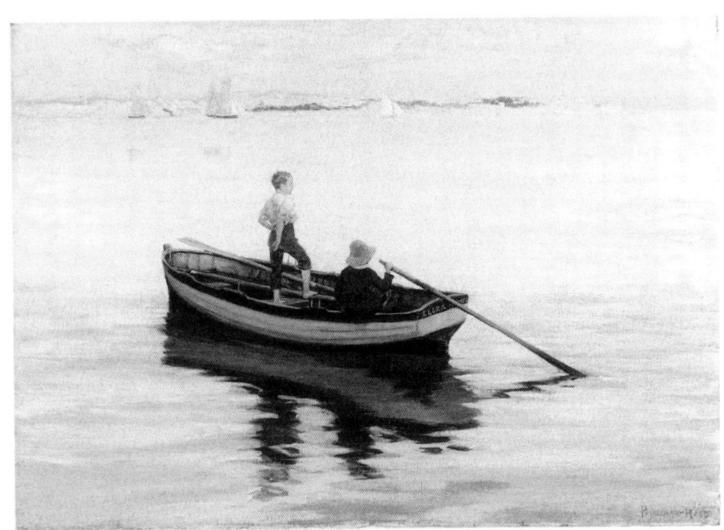

*Two Boys in a Boat* LL 3408

2 The artist usually spent his summers in the 1880s at Torcross and Start Bay in Devonshire (G.P. Jacomb-Hood, *With Brush and Pencil*, 1925, p. 26, and the *Registers of Henry Scott Tuke*, ed. B.D. Price, 1983, R13–R19) but his exhibits at the 1887–8 Royal Society of British Artists exhibition indicate that in 1887 he was in the area around Poole and Bournemouth. The boat in LL 3408 is perhaps situated outside Poole Harbour looking towards Sandbanks (Annette Downing, letter to the compiler, 29 October 1984).

3 Catalogue annotated with MS notes; Hulme Hall was then used by Lever Brothers.

## *Lifeboat*

LL 3414
Canvas[1]: 102 × 127 cm
Signed: *P. JACOMB-HOOD*
Inscribed: *SUNLIGHT LIFEBO / TOIL AND TROUBLE*

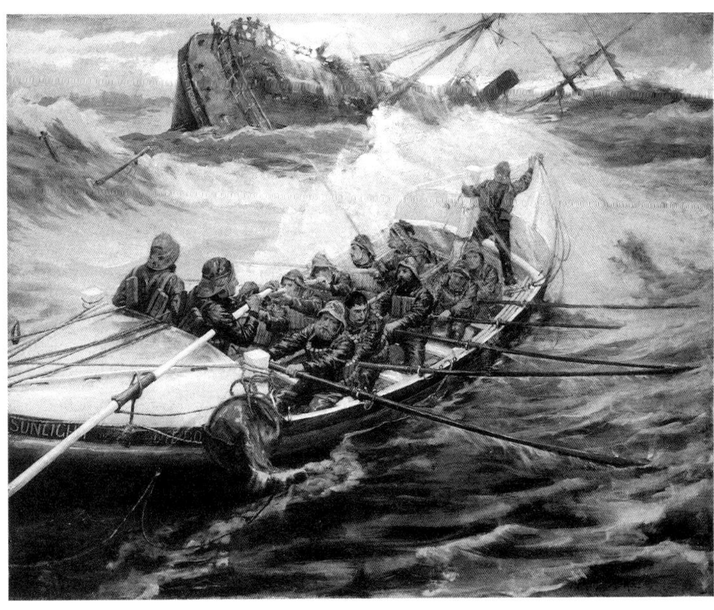

*Lifeboat* LL 3414

This painting was presumably painted for use as an advertisement for Sunlight or Lifebuoy Soap or possibly it was adapted for this purpose by the addition of the inscription. Although noted for his graphic work, Jacomb-Hood does not seem to have been employed extensively by Lever Brothers.[2]

PROV: Presented by Lever Brothers 1983.

1 *ECHERT P.R.B.F. AND CO. 63 REGENT ST., LONDON W* is inscribed on the stretcher.

2 See P. Bradshaw, *Art in Advertising*, 1925, pp. 356 ff., and W. Shaw Sparrow, *Advertising and British Art*, 1924, pp. 173 ff. No advertising directly dependent on LL 3414 has been traced, but the Lifebuoy advertisement in (for example) *Punch*, 25 December 1901, vol. 121, p. iii, has many figures and indeed the whole composition borrowed from LL 3414. The *Illustrated London News*, 19 October 1889, p. 489, contained an engraving signed by H.C. Seppings-Wright showing the rescue of some fishermen by the Llandudno lifeboat; the lifeboat was prominently named on its bows and on the caption *Sunlight No. 1*. The lifeboat image was evidently used widely to publicize Lifebuoy soap and the sponsorship of actual lifeboats was part of this campaign. For Lever's use of paintings in his advertising campaigns, see p. xiii.

## JOPLING, Louise (1843–1933)

### *Blue and White*

LL 3413
Canvas: 123.5 × 84 cm
Signed: *Louise Jopling*

The reviewer of the Royal Academy exhibition in the *Athenaeum*[1] strongly criticized the drawing and painting of the two women 'which are introduced doubtless in order to set off the rawness of a ewer and bowl of Canton enamel'; he then went on to compare the painting unfavourably with the wallpaper 'which it strongly resembles'. The domestic activities of women were a popular subject with female artists in the late 19th century.[2]

REPR: *Royal Academy Pictures*, 1896, p. 158.

PROV: Bought by Lever at the 1896 Royal Academy Exhibition;[3] presented by Lever Brothers 1983.

EXH: Royal Academy 1896 (441).[4]

1 *Athenaeum*, 6 June 1896, p. 752.

2 See Charlotte Yeldham, *Women Artists in 19th Century France and England*, 1984, vol. 2, p. 164 lists pictures with this subject matter painted between 1870 and 1900.

3 Lever lent LL 3413 to the 1897 Liverpool Autumn Exhibition (no. 373). He renamed it *Home Bright*,

*Blue and White* LL 3413

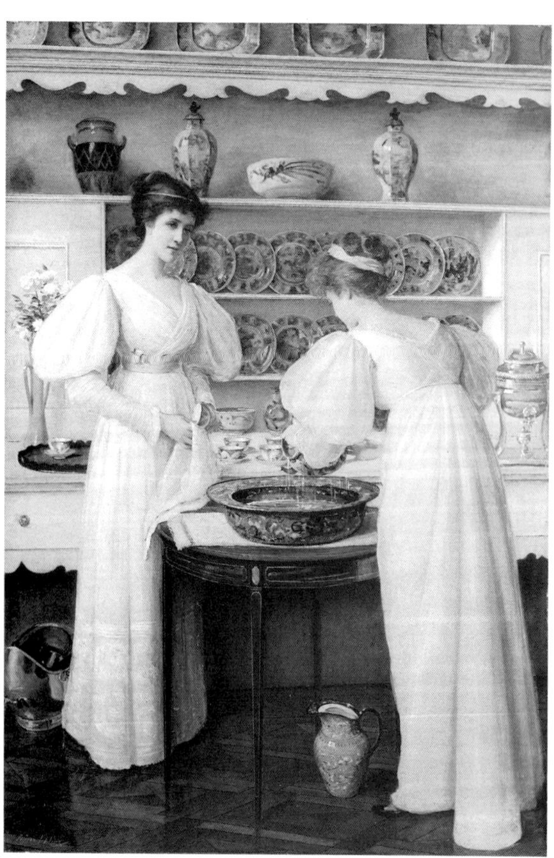

*The Vision* LL 3748

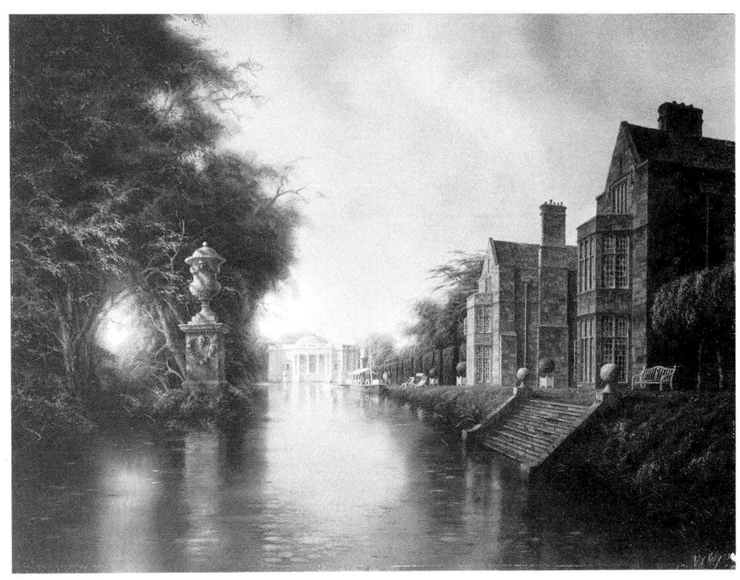

*Hearts Light* and used it for advertising Sunlight Soap; an undated poster reproducing LL 3413 as a Sunlight Soap advertisement is in the Port Sunlight Heritage Centre; in it a carton of Sunlight Soap has been added to the items on the table. For further details about the paintings which he bought for advertising purposes see p. xiii.

4 The Royal Academy picture was described by Henry Blackburn, *Academy Notes*, 1896, p. 16 as 'two girls in white, washing blue china'.

## KELLY, Felix (born 1916)

### *The Vision*

LL 3748 (LP 78)
Board: 56.5 × 77.5 cm
Signed: *Felix Kelly 73*

This painting was commissioned by the Trustees of the Lady Lever Art Gallery in 1972 to commemorate the fiftieth anniversary of the opening of the Gallery.[1] The press release issued on behalf of the Gallery on 18 July 1973[2] states: 'In a fanciful arrangement – professionally referred to as a caprice – the work depicts both the classical exterior of the Gallery and Thornton Manor, home of the Leverhulme family. The two buildings flank the edge of the Manor lake, on which floats a steam launch.'

PROV: Commissioned by the Trustees of the Lady Lever Art Gallery 1972 (£1,545).

1 The artist met the Trustees to discuss the commission on 19 April 1972; he had worked for Unilever Ltd., in London between 1935 and 1938.

2 Published in the *Birkenhead News*, 27 July 1973.

## KNIGHT, Laura (1877–1970)

### *Ballet*

LL 3650 (LP 45)
Canvas: 63.8 × 76.5 cm
Signed: *Laura Knight*

Although some ballet scenes were included in the artist's 1912 exhibition at the Leicester Galleries, most of her ballet paintings date from the years immediately after the First World War. In 1919 she obtained permission to work backstage at the Diaghilev Ballet[1] which had London seasons that year and in 1920, 1921 and each year between 1924 and 1928. This painting is clearly based on a

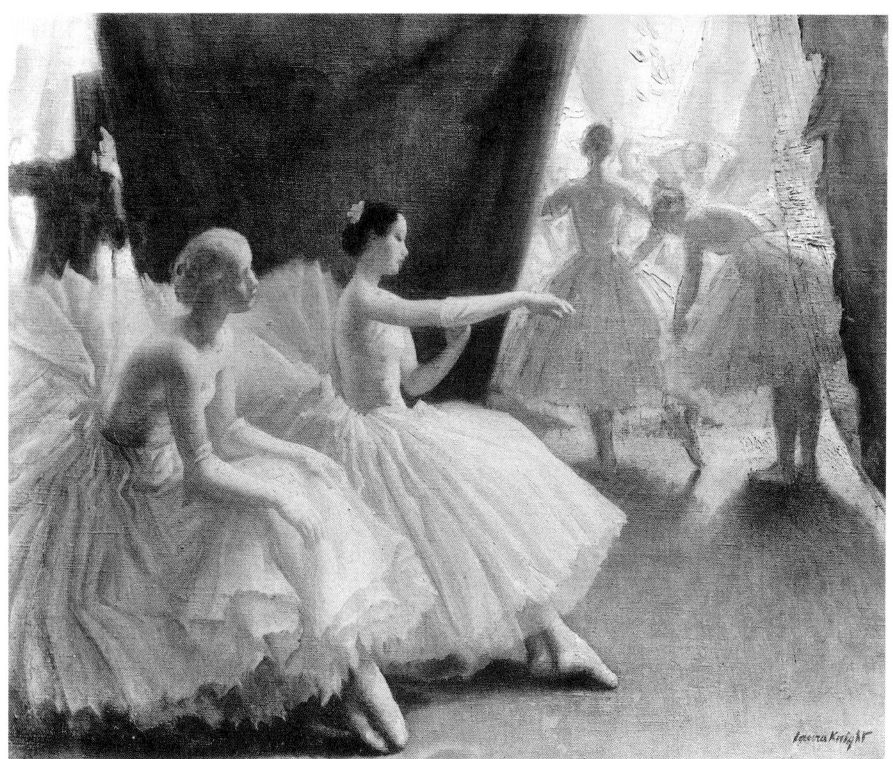


*Ballet* LL 3650

signed but undated drawing inscribed *Diaghilev Ballet, Back Stage*[2] and presumably made by the artist during one of her sketching sessions at that ballet.

Laura Knight became a member of the Royal Academy in 1936 and her paintings at the Academy's summer exhibition that year (including *Ballet*) were generally regarded by the critics as the most remarkable of the exhibition; many of these critics compared *Ballet* with similar subjects by Degas[3] and at least two[4] of them preferred it to her larger and more spectacular works in the same exhibition.

REPR: *Royal Academy Illustrated*, 1936, p. 58.

PROV: Bought from the artist 1936 (£550).

EXH: Royal Academy 1936 (199).

1 Laura Knight, *Oil Paint and Grease Paint*, 1936, pp. 224 ff.; Janet Dunbar, *Laura Knight*, 1975, pp. 99 ff.; Caroline Fox, *Dame Laura Knight*, 1988, pp. 47 ff.

2 Sotheby's sale 26 September 1985, lot 305.

3 H. Granville Fell, 'At the Summer Exhibitions', *Connoisseur*, 1936, vol. 97, p. 342; Douglas Goldring in 'Royal Academy: Summing up', *Studio*, 1936, vol. 112, p. 35.

4 Goldring, *op cit.* and Fell, *op cit.*

## **LE BAS, Edward** (1904–1966)

### ***Dinner at the Garrick***

LL 3914 (LP 65)
Canvas: 76 × 110.5 cm
Signed: *E. le Bas*

This is one of many restaurant scenes painted by the artist in the 1930s and 1940s.[1] The figure seated in the foreground at the right may be the artist's close friend Charles Ginner.[2] The setting is not the Garrick Club[3] but may be the Garrick Hotel and Restaurant which occupied the building at the corner of Irving Street and Charing Cross Road between about 1900 and 1965.[4] The same restaurant appears perhaps in Le Bas's *Barmaid at the Garrick* of 1944[5] and certainly in his *Restaurant*.[6] The artist's diary for 1946[7] notes that he was at the Garrick on 22 March 1946.

REPR: *The Times*, 4 May 1946.

PROV: Bought from the artist 1946 (£200).

EXH: Royal Academy 1946 (230).

1 For a discussion of some of them see Iain Gale, 'The Life, Art and Collection of Edward Le Bas', *Apollo*, 1991, vol. 134, pp. 187–8.

2 Mrs. Ian Langlands-Pearse, conversation with the compiler, 1992.

3 Betty Beesley of the Garrick Club, letter to the compiler, 20 January 1992.

4 This restaurant seems to have been remarkable neither for its food nor for its atmosphere. Its address was 3 and 5 Charing Cross Road and 11–13 Irving Street. The building still stands but the ground floor, where presumably the restaurant was situated, seems to have been totally reconstructed in the 1960s.

5 Reproduced in Herbert Read, *British Contemporary Art*, 1951, plate 40. The picture seems to have been sold to Mrs. Louis Dreyfus in 1954 (artist's register of sales, MSS, the artist's family). The artist's family collection contains a photograph of an entirely different composition by Le Bas also entitled *Barmaid at the Garrick*.

6 A photograph of this painting is in the collection of the artist's family; it was probably exhibited at the Royal Academy 1946 (206). It was photographed by A.C. Cooper and given their negative number 138601; LL 3914 was also

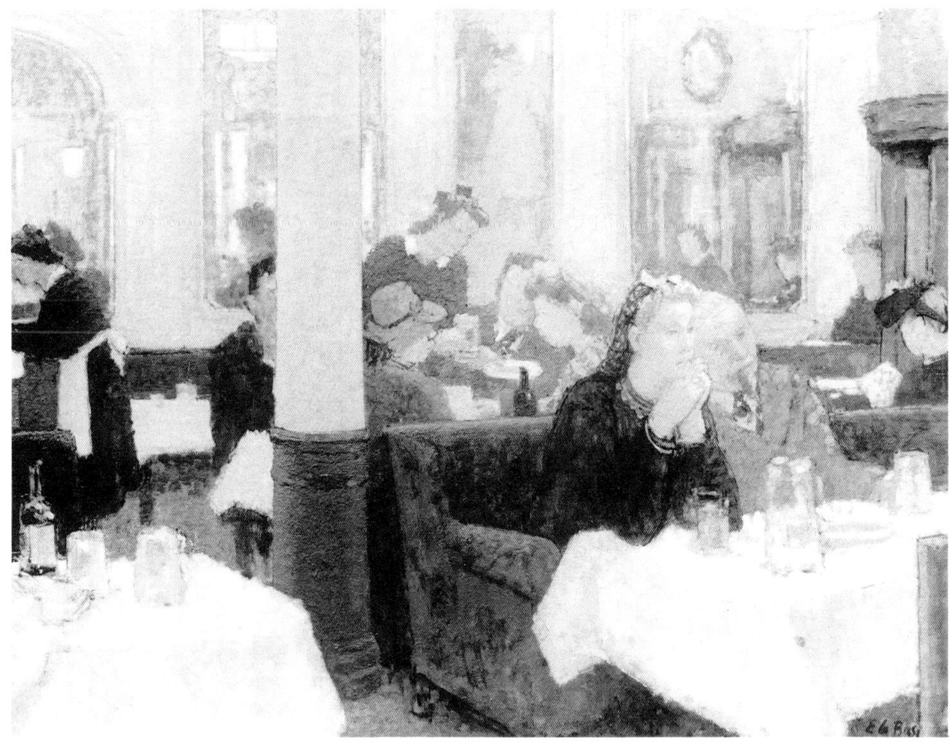

*Dinner at the Garrick*
LL 3914

photographed by A.C. Cooper and given their negative number 138357 indicating that the two paintings were probably painted at about the same time.

7 Still in the possession of the artist's family.

**LEIGHTON, Frederic** (1830–1896)
***The Daphnephoria***
LL 3632 (WHL 1177)
Canvas[1]: 231 × 525 cm

The Daphnephoria was a festival held every ninth year in ancient Thebes (and elsewhere) in honour of Apollo. The Theban ceremony, shown here, originated in a dream of Polemates, general of the Theban (or Boeotian) army during an attack on Thebes by the Aeolians; in his dream Polemates saw a girl (or youth) who gave him a suit of armour (depicted here) and ordered him to institute the Daphnephoria in Thebes. The attack was repulsed and thereafter the Daphnephoria was celebrated there thus: an olive branch was crowned with laurel and flowers; at the top a copper globe (representing the sun or Apollo), with smaller globes (representing planets and stars) hanging from it, was fixed while lower down there was another small globe (representing the moon) with purple garlands (representing the annual risings and settings of the sun) suspended from it. At the bottom the olive branch was wrapped in saffron coloured material; this branch (transformed in this painting into something rather more refined and scientific than the ancient authorities suggest) is carried in front of the Daphnephoros himself who has a golden crown on his head and a rich tunic down to his feet; behind him comes a choir of virgins singing odes by Pindar and others.[2]

Leighton had started work on the subject by January 1874 and a drawing of the entire composition was completed by February of that year. He was then delayed by problems with renting studios, by difficulties with the composition and by concurrent work on his statue, *Athlete Struggling with a Python*, and, although the *Athenaeum* reported in July 1875 that the artist had made considerable progress with the painting, it seems likely that most of the work on it was done over the winter of 1875–6.[3]

Giovanni Costa recorded that studies for the heads were painted in Rome, Capri, Lerici and Venice and that studies for the landscape were made in the pine forests of Pisa.[4] The city just visible to the left of the painting is generally described as ancient Thebes, as Leighton's subject would indicate, but the hill rising sharply over the city surmounted by buildings rather suggests Athens and its Acropolis.[5] The model for the small girls in the procession is generally stated to have been Connie Gilchrist.[6] The figure of the priest leading the chorus may have been taken from the merrymaker in the right foreground of Thomas Couture's *Decadence of the Romans* (Musée du Louvre).[7]

Many drawings and studies survive or are recorded.[8] Studies for the entire composition include one at the Victoria & Albert Museum (E 1841–1910), one reproduced in E. Rhys, *Frederic, Lord Leighton*, 1900, p. 34, one reproduced in Fine Art Society, *Drawings and Studies by the late Lord Leighton*, 1898, plate XVI (then owned by F.A. White, but by 1928 apparently in the collection of James Nicoll) and an oil sketch in the Lady Lever Art Gallery (see below). Despite the size and complexity of the final painting, despite the length of time spent on it by the artist, despite the problems it caused him, its essential composition varied hardly at all as these drawings and sketches were made. Other drawings and studies are: (1) in Leighton House, Royal Borough of Kensington and Chelsea, LH 571–580 and LH 797; (2) in the Museum and Art Gallery, Carlisle, 125–1949.450; (3) in the National Gallery of Victoria, Melbourne, 294/2; (4) in the Ashmolean Museum, Oxford; (5) in the Royal Academy, notebooks XV and XXXV, tracings 11–13, 23, 56, 64; (6) recorded in Fine Art Society, *op. cit.*, plates XIII, XIV and

XV (the drawing appearing as plate XIV was with Powney and Hartnoll in 1979); (7) recorded in the Julian Hartnoll exhibition catalogue, *Victorian Figure Studies*, 1980, no. 23; (8) in the Victoria & Albert Museum, E 1840–1910, 9053–9054 and perhaps 9055; (9) (?) an oil study of pine trees, no. 175, in the Royal Academy, *Winter Exhibition* 1897, then owned by Andrew K. Hichens (lot 182 in the artist's sale, Christie's 11 and 13 July 1896); (10) (?) an oil study of cypress trees, lot 86 in the artist's sale, Christie's 11 and 13 July 1896, bought Earl of Carlisle; (11) reproduced in A.L. Baldry, 'Lord Leighton's Sketches', *Magazine of Art*, 1897, p. 69; (12) recorded in an unidentified reproduction in the Witt Library (the large singing maiden at the front of the group nearest the spectator); (13) exhibited at the Royal Society of British Artists, 1888–9 (157); (14) exhibited at the Grosvenor Gallery, *Winter Exhibition* 1880 (383, 397–399, 402–405); (15) recorded in the F.A. White sale, Christie's 18 December 1925, lots 15 and 16; (16) reproduced in F.G. Dumas, *Modern Artists*, 1896 (*Sir Frederic Leighton* by Lady Dilke), pp. 11–13. Leighton – for the first time in his career – made clay models as studies for some of the figures in LL 3632 and three of these models survive in the Royal Academy.[9]

On its appearance at the Royal Academy in 1876, *The Daphnephoria* received enthusiastic reviews mainly concerned with describing the subject and composition. The *Art Journal* began its review of the Academy exhibition by contrasting Leighton's painting with Luke Fildes's *Widower* (Art Gallery of New South Wales, Sydney) indicating that these two paintings summed up the two essential movements of the 1870s in Britain – classicism and realism. The *Saturday Review*[10] was perhaps the most perceptive:

*Beauty here, as with the Greeks, moves to worship; it is a beauty calm and serene, unshadowed by a cloud, unmarred by violent action. The ancients regarded slow movements as indicative of great minds. In this procession the movement comes out of repose, and to repose it will return. It may be fairly objected that the colour seems to derive its tertiary concords from Germany, with a possible infusion from M. Hamon and other vaporists in France. The generic style also, like the colour, is composite; assuredly it cannot be ranked as strictly Greek; perhaps it may be best designated as Romantic–Classic.*

Among subsequent critics, two artists made notable contributions. William Holman Hunt[11] wrote to *The Times* in 1893 pleading that the painting might be bought for the National Gallery:

*You may look altogether in vain in Continental schools for any work approaching its excellence as to either refinement of expression, appropriateness of action, beauty of form, fertility of invention in incident and decorative feeling or in pictorial subtlety and ability in drawing and colour and the charms of simple, unforced light and shade, with its accumulated difficulty and happily escaped danger.*

Five years later Sir William Blake Richmond[12] had this to say:

*Perhaps 'The Daphnephoria' is the picture of Leighton's that most exhaustively combines the various ideals he set himself to achieve, and, upon the whole, it may be said to be his most homogeneous and consummate performance. The subject chosen was admirably suited to the temperament of the artist, it gave him full scope for the display of a luxurious interpretation of animate and inanimate nature which he relished so keenly: it enabled him to revel in lines of harmony and contrast and to arrange agreeable quantities, while his technique was exactly in sympathy with the pellucid atmosphere of Greece, and the refined and crisp forms of her landscape: it enabled him to suggest the scent of a pine forest, and to colour those young men, maidens and children with a flush of youth, and to figure the serene enjoyment of their lives. It is an idyll, a lyric poem, belonging to a class of painting that Keats's 'Ode to the Grecian Urn' belongs to in poetry. The picture is alive with beauty, it teems with rich associations, with antique life, and yet it is modern. It is a picture that could only have been painted in this century; the classic feeling it demonstrates is of to-day, when the severer forms of classic art appeal to the cultivated with more force than*

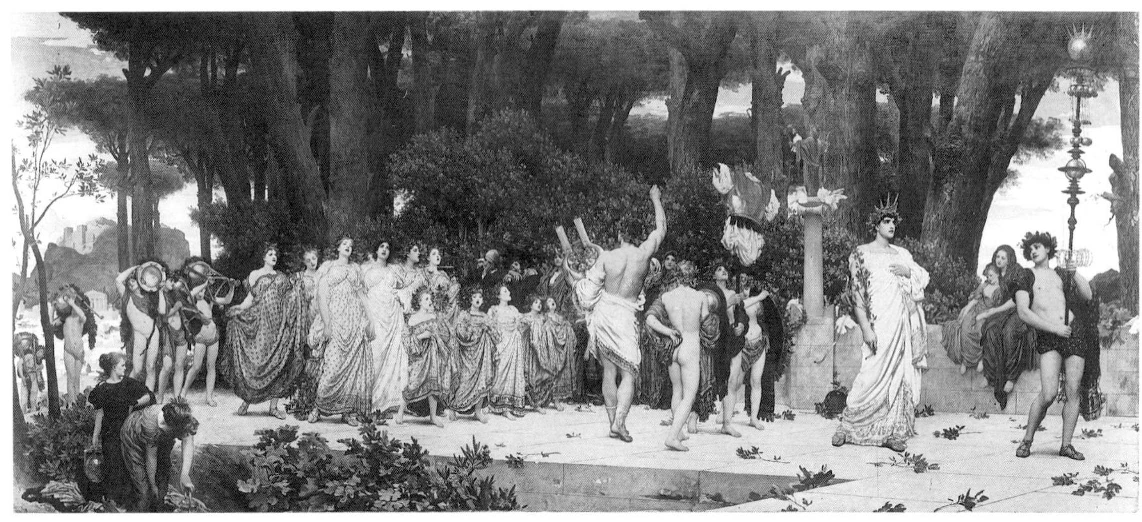

*The Daphnephoria* LL 3632 (colour plate 6)

*formerly. The feeling is Greek, not Roman; more Theocritean than Virgilian; more rustic than urban, yet highly ideal.*

By contrast, E. Chesneau, the French critic, described *The Daphnephoria* as 'purely decorative' and H.H. Statham saw it merely as 'an effective arrangement of figures and colour' with a 'bevy of buxom Greek wenches singing out *ore rotundo* and hitching up their draperies as they walk with an action that has been called ungainly, but which gives a touch of realism to the scene'; George Moore[13] was another hostile critic deploring the large number of figures and the weak design of the central figures; he argued that the spectator's attention was dissipated over the long procession which might have been appropriate for a relief but not for a painting. It is, however, surely both the grandest of Leighton's great ordered processional masterpieces and the culmination of the classical revival in British art of the 1860s and 1870s – despite perhaps a certain Aesthetic languor and decorative over-refinement.

On a more popular level the first act of W.S. Gilbert's *Patience*, first performed in 1881, contained almost a parody of Leighton's painting; towards the end of the act Bunthorne enters crowned with roses and garlands; he is accompanied by a procession of maidens dancing classically, playing archaic musical instruments and singing:

*Let the merry cymbals sound*
*Gaily pipe Pandaean pleasure*
*With a Daphnephoric bound*
*Tread a gay but classic measure.*

The frame is seen by Lynn Roberts[14] as an experimental aedicular frame 'rich, splendid and allusive', but lacking the architectural strength of Leighton's later frames.

REPR: H. Blackburn, *Academy Notes*, 1876, p. 28; E. Chesneau, *Artistes anglais contemporains*, n.d., p. 26 (after a drawing by R.W. Macbeth); Fine Art Society (photogravure) 1888 and 1897 – there is an impression in the Lady Lever Art Gallery (LP 17).

PROV: Commissioned by James Stewart Hodgson in 1873–4 (£1,500);[15] his sale, Christie's 3 June 1893, lot 24, bought Tooth (£3,937.10*s*.);[16] George McCulloch[17] sale, Christie's 23 May 1913, lot 69, bought Sampson (£2,625); bought by Lever from Gooden and Fox May 1913 (£2,850).

EXH: Royal Academy 1876 (241); Manchester, *Royal Jubilee Exhibition*, 1887 (512); Royal Academy, *Winter Exhibition*, 1897 (81); Royal Academy, *Winter Exhibition*, 1909 (100); Liverpool Autumn Exhibition 1913 (82).

1 LL 3632 is painted on a double canvas. Leighton described his working methods for LL 3630 in detail as part of a general survey of Academicians' methods conducted on the occasion of the 1876 Royal Academy Exhibition; he used a semi-absorbent white primed canvas; the composition was first sketched in, in monochrome (brown and white), then thickly scumbled over with a grey tint; this was then painted up with the full colours except for the sky which was laid in, in prime white, and washed over with umber when dry. I am indebted to Helen Valentine for this information; Leighton's account is in the Royal Academy Library; for the background see the Royal Academy, *Annual Report*, 1875, p. 15.

2 The original source for these details is the *Chrestomathia* of Proclus as noted by Mrs. Russell Barrington, *Life, Letters and Work of Frederic Leighton*, 1906, vol. 2, p. 195. Leighton owned a Latin edition of the *Chrestomathia* (his sale, Christie's 15 July 1896, lot 53), but he presumably also relied on dictionaries and encyclopaedias – John Lemprière's *Classical Dictionary*, William Smith's *Dictionary of Greek and Roman Antiquities* and others; the *Dictionnaire des antiquités grecques et romaines* of C. Daremberg and E. Saglio gives a French translation of the appropriate passage from Proclus with references to this and other sources; the tripods being carried at the back of the procession are presumably those described by Pausanias as consecrated to Apollo (*Description of Greece*, Loeb edition, 1917–35, vol. 4, p. 225 (IX, 10)) – Leighton owned another translation of the *Description of Greece* (see his sale, Christie's 15 July 1896, lot 85). The details given in the various dictionaries and other sources are not entirely consistent and Barrington, *op. cit.*, p. 196 rightly emphasized that Leighton's approach to LL 3632 was not archaeological, but he has broadly followed the various accounts fairly carefully – except that the suit of armour seen by Polemates in his dream is not recorded as part of the procession. According to Barrington, *op. cit.*, p. 196, it was 'a written account of what took place' that first inspired the artist to paint LL 3632 but the event was thought to be depicted on some Greek vases (see Daremberg and Saglio, *op. cit.*) and the armour carried aloft in the procession was probably taken from a Greek vase (Ian Jenkins, conversation with the compiler, 15 January 1986); for Leighton's interest in Greek vases generally, see Ian Jenkins, 'Frederic Leighton and Greek Vases', *Burlington Magazine*, 1983, vol. 125, pp. 597 ff.; there are no other representations of this scene in post-classical art known to the compiler.

3 *Athenaeum*, 17 January 1874, p. 100, and 7 February 1874, p. 201; the description of the drawing in the 7 February *Athenaeum* indicates that the broad outlines of the final composition were already established. Work on the statue was finally suspended in November 1875 in favour of work on LL 3632; there are five letters from Leighton to Hodgson about progress on LL 3632 in the Royal Borough of Kensington and Chelsea Libraries and Arts Service (see B. Curle, *Lord Leighton, a Catalogue of Letters*, Royal Borough of Kensington and Chelsea Libraries and Arts Services, 1983, cat. nos. 145–149, inv. nos. 12617, 12620, 12622, 12628, 12638); *Athenaeum*, 31 July 1875, p. 157. F.G. Cotman was assisting Leighton with the painting of LL 3632 during 1875–6 (Norma Watt, 'F.G. Cotman', *Norfolk Fair*, May 1984, p. 57, and A.L. Baldry, 'Frederick George Cotman', *Studio*, 1909, vol. 47, p. 170).

4 G. Costa, 'Notes on Lord Leighton', *Cornhill Magazine*, 1897, p. 378. Leighton went to Italy during most summers partly for making sketches for his paintings; he often met Costa there.

5 Ian Jenkins, conversation with the compiler, 15 January 1986; Leighton visited Athens in 1867 (Barrington, *op. cit.*, vol. 2, p. 130).

6 This observation first appears in Fine Art Society, *Drawings and Studies by the late Lord Leighton*, 1898, plate XIII. Connie Gilchrist, 1865–1946, was a child dancer and later an actress; she married the Earl of Orkney in 1892 and retired

from the stage; she is said to have acted as a model for a number of Leighton's works between about 1871 and 1877 (Barrington, *op. cit.*, vol. 2, pp. 197, 268, and L. and R. Ormond, *Lord Leighton*, 1975, pp. 98, 133). She was certainly the model for J.M. Whistler's *Harmony in Yellow and Gold: The Gold Girl* of about 1876 (now Metropolitan Museum, New York) as her name is inscribed on the canvas.

7 A. Boime, *Thomas Couture and the Eclectic Vision*, 1980, p. 555. There are probably other more general borrowings in LL 3632 from classical sculpture – in particular from the Parthenon frieze (Ian Jenkins, conversation with the compiler, 15 January 1986).

8 Stewart Hodgson, who commissioned LL 3632, is stated to have acquired all the drawings and studies for it at the same time (Edgcumbe Staley, *Lord Leighton*, 1906, p. 106).

9 Staley, *op. cit.*, p. 254, lists these models; see also E. Rhys, *Frederic Lord Leighton*, 1900, p. 68, and Ormond, *op. cit.*, pp. 92 and 163. There were models for the two girls on the wall, for three of the singing maidens, for one of the boys with a tripod and for the male leader of the choir. The Royal Academy still has bronze and plaster versions of the singing maidens and of the leader of the choir together with a bronze version of a boy with a tripod. A bronze version of the three singing maidens was formerly owned by the Fine Art Society.

10 *Art Journal*, 1876, p. 189 – Rhys, *op. cit.*, p. 111, observed that before 1876 the *Art Journal* had often been hostile to Leighton; *Athenaeum*, 29 April 1876, pp. 600–1 (see also *Athenaeum*, 7 February 1874, p. 201, for an earlier review based on a drawing for the composition); *Saturday Review*, 20 May 1876, p. 649. J. Comyns Carr in the *Academy*, 1 April 1876, p. 318, described LL 3632 as 'one of the most considerable works yet produced by the English School'. H.H. Statham in 'Reflections at the Royal Academy', *Fortnightly Review*, July 1876, vol. 26, pp. 60 ff., admired Alma-Tadema's archaeological approach to antiquity rather than the more decorative and aesthetic attitude adopted by Leighton in LL 3632. Other reviews and descriptions are quoted in Staley, *op. cit.*, pp. 105–6.

11 *The Times*, 5 June 1893.

12 Sir William Blake Richmond, *Leighton, Millais and William Morris*, 1898, pp. 19–20. Even the young Roger Fry was enthusiastic about LL 3632 – see *Letters of Roger Fry*, ed. Sutton, 1972, p. 117, but his comments in his introduction to R.R. Tatlock's 1928 Lady Lever Art Gallery *Catalogue* are much less favourable (p. 30).

13 E. Chesneau, *English School of Painting*, 1885, pp. 262–3. In his *Artistes anglais contemporains*, n.d., Chesneau found in LL 3632 'gaucheries d'attitude, mollesses dans le dessin des draperies' and he asked for 'légers traits d'un réalisme innocent'. H.H. Statham, *op. cit.*, p. 61; George Moore, 'Lord Leighton', *Cosmopolis*, 1896, vol. 1, pp. 719–20.

14 Lynn Roberts, 'Nineteenth Century English Picture Frames', *International Journal of Museum Management and Curatorship*, 1986, vol. 5, p. 279.

15 Staley, *op. cit.*, p. 106; *Athenaeum*, 17 January and 7 February, 1874, pp. 100 and 201; Ormond, *op. cit.*, p. 92; Barrington, *op. cit.*, vol. 1, p. 275. LL 3632 was painted for and hung in the dining room of Hodgson's house, Lythe Hill, near Haslemere, Surrey. The drawing room contained W.B. Richmond's four frescoes of 1873–4 entitled *The Duties of Women* and there were other murals by S. Pepys Cockerell and Stacy Marks – see E.W. Stanton, *Bygone Haslemere*, 1914, pp. 272–4; the Stacy Marks murals depicted haymaking, ploughing, angling and driving home the cows – see H.S. Marks, *Pen and Pencil Sketches*, 1894, p. 210; Hodgson bought the Lythe Hill estate in 1867 and the new Lythe Hill was then designed for him by his friend Fred Cockerell; the house seems to have been demolished in about 1980. Hodgson (1827–99) was a partner in the London merchant house of Finlay, Hodgson and Co. and in 1867 became a partner in the banking firm Baring Brothers and Co. following a merger between the two firms

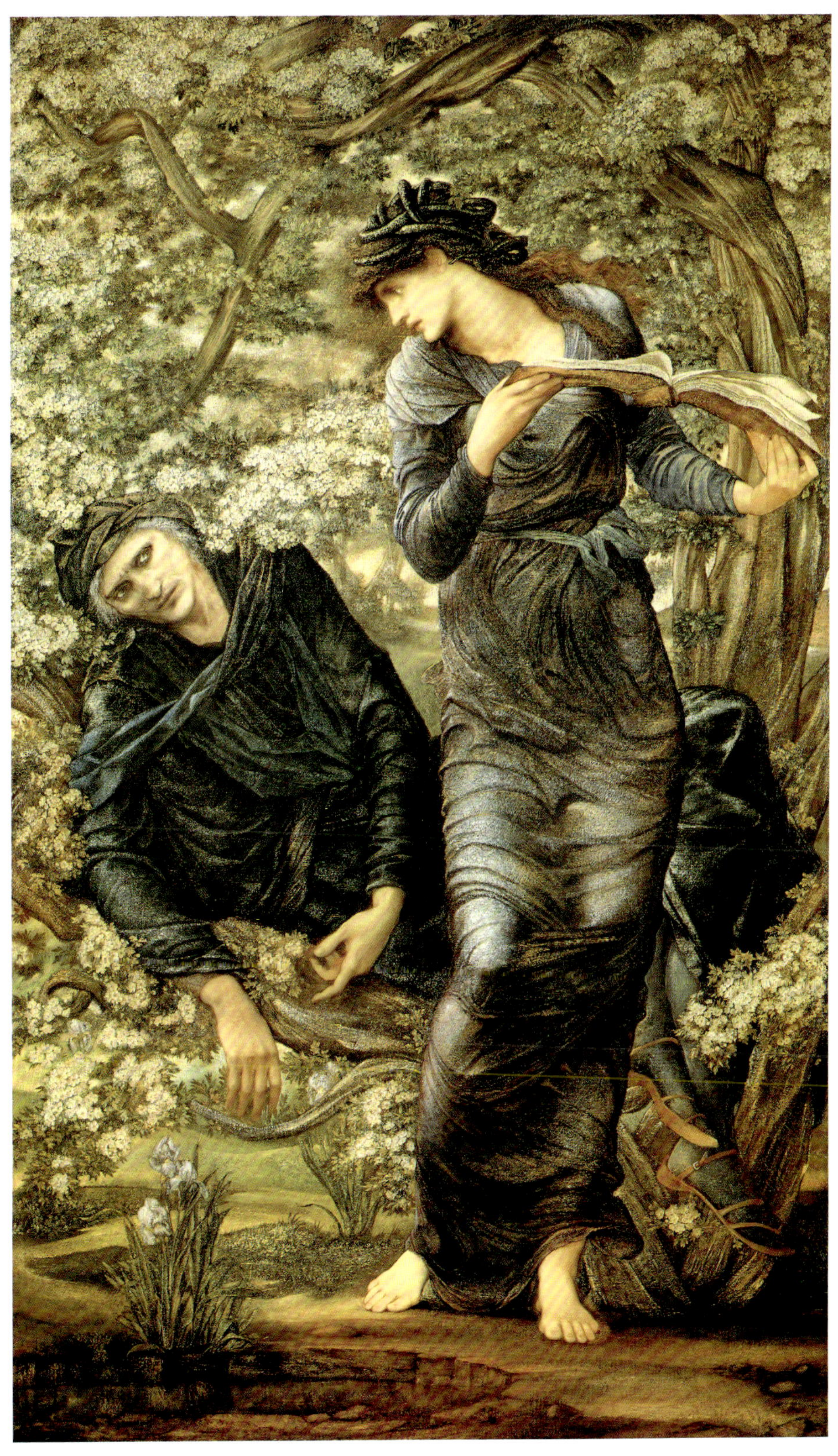

1 Edward Burne-Jones, *The Beguiling of Merlin* LL 3121

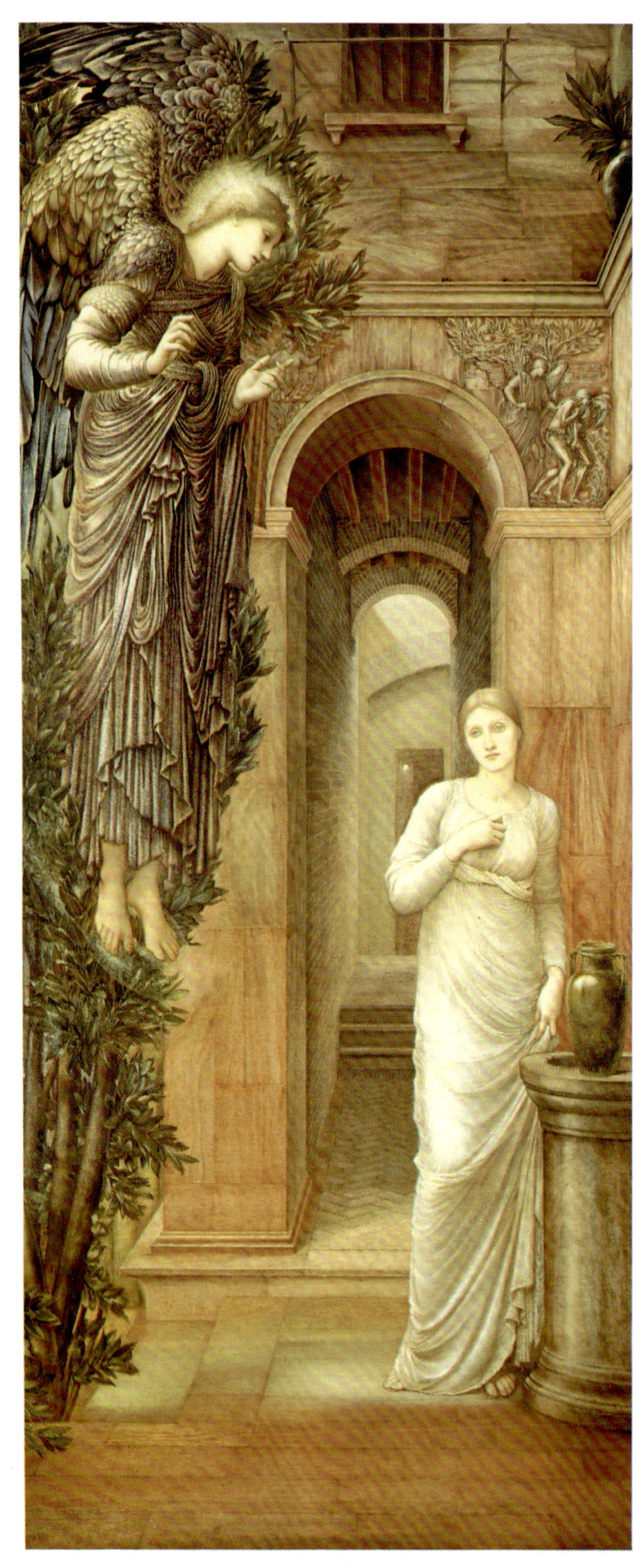

2 Edward Burne-Jones, *The Annunciation* LL 3634

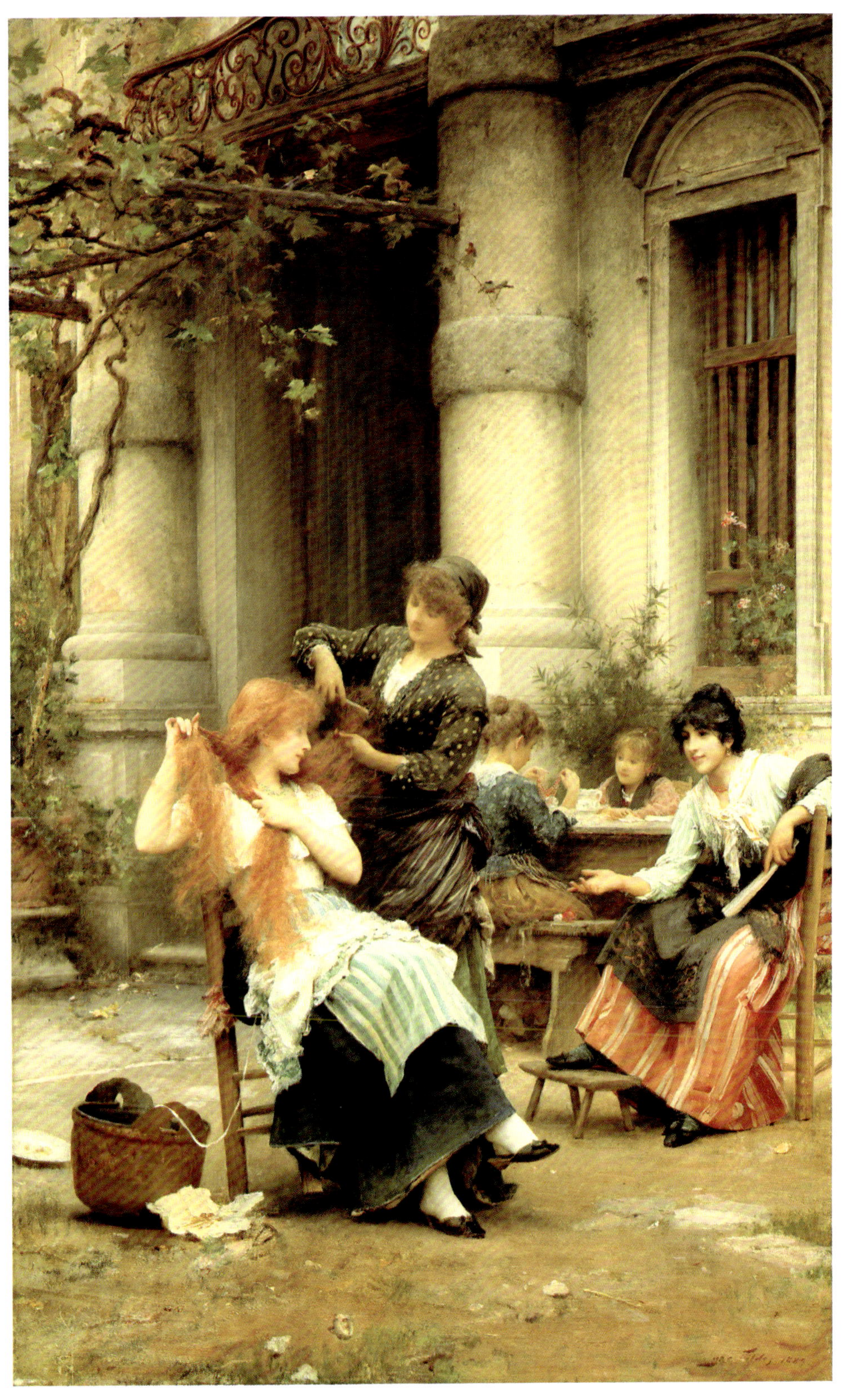

3 Luke Fildes, *An Al-fresco Toilette* LL 3621

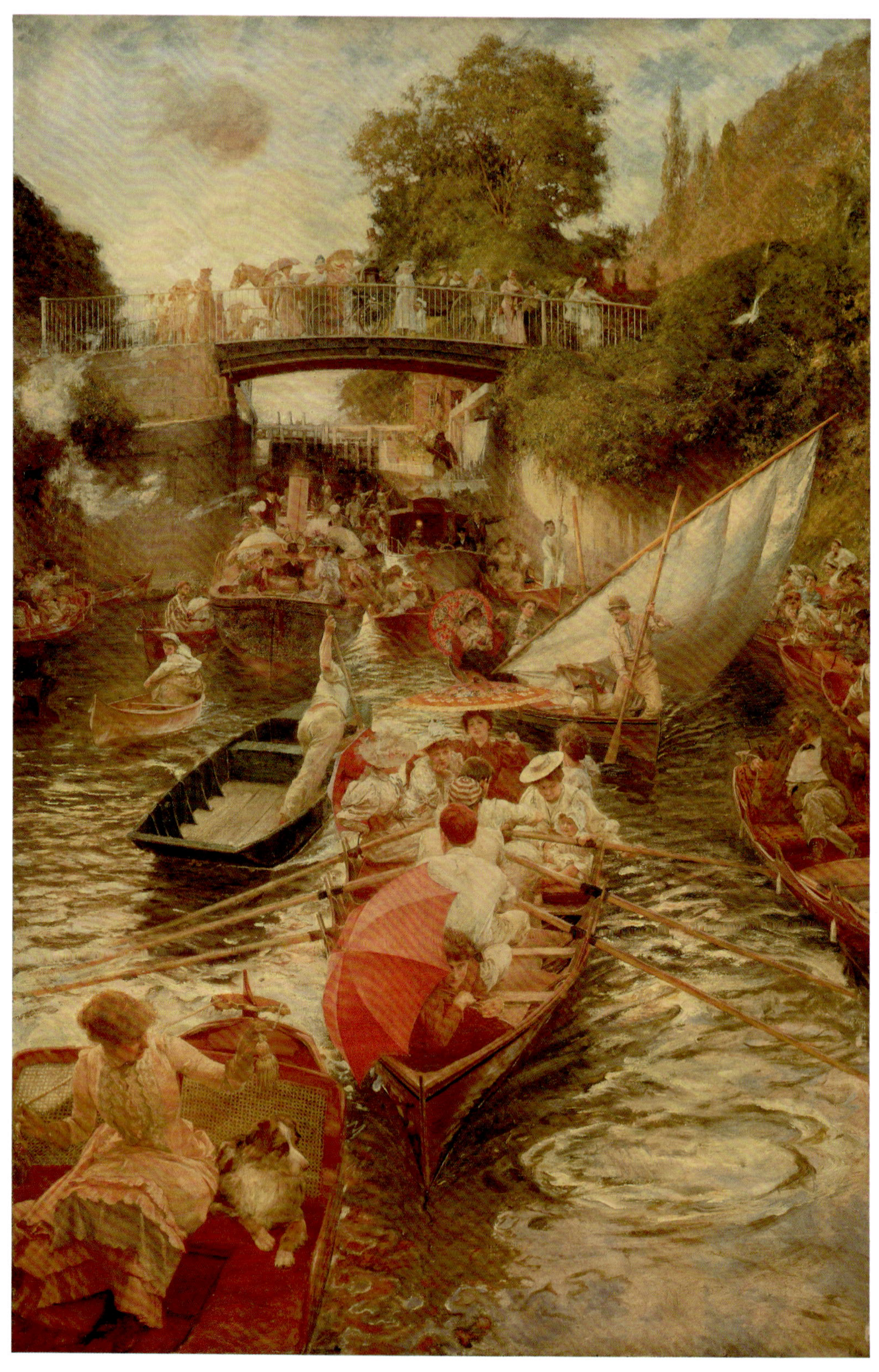

4 Edward John Gregory, *Boulter's Lock, Sunday Afternoon* LL 3149

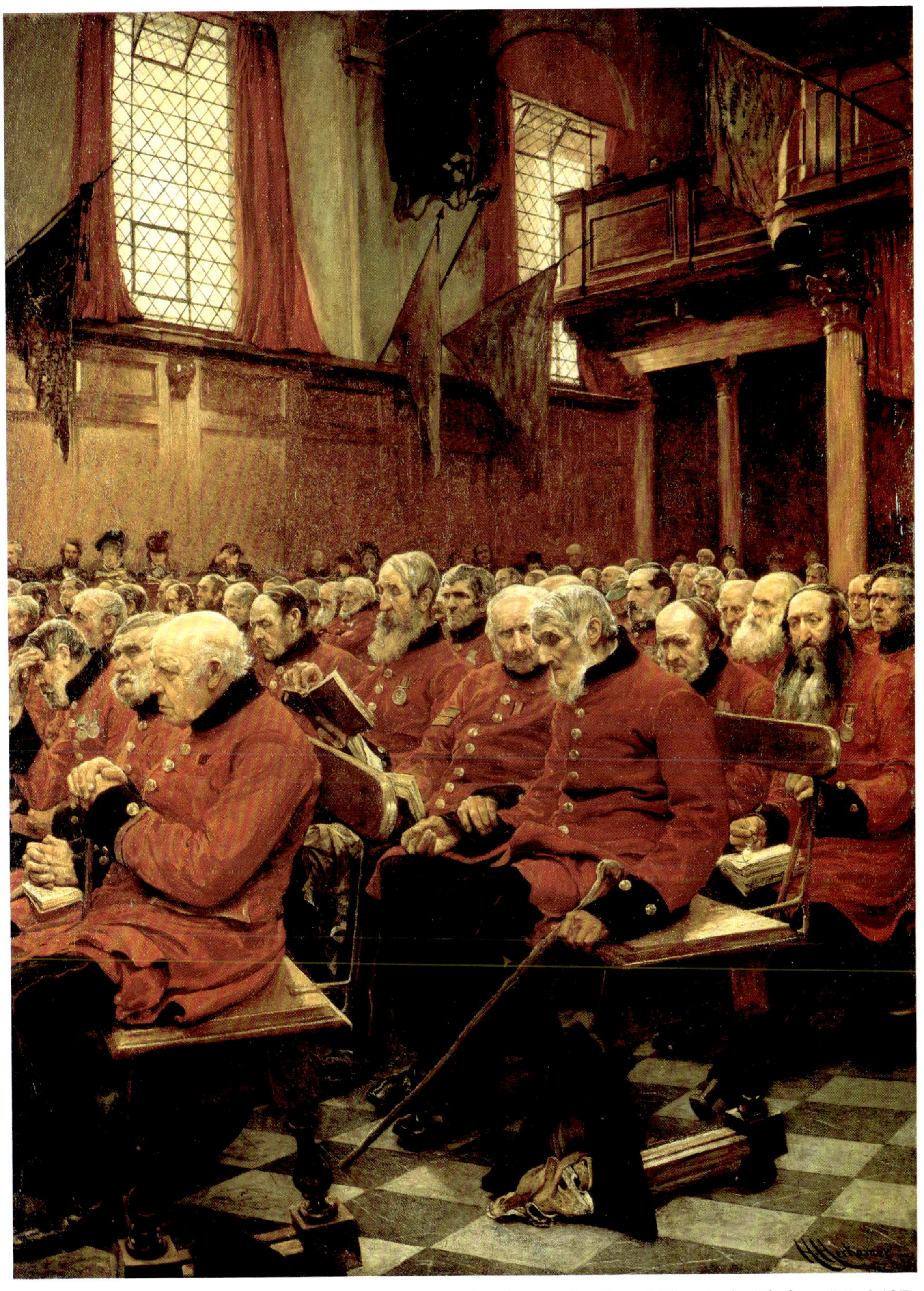

5 Hubert von Herkomer, *The Last Muster – Sunday at the Royal Hospital, Chelsea* LL 3627

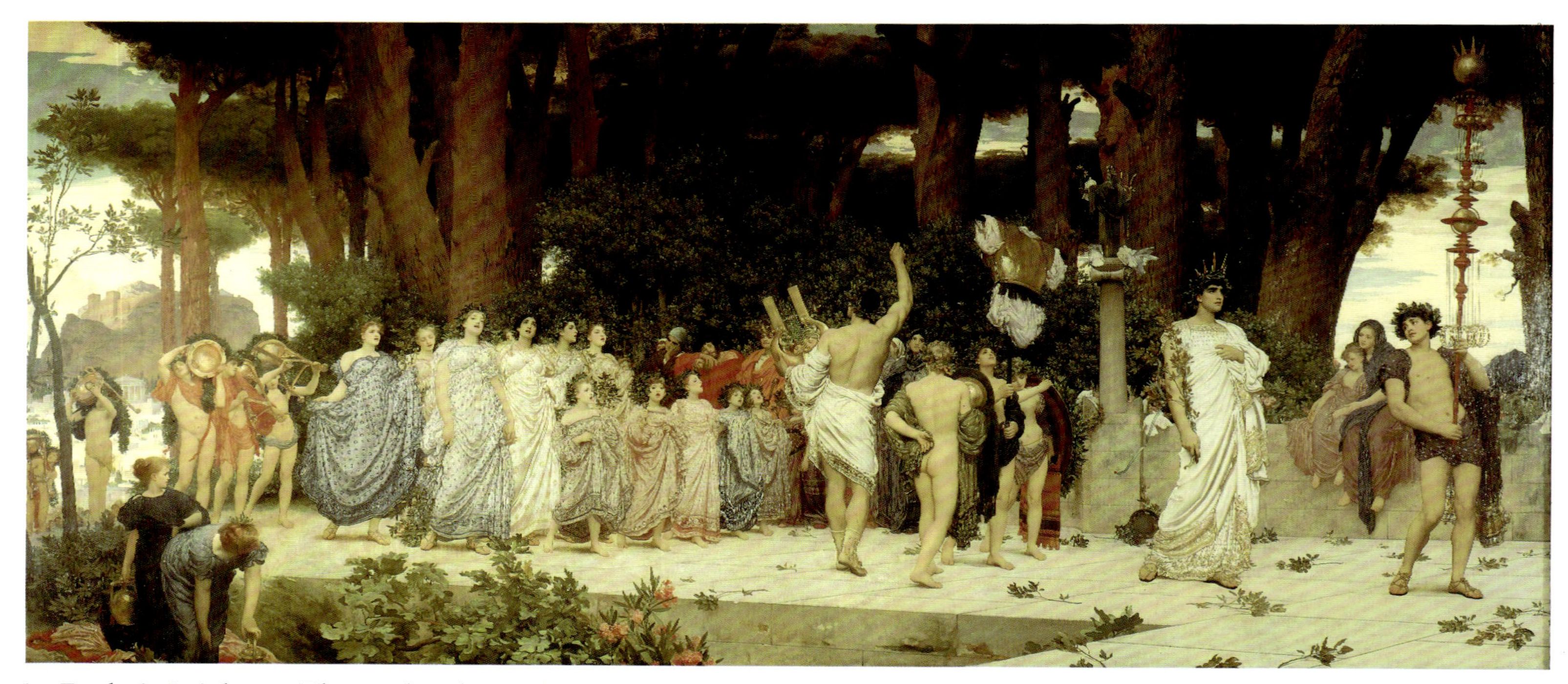

6 Frederic Leighton, *The Daphnephoria* LL 3632

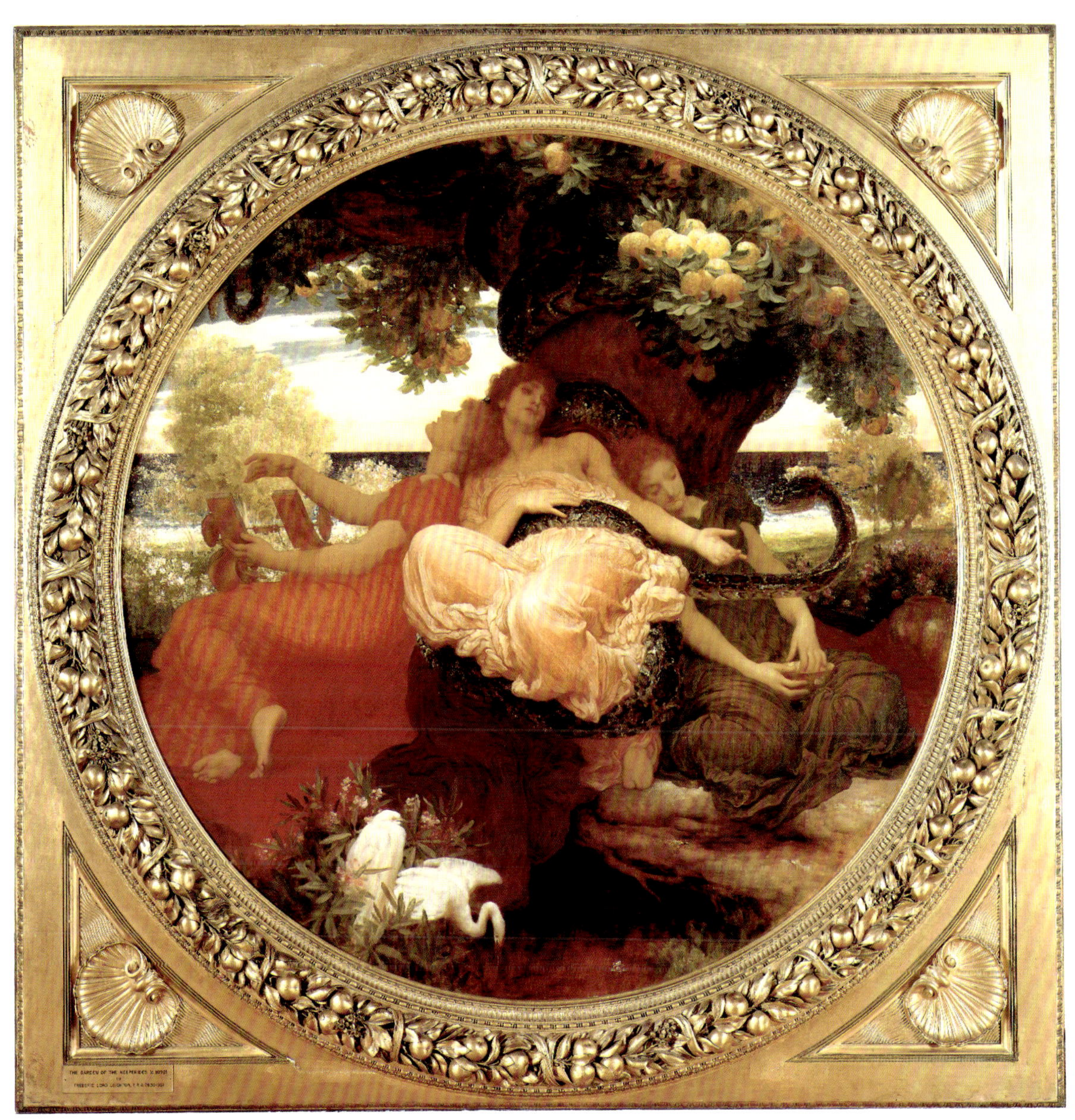


7 Frederic Leighton, *Garden of the Hesperides* LL 3139

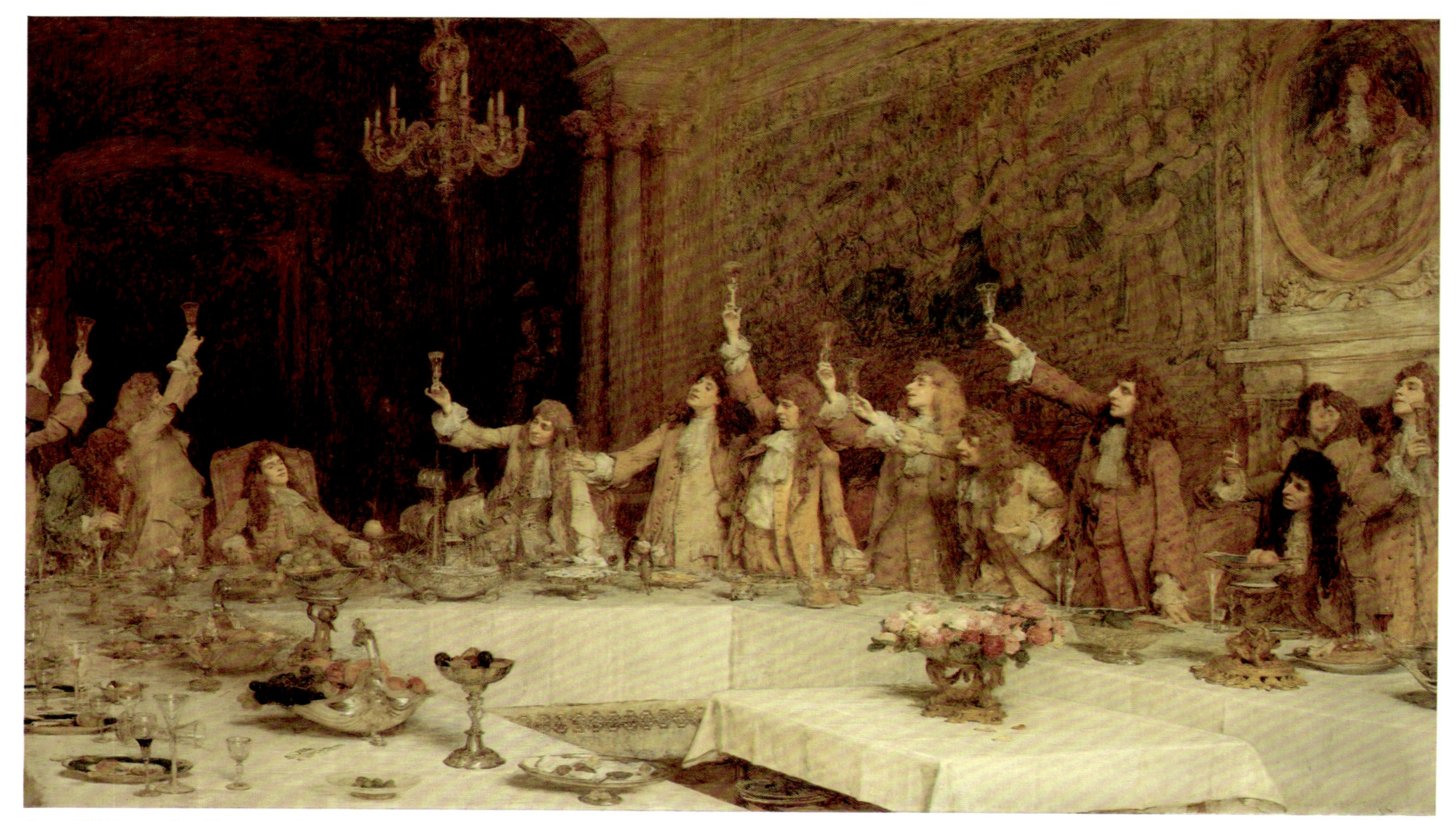

8 William Quiller Orchardson, *The Young Duke* LL 3612

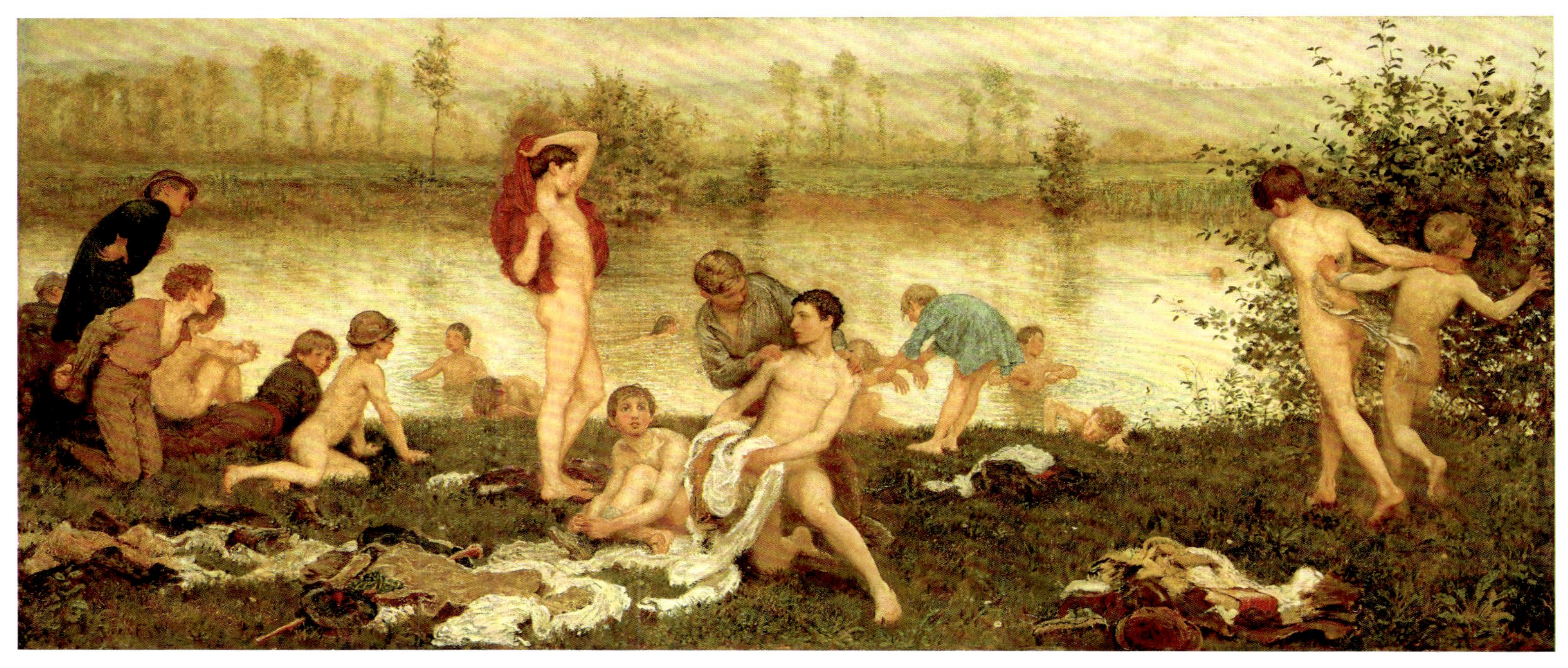

9 Frederick Walker, *The Bathers* LL 3143

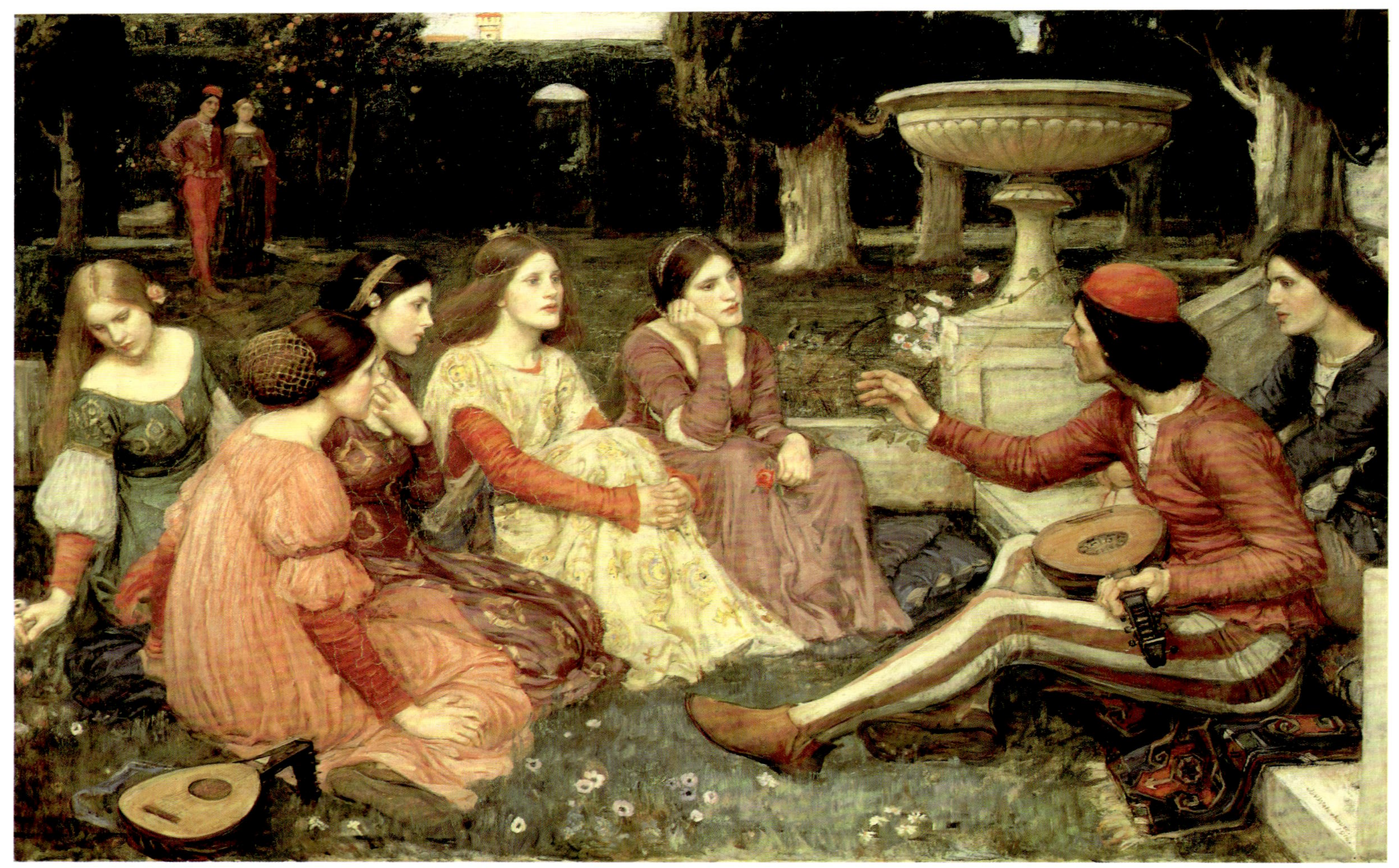

10 John William Waterhouse, *The Decameron* LL 3133

(M.J. Orbell, letter to the compiler, 11 November 1985). He was a major patron of Leighton, having bought his *The Sisters* and *Lieder ohne Worte* in the early 1860s; see Ormond, *op. cit.*, nos. 39, 253, 292, 309, 314, 336, 349, 361 for other works by Leighton in Hodgson's collection; the two men probably met at the Hogarth Club, where they were both members, in 1860 (Ormond, *op. cit.*, p. 52; Deborah Cherry, 'The Hogarth Club, 1858–1861', *Burlington Magazine*, 1980, vol. 122, p. 242); Hodgson may well have been responsible for the extensive patronage Leighton received from some financiers (see Ormond, *op. cit.*, p. 119); among them was Lord Revelstoke, another partner in Baring Brothers and Co. Hodgson's friendship with Leighton is documented by a series of letters from Leighton to him in the Royal Borough of Kensington and Chelsea Libraries and Art Service (Curle, *op. cit.*, cat. nos. 130–162).

16 Hodgson had to sell his collection following the near collapse of Baring Brothers and Co. in 1890 in order to pay off the debts of that company; Baring Brothers was reconstituted as Baring Brothers and Co. Limited, and Hodgson ceased to be a director (Orbell, *op. cit.*, and see A.C.R. Carter, *Let me tell you*, 1940, p. 80); Lord Revelstoke's paintings, including his *Golden Hours* by Leighton, were sold at the same sale.

17 McCulloch had acquired LL 3632 by 1897; see A.L. Baldry, 'The Collection of George McCulloch', *Art Journal*, 1897, p. 376.

## *Sketch for Daphnephoria*

LL 3116
Board: 26.2 × 60 cm

This sketch is very close to the 'original sketch' for *The Daphnephoria*, reproduced by the Fine Art Society in 1898;[1] in common with this sketch it has for example the old man seated at the base of the column and the bystander at the extreme right, both of whom were omitted in the final composition; in general, however, it differs only slightly from this final composition for which see p. 62.

PROV: Mrs. Eustace Smith;[2] by descent to Charles C. Smith from whom purchased 1979.

1 Fine Art Society, *Drawings and Studies by the late Lord Leighton*, 1898, plate XVI, then owned by F.A. White but by 1928 apparently in the collection of James Nicoll. This was perhaps the drawing discussed at length by the *Athenaeum*, 7 February 1874, p. 201. Another sketch for *The*

*Sketch for Daphnephoria* LL 3116

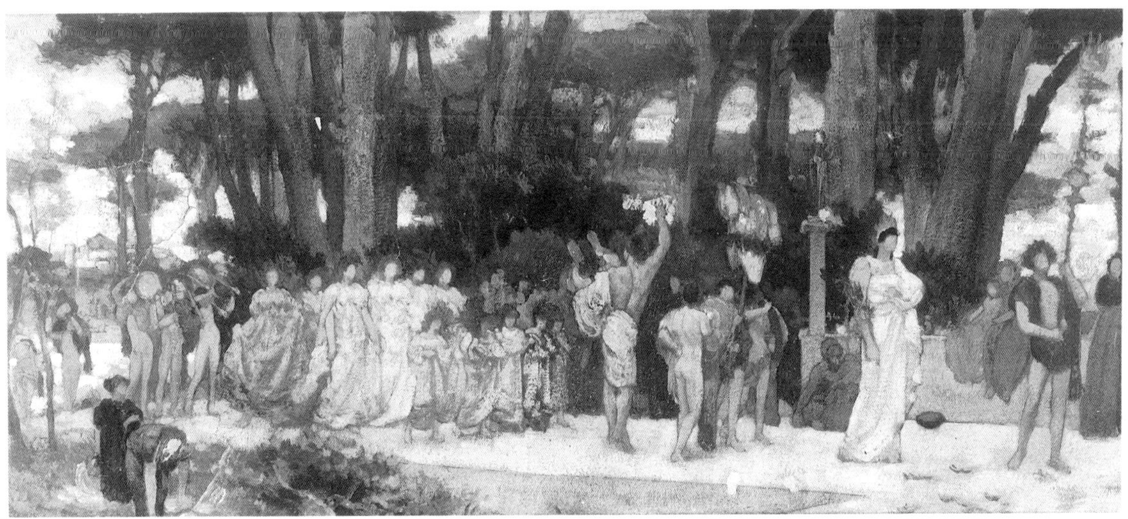

*Daphnephoria* also apparently in oil and very similar to LL 3116, but rather more finished than it, is reproduced in E. Rhys, *Frederic, Lord Leighton*, 1900, opp. p. 34. LL 3116 is not listed by L. and R. Ormond, *Lord Leighton*, 1975, p. 163 among the sketches for *The Daphnephoria*.

2 She was a friend of the artist around the 1870s and Leighton painted her portrait which was lot 43 at Sotheby's Belgravia sale, 6 October 1980 – see Ormond, *op. cit.*, pp. 72, 174 and Timothy Wilcox, 'The Aesthete Expunged', *Journal of the History of Collections*, 1993, vol. 5, p. 52, who notes that LL 3116 was probably given to her by the artist.

## *Psamathe*

LL 3630 (WHL 1175)
Canvas[1]: 85 × 66.5 cm

Psamathe was one of the fifty Nereids, the female tutelary deities of the sea shore; they are particularly identified with the Aegean, the favoured residence of their father Nereus. This painting was begun in 1879 and completed in 1880.[2]

Contemporary critics saw *Psamathe* as primarily an academic exercise; the *Magazine of Art*[3] described it as 'a fine study of the nude, with a background of sea and the hills of Capri on the horizon', but criticized the flesh as too violent in colour and cold in tone; for the *Art Journal*,[4] it was 'a surpassing piece of craftsmanship'. The *Athenaeum*[5] observed: 'The contours of the figure are exuberant, and therefore not severe in their character; they have been studied from life, and are less classical than those usually affected by Sir F. Leighton.' Later commentators were less technical in their approach; Mrs. Lang[6] found much expression in Psamathe's back and imagined what her face must be like while Rhys[7] referred to her 'dreamy loveliness'; the Ormonds[8] went further, investing the figure with the same symbolic and archetypal value that critics of the later 19th century attributed to Hippolyte Flandrin's *Jeune Homme nu, assis sur un Rocher* (Musée du Louvre); certainly *Psamathe* is very much more evocative than Leighton's much earlier Nereid picture, the rather prosaic *Actaea* of about 1868 (National Gallery of Canada, Ottawa). By contrast, for Adrienne Munich the massiveness of *Psamathe* appears 'ominous, disturbing and even grotesque'.[9]

A drawing for the composition is now in a New York private collection.[10] J.P. Russell's *Etude de nu: Madame Russell* (Musée Rodin, Paris) of 1887 seems to have been based on *Psamathe*.

REPR: H. Blackburn, *Academy Notes*, 1880, p. 58; G.R. Halkett, *Notes to the Walker Art Gallery*, 1880, p. 43.

PROV: Painted for Benson Rathbone[11] at a price of £630;[12] bought by Lever from H.E. Kidson 5 July 1893 (£315).[13]

EXH: Royal Academy 1880 (614); Liverpool Autumn Exhibition 1880 (348); Hulme Hall, Port Sunlight, *Autumn Art Exhibition*, 1902 (176).

1 Canvas stamp: Charles Roberson, 99 Long Acre, London. Roberson label also on stretcher. LL 3630 is painted on a double canvas. Leighton described his working methods for LL 3630 in detail as part of a general survey of Academicians' methods conducted on the occasion of the 1880 Royal Academy exhibition; he used a primed canvas tinted with yellow watercolour; the figure was first underpainted in cool colours with the draperies omitted, while the sky was prepared in a salmon colour with the sea in orange red; much of the work was done using thumb and fingers. I am indebted to Helen Valentine for this information; Leighton's account is in the Royal Academy Library; for the background see the Royal Academy, *Annual Report*, 1875, p. 15.

2 See Leighton's account of his working methods in LL 3630 (note 1).

3 *Magazine of Art*, 1880, p. 313.

4 *Art Journal*, 1880, p. 187.

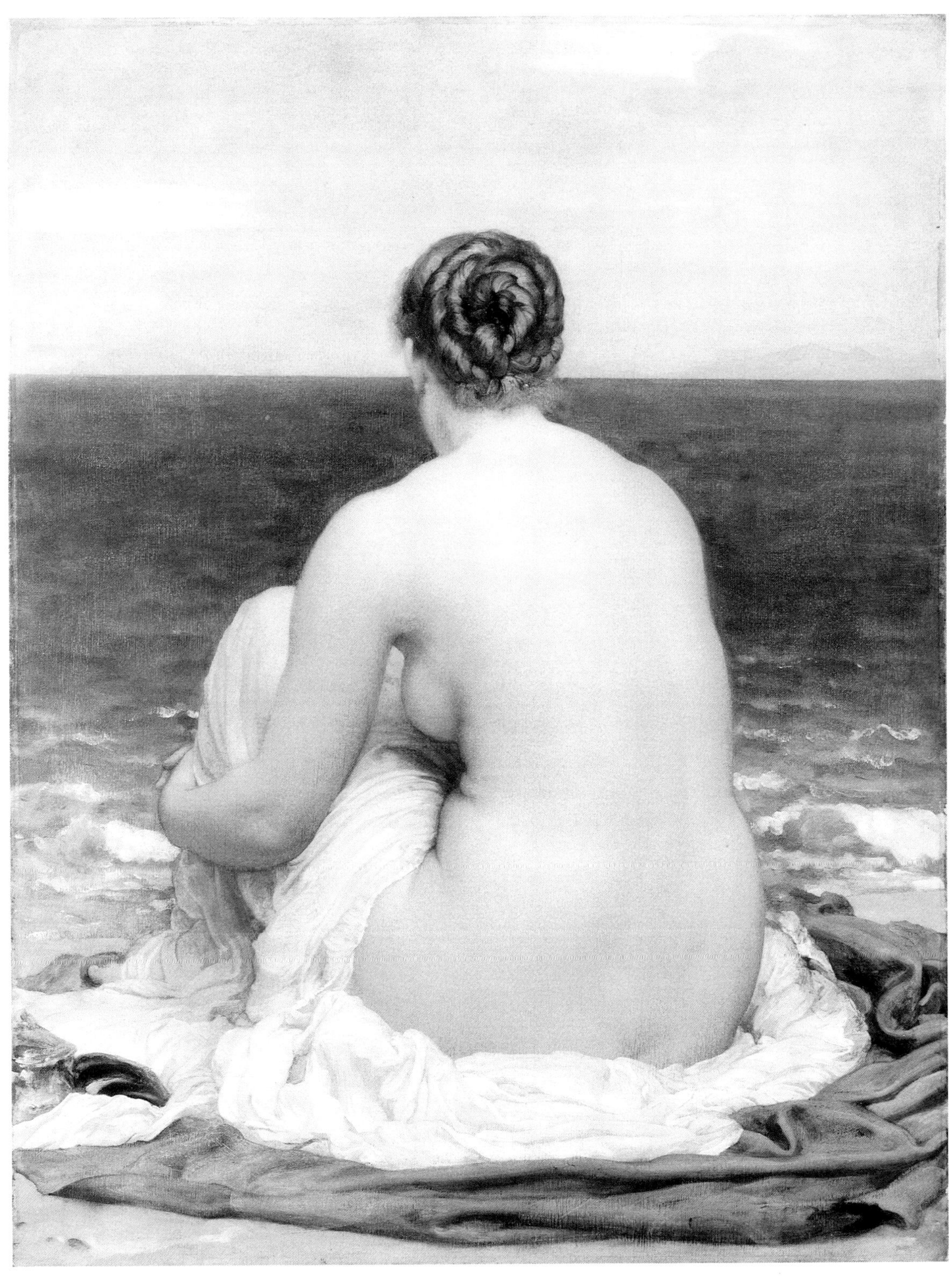

*Psamathe* LL 3630

5 *Athenaeum*, 1 May 1880, p. 572. Indeed, the realism of LL 3630 so upset Lord Ronald Gower that he described it and Leighton's other pictures at the 1880 Royal Academy as indecent; see *Academy*, 22 May 1880, p. 391. Millais on the other hand much admired the finish of LL 3630, see V.C. Prinsep, *Royal Academy Lectures*, 1901, p. 181.

6 Mrs. A. Lang, 'Sir Frederic Leighton', *Art Annual*, 1884, p. 16.

7 E. Rhys, *Frederic Lord Leighton*, 1900, pp. 41–2.

8 L. and R. Ormond, *Lord Leighton*, 1975, p. 128; Flandrin's painting was certainly conceived simply as an academic exercise. R. Jenkyns in *Dignity and Decadence*, 1991, p. 227, notes the sculptural quality of LL 3630. The *Baigneuse de Valpinçon* by Ingres, which entered the Louvre in 1879 the year before LL 3630 was painted, might have been another of Leighton's sources.

9 A.A. Munich, *Andromeda's Chains*, 1989, p. 164.

10 No. 24 in the Julian Hartnoll, *Victorian Figure Studies* exhibition, 1980; the same drawing was probably no. 242 at the 1897 Royal Academy *Winter Exhibition*.

11 There is an MS label on the back of LL 3630: 'Aug 188[?]. This picture Psamathe (Nymph / of the Sands) was painted by me / for my old and much valued / friend Benson Rathbone / Fred. Leighton.' Benson Rathbone (died 1892) was senior partner in the Liverpool cotton brokers Messrs. Rathbone, Duckworth and Co.; he was President of the Liverpool Cotton Brokers Association in 1871 (J. Wallace Coop and Seymour Taylor, *Bulls and Bears*, 1908, no. 67); he was also a considerable collector, particularly of landscapes and watercolours, and lent extensively to the Walker Art Gallery, Liverpool, *Grand Loan Exhibition*, 1886.

12 H.E. Kidson, letter, 1901.

13 Lever's diary, *Liverpool Echo*, 24 September 1952. LL 3630 was the first major painting bought by Lever for his private collection at Thornton Manor – as opposed to the pictures he purchased for use as soap advertisements, see Royal Academy, *Lord Leverhulme*, 1980, pp. 14 ff.

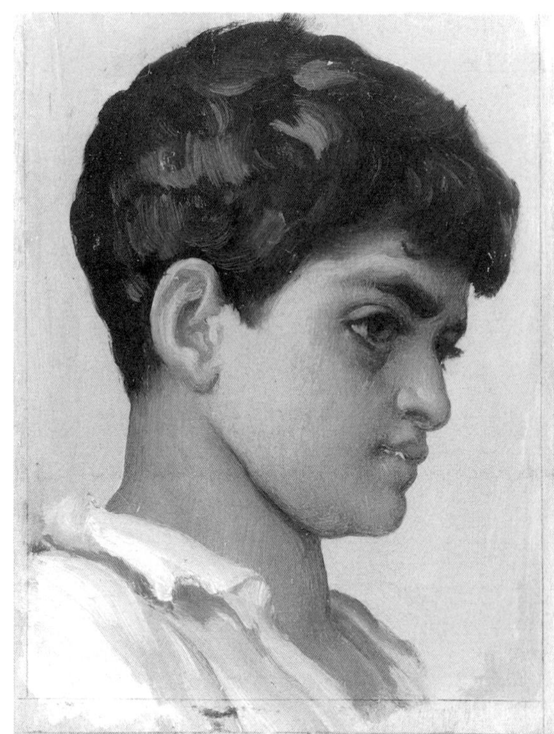

*Head of a Spanish Boy* LL 3742

*Head of a Spanish Girl* LL 3740

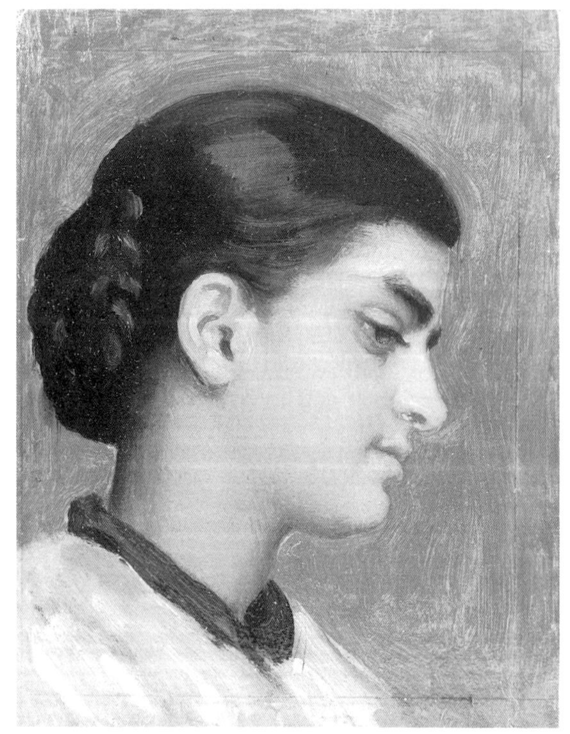

### *Head of a Spanish Boy*

LL 3742 (WHL 1436, TM 28)
Canvas: 14 × 11 cm

### *Head of a Spanish Girl*

LL 3740 (WHL 1438, TM 30)
Canvas: 12 × 10 cm

Leighton made studies of this nature on his many summer excursions to southern Europe. A *Head of a Girl* very similar to the *Head of a Spanish Girl* is now in the Montreal Museum of Fine Arts (inv. 964.1463) and *Paolo, Head of a Capri Boy*, 26.5 × 21 cm, Christie's 24 October 1975, lot 100, apparently represents the same model used in the Lady Lever Art Gallery male head. *Paolo, a Capri Boy*, 30.1 × 22.2 cm was formerly owned by the Fine Art Society; this and the head at Christie's may have been related to Leighton's *Paolo* exhibited at the 1876 Royal Academy but now lost.

PROV: The artist's sale, Christie's 11 July 1896, lot 1, bought Agnew (£45.3*s*.) for Lever (£47.8*s*.).

EXH: Oldham, *Exhibition of Modern Paintings*, 1889 (75).[1]

1 This exhibition was devoted mainly to contemporary paintings (Aileen McEvoy, letter to the compiler, 10 March 1986), indicating perhaps that LL 3742 and LL 3740 dated from the 1880s.

### *Garden of the Hesperides*

LL 3139 (WHL 29)
Canvas: 169.5 × 169.5 cm

The Hesperides were the guardians of the golden apples given to Juno, or to Jupiter, on the day of their marriage; they were the daughters of Hesperus, the god of evening, and resided in a magnificent garden of uncertain location; their singing was especially remarkable and they were assisted in looking after the apples by the dragon Ladon who never slept. The dragon was eventually killed by Hercules who then stole the apples.[1] Leighton has changed the dragon into a snake as Edward Burne-Jones did for his painting of this subject (now Hamburger Kunsthalle)[2] and the twining of the snake around the central figure may have been inspired by a notorious passage in Flaubert's novel *Salammbô* or by one of the numerous paintings and sculptures representing that passage.[3] The Ormonds argue that LL 3139 is deeply symbolic suggesting in particular that there are conscious references to the Garden of Eden and that therefore this painting represents a precarious and secure golden age before a pagan Fall of Man.[4]

R. Jenkyns[5] observes that the *Garden of the Hesperides* (with Leighton's *Flaming June* and other works of this period) showed a marked departure from his earlier Hellenism: 'mannered in composition, oppressive in colouration they convey a strong sense of heavy and even sinister languor'. Certainly the compressed foreground space and repeated sinuous, linear curves show the artist abandoning classicism in favour of (broadly speaking) *art nouveau* principles or at least of a new interest in problems of flat, formal design.[6]

Most reviewers, when they saw this painting at the Royal Academy in 1892, concentrated on its formal qualities. The *Saturday Review*[7] was judicious:

*'The Garden of the Hesperides' is very different. The space is admirably filled; in fact, this is one of the best compositions out of the many ideal arrangements that this artist has imagined. The beauty of the thing is so patent, that it gives a thrill of satisfaction at first sight. Then, after closer looking, it is impossible, in these days of naturalism, not to think what the motif might be with a modern half-decorative, half-realistic treatment, which would give us a sentiment of coolness, freshness, and space, a suggestion of mystery in the trees and shadows, of light on the sea, of air in the sky. One has seen of late, chiefly abroad, attempts at a classic-impressionist mixture. It is very effective, and promises much, though it has seldom been executed with Sir Frederic's stateliness of manner and traditional harmony of composition. However, this is to ask Sir Frederic for what is outside his ideal; it is to expect from Guido the qualities of Velasquez's*

*'Spinners'. Accepting, then, this aspect of the decorative work, what can we say of the colour? It is infinitely better than that of the other picture, and yet to some tastes it will seem brilliant and gay rather than rich; pretty doubtless, but shallow. There is a brown pinkiness about the deep hole at the bottom, a salmon pinkiness about the dresses above it that sound the keynote of this bright morbidness. The rich, the resonant deep notes of low orange, cherry, and allied scales seem lacking.*

George Moore in the *Speaker*[8] followed a similar line:

*The place of honour has been given to the President's 'Garden of the Hesperides'. The striking merit of the picture is in the arabesque, which is charming and original . . . The brown water in the foreground balances the white sky, and the white birds in it – diminutive swans – are most happy. The faces of the women are charming in colour and were it not for the strawberry-cream garment in the middle of the picture, I would feel inclined to say that this picture is as good as anything Sir Frederic has done.*

The *Athenaeum*,[9] having described the subject of LL 3139, also went on to the colour and composition:

*the atmosphere, to be in keeping with the subject, is pure and bright; the colours are sumptuous; the composition is as simple as it is massive; and the lines of the limbs of the Hesperides, in their flowing completeness and elegance, harmonize with the folds of the snake's body in a manner which evinces at once the care and the resources of the artist, who, with singular judgment, has framed his composition in a circle.*

An earlier description in the same periodical[10] was again concerned primarily with LL 3139 as a flat design:

*The art of the painter is manifest in the choiceness, harmony, and subtlety of the 'serpentining lines on lines' which the design involves, and which are traceable in the convolutions of the snake, the elegant and flowing ordonnance of the forms of the women, their graceful limbs, and the, so to say, sympathetic symmetry and balance of their attitudes. All these elements are in harmony with the circle which encloses them and with the arrangement of the boughs of*

*. . . the fair Hesperian tree*
*Laden with blooming gold*

*which crowns the composition, while, under its branches, the dark blue and purple levels of that magic ocean which enshrined the garden of the Hesperides are visible as far as the eye can reach. As with the ordering of the lines of this composition, so its coloration has been contrived. The central figure is clad in rose-amber of a pure and rather light hue, the maiden with the lyre wears a deeper rose, and the third daughter's dress is a warm green, neither light nor dark. The tonality of the picture is in keeping with the amenities of its formative and chromatic qualities, and loses nothing of simplicity in being at once soft, homogeneous, and brilliant.*

*The Times*[11] put especial emphasis on the absence of action or incident, observing first that 'to the modern English artist painting scenes of Greek literature and life, every detail is a pitfall, every incident a snare'; the writer continued:

*He has painted not the garden invaded or the dragon destroyed but the three beautiful maidens grouped round the foot of the orange tree with the mystic serpent turning around and among them. In other words we have here very little more than an exquisite study of line and colour with no more story than is required to give consistency to the composition. How perfectly the lines of the figures and the draperies fit into the circular composition and with what consummate knowledge the painter had harmonized the green, the red, the faint flame colour of the dresses, the orange of the golden fruit and the enamel blue of the serpent may easily be imagined.*

The *Art Journal*[12] criticized the arbitrary character of the 'intricate bunches of artfully crumpled tissues in which the President has revelled'.

Dorothy Dene is said to have been a model for one or all of the figures[13] and the sky was painted from a landscape sketch made in Ireland some years earlier.[14]

There is an oil sketch in a private

collection[15] and a model for it in bronze and plaster at the Royal Academy.[16] There are drawings at Leighton House, Royal Borough of Kensington and Chelsea (LH 699–700, 704–705 and perhaps 708 and 1106), in the Walker Art Gallery, Liverpool (inv. 9351), in the Art Museum, Princeton University (48–172), in the National Gallery of Canada, Ottawa (inv. 4458 and 4462)[17] and in the Royal Academy (tracings 41); drawings were also sold at Christie's 23 April 1974, lots 23 and 24; 14 May 1985, lot 189 and a drawing was reproduced in the Pall Mall Gazette, *Pictures of 1892*, p. 20. A study was exhibited at the Royal Society of British Artists 1892 (14). A copy after the painting by Frank Salisbury was in the sale of his studio, Christie's 25 September 1985, lot 8; Salisbury admired Leighton's painting above all others – even including Michelangelo's Sistine Chapel ceiling.[18] According to the Ormonds[19] the frame with mouldings

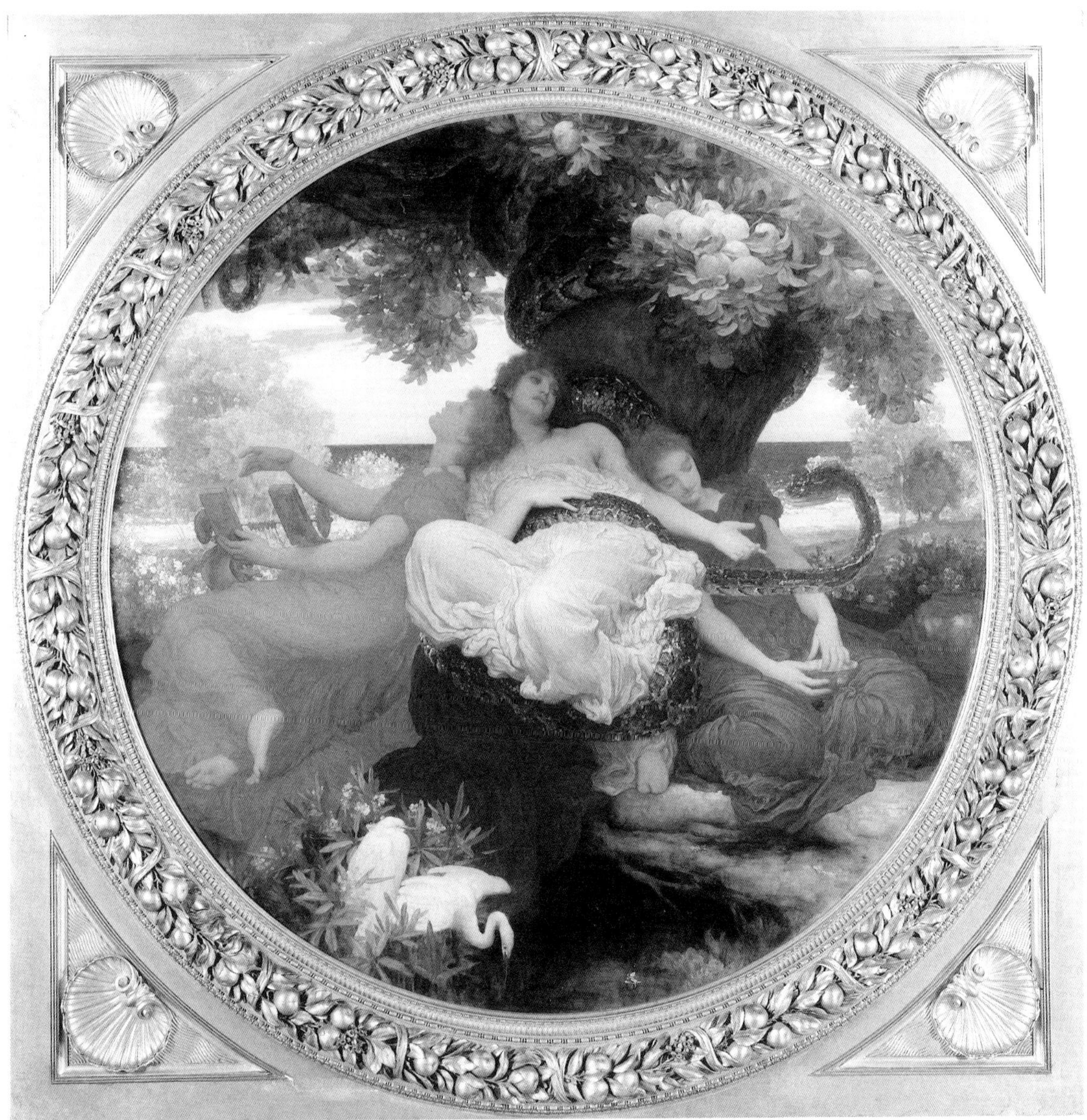

*Garden of the Hesperides* LL 3139 (colour plate 7)

of fruit and foliage was 'devised' by Leighton.

The artist had made 'good progress' with the painting of the *Garden of the Hesperides* by 8 August 1891 and by 15 August 1891, the *Athenaeum*[20] was able to describe it in detail.

REPR: H. Blackburn, *Academy Notes*, 1892, p. 58; photogravure published by Arthur Tooth and Sons 1893 – there is an impression in the Lady Lever Art Gallery (LP 18).

PROV: Bought by George McCulloch in August 1891;[21] his sale, Christie's 23–30 May 1913, lot 70, bought Gooden and Fox (£2,625) for Lever (£2,690.12*s*.6*d*.).

EXH: Royal Academy 1892 (204);[22] Liverpool Autumn Exhibition 1892 (994); Chicago, *World's Columbian Exhibition*, 1893; Guildhall Art Gallery, *Loan Exhibition*, 1895 (24); Royal Academy, *Winter Exhibition*, 1897 (39) and 1909 (41).

1 There are many different versions of the myth and no firm evidence about which source Leighton was using. F.G. Stephens in the *Athenaeum*, 30 April 1892, p. 569 pointed out that Milton's *Comus* (lines 980–2) describes 'the liquid air / All amidst the Gardens fair / Of Hesperus, and his daughters three / That sing about the golden tree'. In one version of the myth the Hesperides assisted Hercules to steal the apples by making Ladon drunk and sending him to sleep; this may be the event depicted in LL 3139; this interpretation of the picture has not, however, been advanced by any commentator so far. If this is indeed the subject of LL 3139 there is more drama and less languid repose in the picture than has hitherto been supposed. For J.A. Kestner, however, in his *Mythology and Misogyny*, 1989, p. 160, LL 3139 represents 'a female community before the irruption of man' – that is, Hercules.

2 The review of LL 3139 in the *Art Journal*, 1892, p. 188 mentioned a Graeco-Roman low relief of Hercules and the Hesperides in which the dragon is also shown as a snake. This relief was reproduced in the various editions of the *Dictionnaire des antiquités grecques et romaines* of C. Daremberg and E. Saglio, 1877–1919. This substitution was also noted in the *Academy*, 7 May 1892, p. 450 by Claude Phillips.

3 *Academy*, 7 May 1892, p. 450 in its review of LL 3139 compared it with the heroine of Flaubert's novel. Paintings by Gabriel Ferrier of 1880 and Jules Toulot of 1886 show the nude Salammbô with the snake around her; D.M. Ferrary's marble *Salammbô* is in the Lady Lever Art Gallery and represents the same scene; see Lady Lever Art Gallery, Port Sunlight, *Catalogue of Foreign Paintings, Drawings, Miniatures, Tapestries, Post Classical Sculpture and Prints*, 1983, pp. 113–14 with a list of other Salammbô sculptures and paintings; R. Ormond (unpublished catalogue entry, July 1978) suggested as possible sources for LL 3139 the 'entwined sea nymphs and sea serpents' of Arnold Böcklin and the 'more perversely sexual snake phantasies' of Franz von Stuck. Other sources may have included the *Doni Tondo* by Michelangelo (R. Jenkyns, *Dignity and Decadence*, 1991, p. 227) or various representations of Lilith, for example the Hon. John Collier's painting of 1887 (Grosvenor Gallery 1887, no. 24, reproduced in Pall Mall Gazette, *Pictures of 1887*, p. 68) and Albert Toft's sculptures of 1889 (Royal Academy 1889, no. 2112, reproduced in H. Blackburn, *Academy Notes*, 1889, p. 100).

4 See L. and R. Ormond, *Lord Leighton*, 1975, pp. 131–2; they also suggest similarities between LL 3139 and Tennyson's poem *The Hesperides*; both painting and poem, it appears, suggest a state of dream-like suspended animation. R.D. Altick, *Paintings from Books*, 1985, p. 236, however, repudiates any connections between LL 3139 and Tennyson's poem. In fact Burne-Jones's 1873 *Garden of the Hesperides* (Hamburger Kunsthalle), inspired by the account of the Hesperides in William Morris's *Earthly Paradise* of 1868–70, is much closer to traditional renderings of the *Garden of Eden*. J.M.W. Turner's *Goddess of Discord Choosing the Apple of Contention in the Garden of the Hesperides* of 1806 also certainly refers to the Garden of Eden more directly than does LL 3139 (see John Gage, *Colour in Turner*,

1969, pp. 137–8); Ruskin discussed Turner's painting and gave a long account of the Hesperides myth in *Modern Painters*, 1860, vol. 5, part 9, chapter 10; Ruskin's analysis has no direct similarities with LL 3139 but Leighton presumably read it.

5 R. Jenkyns, *The Victorians and Ancient Greece*, 1980, p. 308. See also R. Jenkyns, 'Hellenism in Victorian Painting' in *Rediscovering Hellenism*, ed. G.W. Clarke, 1989, p. 98.

6 E. Rhys, *Frederic Lord Leighton*, 1900, pp. 49–50 described LL 3139 as 'the most sumptuous piece of decoration [Leighton] ever achieved' and as 'an example of elaborately artificial composition'.

7 *Saturday Review*, 7 May 1892, p. 535.

8 *Speaker*, 30 April 1892, p. 528. Moore wrote a very similar review of LL 3139 for the 1892 *Fortnightly Review*, reprinted in his *Modern Painting*, 1893, 'Sir Frederic is himself, and nothing but himself. And the picture is so incontestably the work of an artist that I cannot bring myself to inquire too closely into its shortcomings'. In the same way Moore exempted LL 3139 from his general attack on Leighton's work in his article 'Lord Leighton', *Cosmopolis*, 1896, vol. 1, pp. 717–18; there he praised the poses of the female figures, the drama, the design and the expressive lines of the composition, but deplored the bright prosaic colours.

9 *Athenaeum*, 30 April 1892, p. 569.

10 *Athenaeum*, 15 August 1891, p. 234.

11 *The Times*, 30 April 1892.

12 *Art Journal*, 1892, p. 188; for other reviewers see *Magazine of Art*, 1892, p. 221; Pall Mall Gazette, *Pictures of 1892*, p. 2; *Academy*, 7 May 1892, p. 450; Claude Phillips in the *Academy* saw LL 3139 as 'pure decoration'. The young D.H. Lawrence admired LL 3139, see Nottingham Castle, *Young Bert*, 1972, p. 36.

13 L. and R. Ormond, *op. cit.*, p. 135.

14 R. Ormond, *op. cit.*

15 L. and R. Ormond, *op. cit.*, p. 171, no. 365, plate 188.

16 Reproduced in L. and R. Ormond, *op. cit.*, plate 186; the original plaster or clay version is reproduced in *Magazine of Art*, 1892, p. 217.

17 Inv. 4458 is reproduced in L. and R. Ormond, *op. cit.*, plate 187.

18 Frank Salisbury, *Sarum Chase*, 1953, p. 7.

19 L. and R. Ormond, *op. cit.*, p. 123. No frame maker's label survives on the back of LL 3139. Lynn Roberts in 'Nineteenth Century English Picture Frames', *International Journal of Museum Management and Curatorship*, 1986, vol. 5, p. 289, describes how the frame of LL 3139 differs from its Renaissance prototypes and how it complements the picture.

20 *Athenaeum*, 8 August 1891, p. 200 and 15 August 1891, p. 234.

21 *Athenaeum*, 29 August 1891, p. 299.

22 At the 1892 Royal Academy, LL 3139 hung opposite *Distraction* by Bouguereau – the French artist with whom Leighton was frequently compared.

## *Fatidica*

LL 3142 (WHL 1435, TM 27)
Canvas[1]: 153 × 111 cm

Fatidica (or Fauna or Fatua) was a Roman goddess notable for her prophetic powers which she exercised on behalf of women.[2] Leighton's sources plainly include the Prophets and Sibyls of Michelangelo's Sistine Chapel ceiling and perhaps Edward von Steinle's *Tiburtine Sibyl* now in the Stadelsches Kunstinstitut, Frankfurt. He does not seem to have been inspired by H.A. Pegram's *Sibylla Fatidica*, a sculpture exhibited at the 1891 Royal Academy.[3]

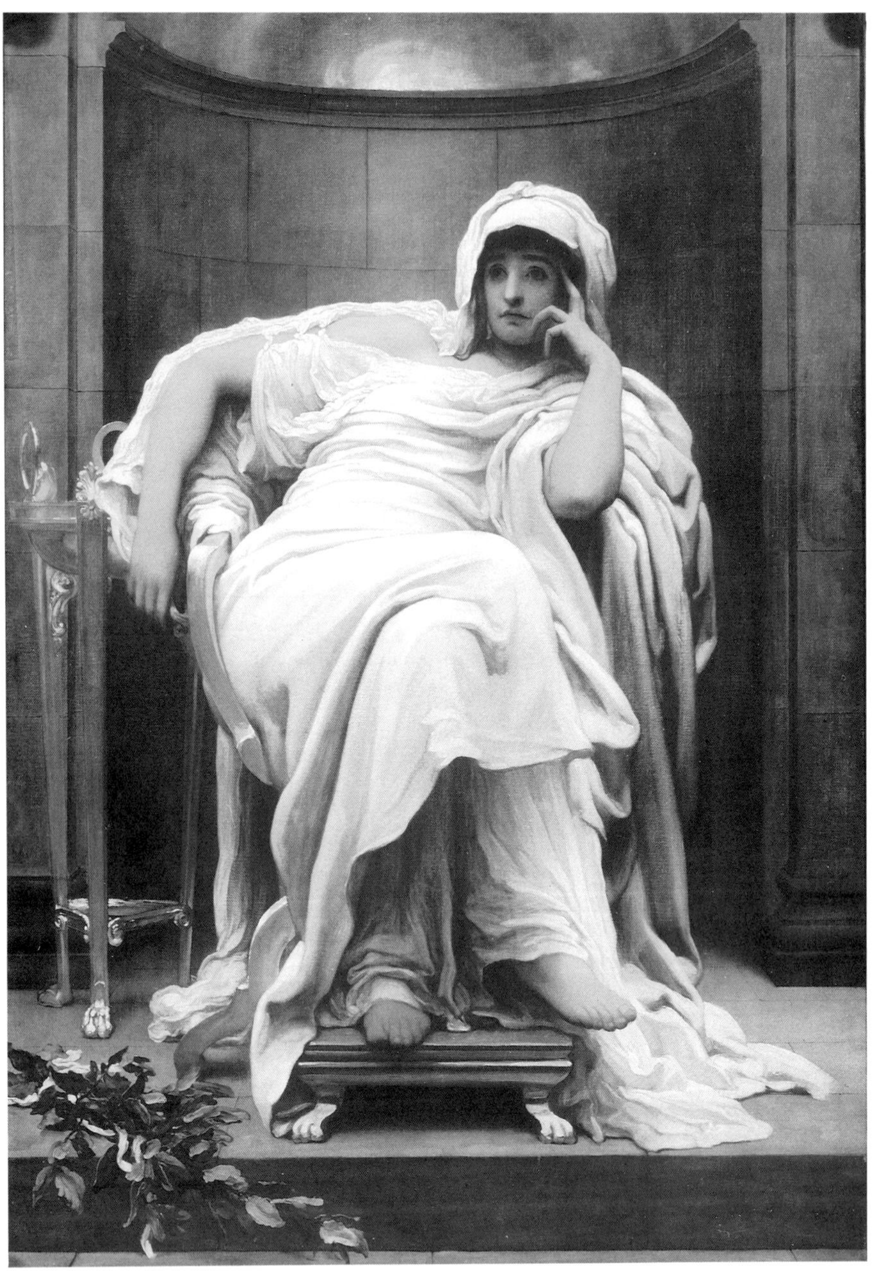

*Fatidica* LL 3142

Pegram is much more overtly symbolist than Leighton.

The *Athenaeum*[4] explained the subject of *Fatidica*:

*Warm as it is, 'Summer Slumber' is not less harmonious than* Fatidica, *an exercise in pure marble-white which depicts a stately dame, half reclining and half sitting in a silver chair upon one of the elbows of which one arm rests, while the other arm supports her head. Her pale face and its abstracted air suggest that she is brooding over the future. She sits on a platform set in a large niche or the ambo of a temple, and the walls behind her are covered with silver, where pallid gleams and shadowy reflections seem to play, adding to the mystery of the design. A silver tripod at her side sustains a sullen, slowly burning fire. At her feet lies a long branch of golden laurel appropriate to the divinity whose minister and mouthpiece she is.*

Other reviews were, however, very much more perfunctory – indicating perhaps that classical exercises like this no longer interested the public in the 1890s.

Drawings for *Fatidica* are (1) reproduced in M.H. Spielmann, 'The Royal Academy', *Magazine of Art*, 1894;[6] (2) reproduced in Pall Mall Gazette, *Pictures of 1894*;[7] (3) reproduced in Fine Art Society, *Drawings and Studies by the late Lord Leighton*;[8] (4) in Leighton House, Royal Borough of Kensington and Chelsea, LH 732–733, 735, 741; (5) in the Royal Academy, tracing 60; (6) in the City Museum and Art Gallery, Birmingham, 220'33; (7) recorded in the Lever sale, Knight, Frank and Rutley 8 July 1926, lot 476.

REPR: H. Blackburn, *Academy Notes*, 1894, p. 31; *Royal Academy Pictures*, 1894, frontispiece; photo engraving published by the Berlin Photo Company for T. Agnew and Sons 1894 – there is an impression in the Lady Lever Art Gallery (LP 20).

PROV: Bought from the artist by T. Agnew and Sons 3 April 1894; bought by Lever[9] June 1895 (£1,050).

EXH: Royal Academy 1894 (20); Royal Academy, *Winter Exhibition*, 1897 (54); Hulme Hall, Port Sunlight, *An Exhibition to Celebrate the Coronation*, 1902 (148) and *Autumn Art Exhibition*, 1902 (168).

1 There are labels on the back from Foord and Dickinson, 129 Wardour Street, London, frame makers, and from Charles Roberson and Co., 99 Long Acre, London.

2 L. and R. Ormond, *Lord Leighton*, 1975, p. 124: 'Fate and the transience of life are expressed by this mysterious demi-goddess who looks abstractedly into the past and the future.' The Ormonds also list other 'sibyl-like' figures by Leighton from his last years. See also Royal Academy, *Lord Leverhulme*, 1980, p. 62.

3 Reproduced in *Royal Academy Pictures*, 1891, p. 79. The marble version of 1904 is now in the Tate Gallery.

4 *Athenaeum*, 5 May 1894, p. 583.

5 *Academy*, 12 May 1894, p. 400; *The Times*, 5 May 1894; *Art Journal*, 1894, p. 211 (by R.A.M. Stevenson); *Magazine of Art*, 1894, p. 272 (by H.M. Spielmann). See, for example, the *Speaker*, 5 May 1894, p. 500 (by George Moore): 'This year I confess that Sir Frederic Leighton frankly bores me. His work is no worse than usual; it flows on very much as usual, very much as Mr. Swinburne's poems flow on – admirable metre signifying nothing . . . In this room the lady sits in canonical draperies in an arm chair.' Claude Phillips in the *Academy* criticized the arbitrary lighting in *Fatidica*.

6 *Magazine of Art*, 1894, pp. 217–18.

7 *Pictures of 1894*, p. 80.

8 *Drawings and Studies by the late Lord Leighton*, 1898, plate 31 – this drawing was then owned by Val Prinsep and dated 1893.

9 For Lever's patronage of Leighton, see Royal Academy, *op. cit.*, pp. 16, 62.

## *Clytie*

LL 3739 (WHL 1427, TM 14)
Canvas: 17.2 × 19 cm

LL 3739 is a sketch for the *Clytie* of 1895–6 now in an Indian private collection.[1] The artist was making studies for *Clytie* in October 1895 while staying with Giovanni Costa at Rome in the Palazzo Odescalchi.[2]

PROV: Bought by Lever from the Fine Art Society 2 May 1896 (£47.5*s*.).[3]

1 L. and R. Ormond, *Lord Leighton*, 1975, p. 173, nos. 396–7, plate 192. An oil study of altar and fruit for *Clytie* is now at the Victoria & Albert Museum (Ormond, *op. cit.*, p. 173, no. 398).

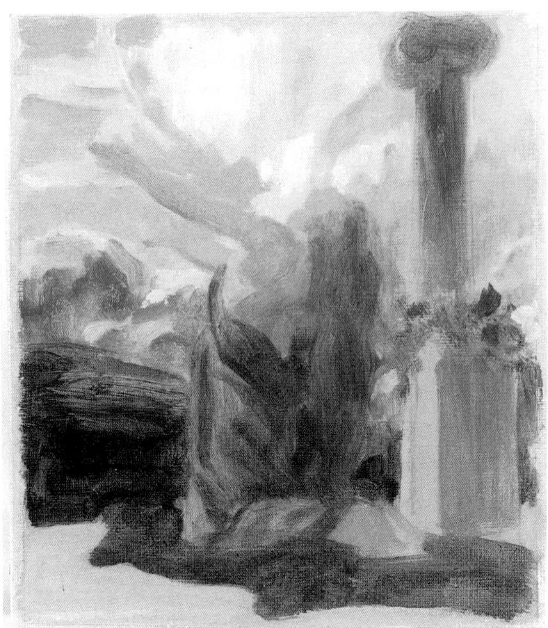

*Clytie* LL 3739

2 O.R. Agresti, *Giovanni Costa*, 1904, p. 260.

3 LL 3739 cannot have been in the artist's sale which took place on 11–13 July 1896; he died 25 January 1896. The Fine Art Society published a photogravure of the 1895–6 *Clytie* in 1897, and may have had LL 3739 in this connection.

## **LESLIE, George Dunlop** (1835–1921)
### ***This is the Way we Wash our Clothes***

LL 3410
Canvas: 61 × 46 cm

The critic of the *Athenaeum*[1] wrote:

*A smaller picture is called* This is the Way we wash our Clothes. *A little girl of eight years of age stands on a chair in her nursery, and according to the ancient rhyme, is busily washing a little garment in a white basin. Mr. Leslie has made no attempt to beautify the bright and intelligent child, but her expressive and natural look will touch the hearts of all mothers and lovers of infancy. We like the picture because it is quite unpretentious.*

This painting must be closely related to James Hayllar's *Soap Suds*;[2] Leslie and Hayllar were close friends and lived next door to each other in Wallingford during the 1880s;[3] both paintings are very similar in conception and in composition; both were used as soap advertisements – Leslie's painting by Lever for Lever Brothers[4] and *Soap Suds* by T.J. Barratt for A. and F. Pears.[5] *Soap Suds* is now lost and cannot be dated from exhibition catalogues; it is therefore unclear whether Leslie was imitating Hayllar, or Hayllar Leslie, in the subject and treatment of the pictures and also uncertain whether Lever was following Barratt, or Barratt Lever, in the use of the very similar images for advertising soap and in the employment of almost identical titles in their advertisements.[6]

Some artists, notably W.P. Frith and J.E. Millais (see p. 38) objected to the use of their paintings for advertising soap, but the editor of the *Magazine of Art* observed that Leslie's painting could not be degraded by such use.[7]

REPR: H. Blackburn, *Academy Notes*, 1887, p. 106; Pall Mall Gazette, *Pictures of 1887*, p. 52.

PROV: Presented by Lever Brothers 1983.

EXH: Royal Academy 1887 (859).

1 *Athenaeum*, 30 April 1887, p. 581; LL 3410 was also noticed by the *Art Journal*, 1887, p. 278.

2 Reproduced from the Hayllar family photograph albums in C. Wood, 'The Artistic Family Hayllar', *Connoisseur*, 1974, vol. 185, p. 272 fig. 11.

3 Wood, *op. cit.*, pp. 271–2.

4 LL 3410 was reproduced as part of a soap advertisement by Lever Brothers; there is an example in the John Johnson Collection, Bodleian Library, Oxford, inscribed *SUNLIGHT SOAP / This is the way we wash our clothes / From the painting by G.D. Leslie R.A. Exhibited in the Royal Academy, London, 1887*; LL 3410 was probably one of the pictures bought directly from the artist

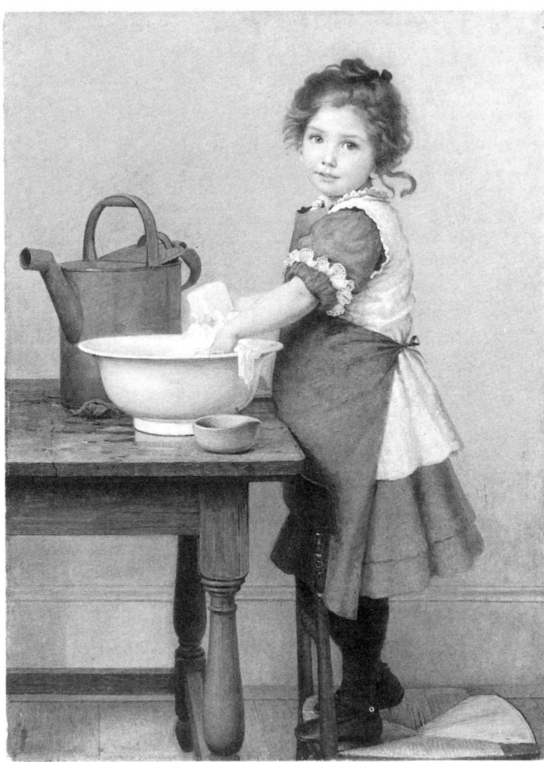

*This is the Way we Wash our Clothes* LL 3410

by Lever for advertising purposes – for further details about these pictures see Royal Academy, *Lord Leverhulme*, 1980, pp. 14 ff;, 53; LL 3410 must have been one of the first paintings bought by Lever for this purpose – if he acquired it at the 1887 Royal Academy Exhibition; perhaps its obvious utility as a soap advertisement suggested to Lever the exploitation of contemporary paintings for this purpose. See above p. xiii.

5 A. and F. Pears bought *Soap Suds* from Hayllar in May 1887 for £33.15*s*. (A. and F. Pears Ltd., Works of Art, MSS p. 10, Unilever Historical Archives, Port Sunlight); both pictures therefore appear to date from 1887; M. Dempsey and T. Shackleton, *Bubbles: Early Advertising Art from A. and F. Pears Ltd.*, 1978, p. 5 reproduce a Pears Soap handbill of about 1893 containing a reproduction of *Soap Suds* with its new title: *This is the way we wash our hands.*

6 Lever used Leslie's original title for his advertisement, whereas Barratt created a new title for his handbill; this might indicate priority for Lever, but generally speaking, Barratt was the pioneer – see Royal Academy, *op. cit.*, p. 14 and Edward Morris, 'Advertising and the Acquisition of Contemporary Art', *Journal of the History of Collections*, 1992, vol. 4, pp. 196–7.

7 'Artistic Advertising', *Magazine of Art*, 1889, pp. 423 ff.

## *September Sunshine*

LL 3631 (WHL 1432, TM 23)
Canvas[1]: 95.5 × 130.5 cm

This landscape was well received at the 1896 Royal Academy and was generally described as a view on the Thames – or upper Thames.[2] A more critical review appeared in the *Academy*, written by Claude Phillips:[3]

*The tender, peaceful beauty of home scenery is evidently felt by Mr. G.D. Leslie, whose 'September Sunshine' has, moreover, certain decorative qualities, which we should be better able to appreciate did the artist not so completely ignore the atmospheric garment with which, especially in England, nature enwraps even her sunniest scenes.*

The *Art Journal*[4] was also probing:

*Mr. G.D. Leslie has achieved an effect of the same sort in his 'September Sunshine', but he has adopted a more precise and mannered style of handling which gives a somewhat different character to the picture. His aim has seemingly been to give the definiteness of relief and smooth evenness of lighting which is presented by a landscape viewed from a point of view which brings the sun directly behind the spectator. He has avoided in this way any large surfaces of shadow, and depends for what modelling he requires upon the smallest possible touches of darker colour.*

*September Sunshine* is among the artist's earlier landscapes and his motives for taking up this subject matter are worth quoting:[5]

*Coincidentally with the invasion of the line [at the Royal Academy Summer Exhibitions] by the life-sized portraits, the patronage hitherto given to subject-pictures began to fall off lamentably, and in consequence of this a great number of distinguished painters, who formerly produced important works of figure subjects, began to take to portraiture. Prominent among such painters were Millais, Holl, Orchardson, and Pettie. But numerous other examples of men who likewise did so may be found among members of the Academy who are still living. I should have taken to portrait painting myself, but, unfortunately, I never could work well in harness, feeling miserable unless I have absolute freedom to choose my own models and my own subjects. There is still some patronage, though at a very moderate remuneration, for landscapes, and accordingly I have chiefly occupied my old age with that delightful branch of painting.*

REPR: *Art Journal*, 1896, p. 176; *Handbook to the Royal Academy*, published by Black and White, 1896; Pall Mall Gazette, *Pictures of 1896*, p. 6; H. Blackburn, *Academy Notes*, 1896, p. 64; *Royal Academy Pictures*, 1896, p. 150.

PROV: Bought by Lever from the artist through Thomas Agnew and Sons, 4 May 1896 (£210).

EXH: Royal Academy 1896 (281); Carnegie Art Galleries, Pittsburgh, *International Exhibition*, 1897 (260); Hulme Hall, Port Sunlight, *Autumn Art Exhibition*, 1902 (106).

1 Label on the back: *W.R. Smith, Carver and Gilder, 20–22 Mortimer Street, London W.1.*

2 M. Phipps Jackson in the *Magazine of Art*, 1896, p. 356; *Athenaeum*, 4 July 1896, p. 39.

3 *Academy*, 6 June 1896, p. 474.

4 *Art Journal*, 1896, p. 180. LL 3631 is not related in composition to the artist's *November Sunshine* of 1895.

5 G.D. Leslie, *The Inner Life of the Royal Academy*, 1914, pp. 132–3.

## *Midsummer Morn, Bushey Park*

LL 3633 (WHL 2, TM 25)
Canvas[1]: 97.5 × 138.5 cm

The subject of LL 3633 is the Diana Fountain in Bushey Park near Hampton Court, Middlesex.[2]

REPR: *Royal Academy Pictures*, 1905, p. 66; *Handbook to the Royal Academy*, published by Black and White, 1905, p. 10; Pall Mall Magazine, *Pictures of 1905*.

PROV: Bought from the artist by Lever, 8 August 1905 (£200).

*September Sunshine* LL 3631

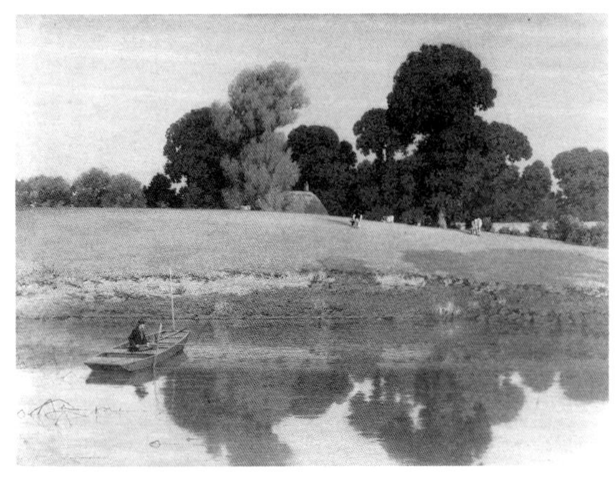

*Midsummer Morn, Bushey Park* LL 3633

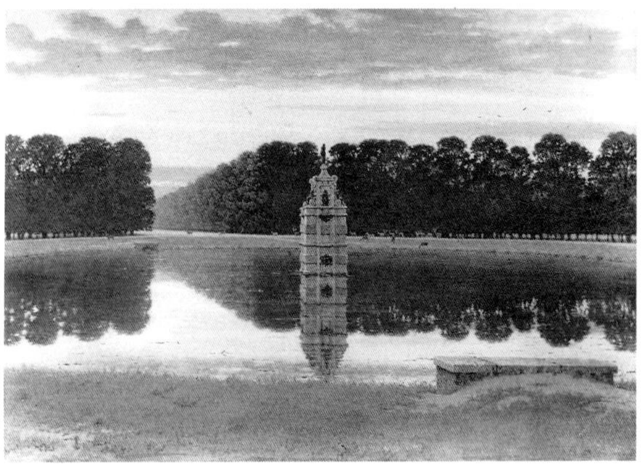

EXH: Royal Academy 1905 (175); Royal Academy, *Winter Exhibition*, 1922 (99).

1 Frame maker's label: *R. Dolman and Co., New Compton Street, London WC.*

2 The artist spent some time as a young man staying with his family in a house overlooking Bushey Park during 1857 – see C.R. Leslie, *Autobiographical Recollections*, 1860, vol. 2, p. 313.

## **MASON, George** (1818–1872)
### ***The Gander***

LL 3146 (WHL 4112)
Canvas: 48.5 × 83.6 cm

The artist moved away from Wetley, Staffordshire to London in 1864 and this painting was painted in London[1] in 1864 or 1865, although Wetley Rocks can be seen in the background.[2] G.A. Simcox[3] rightly saw it as a key work in Mason's development of a poetic and idealised rendering of the mudane aspects of rural life:

*The most characteristic of his single pictures, the one in which we see most aspects of his genius at their culminating point is* The Gander. *There we have in the girl's figure the perfection of homely grace though she is only trying to scare the ganders while she is half scared herself; and we have the perfection of the passion of twilight brought to the focus in the marvellous glow of the sky reflected in the pool . . . charged with passion and sentiment but the passion and sentiment do not centre in the human figure.*

This was one of three paintings by Mason exhibited at the 1865 Royal Academy after a period of relative inactivity; they were reviewed very favourably and the artist's high reputation at least within a certain circle[4] was established. *The Times*[5] described it as 'one of the most lovely pictures of its class in the exhibition', complaining only of a 'want of solidity in the relief of the figures against the sky or ground'; each of Mason's paintings at the 1865 Royal Academy was 'a painted poem thanks to the exquisite innate refinement . . . Nothing can be truer to nature but it is truth which has passed through the medium of a pure and delicate conception kindled by an intense sympathy with the nature he paints.'

The critic of the *Athenaeum*[6] wrote:

*There is much that is delicious to the lover of colour and of the sober aspects of nature in Mr. Mason's quaintly styled pair of pictures,* The Gander *and* The Geese. *The delicacy, breadth, and truth of these lovely studies merit the greatest care and regard from painters. In their subjects there is a dash of quiet humour. In that of the first we have a girl repulsing an irate gander; in the second picture she drives geese along a windy moor. The effect – grey twilight over a moorland, which supplies a landscape of exquisite beauty to the first, shows a mastery not often surpassed.*

F.T. Palgrave[7] contributed a very similar review:

*Mr. Mason, like Mr. Whistler, seems to us to reach poetry on canvas through the harmonious unity which marks each of his three scenes. All these have the air of effects at morning or at twilight taken from the same wild piece of nature. They appear to stop a little short of completion, as if the gifted painter had feared lest the bloom of his delicate transparent atmosphere should be injured by further touches. The figures – children in two of the pieces, a traveller with a pony in the third – are sketched with singular beauty, truth, and refinement; we doubt whether anything in the Exhibition fully equals them in this respect . . . It is pleasant to see that Mr. Mason, whose merits were long neglected, has now found admirers both among the public and his fellow-artists. Few landscapes will be more sought after than his in future years.*

Only the *Art Journal*[8] was more reserved:

The Gander, *the artist's best work, has colour, character, action, and a vague and suggestive grandeur; it, however, lacks completeness. It is more the indication of a purpose than the consummation of a picture.*

A *Study for Figure in the Gander* was lent by the artist's widow to the 1895 Birming-

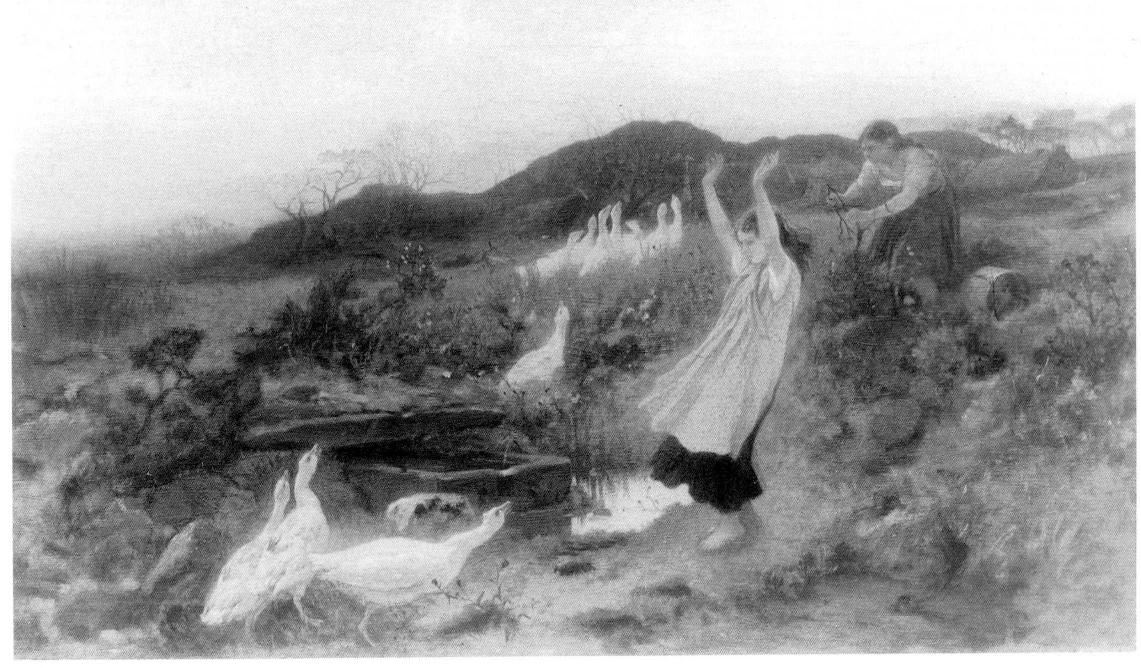

*The Gander* LL 3146

ham Royal Society of Artists exhibition, *Pictures and Sketches by George Mason and George Pinwell* (486) and a *Gander: Study from Nature* was lent by the Hon. Percy Wyndham to the Burlington Fine Arts Club, *George Mason* exhibition of 1873 (67).

PROV: J. Tong; William Coltart;[9] his sale, Christie's 11 April 1904 did not, however, include LL 3146. R.E. Tatham sale, Christie's 7 March 1908, lot 97, bought Agnew (£1,995); Sir William Agnew. Anon. sale, Christie's 27 February 1920, lot 134, bought Gooden and Fox[10] (£1,575) for Lever (£1,616.7*s*.).

EXH: Royal Academy, 1865 (31); Burlington Fine Arts Club, *George Mason*, 1873 (36); Liverpool, *Grand Loan Exhibition*, 1886 (819); Manchester, *Royal Jubilee Exhibition*, 1887 (658); Guildhall Gallery, London, 1894 (123); Birmingham, Royal Society of Artists, *Pictures and Sketches by George Mason and George Pinwell*, 1895 (460); New Gallery 1897–8 (153); Royal Academy, *Winter Exhibition*, 1901 (45); Glasgow, *International Exhibition*, 1901 (322).

1 Alice Meynell, 'George Mason', *Art Journal*, 1883, p. 187.

2 Stoke-on-Trent City Museum and Art Gallery, *George Heming Mason*, 1982, nos. 33 and 34. The Victoria & Albert Museum has *At Wetley Rocks, Staffordshire*, 17.8 × 33 cm, (inv. 309–1887) which is related to LL 3146; it has the foreground well (or pool) and rocks of LL 3146 but a different background.

3 G.A. Simcox, 'Mr. Mason's Collected Works', *Portfolio*, 1873, pp. 40–3. A. Staley, *The Pre-Raphaelite Landscape*, 1973, p. 177, also argues that LL 3146 is typical of Mason's work and offers an analysis of it similar to that of Simcox, but he insists on the influence of Giovanni Costa in the 'careful spacing and strong linear axes', and notes that Mason painted 'rustic idylls' not 'pure landscapes'.

4 See Meynell, *op. cit.*, p. 187: 'it is clear that the prosaic kind of landscape painting then prevalent has become distasteful to all who had made their artistic education in any degree liberal by that

better knowledge of Continental Art which was at that time beginning to work changes in England.'

5 *The Times*, 29 April 1865.

6 *Athenaeum*, 6 May 1865, p. 628. Frederic Leighton asked F.G. Stephens in 1863 to look at Mason's paintings at the Royal Academy (L. and R. Ormond, *Lord Leighton*, 1975, p. 47) – Stephens usually wrote art criticism for the *Athenaeum*.

7 F.T. Palgrave, *Essays on Art*, 1866, p. 116. The *Reader*, 24 June 1865, p. 718 also commented on the poetry in LL 3146; W.M. Rossetti in *Fraser's Magazine*, 1865, p. 749 found LL 3146 the best of Mason's exhibits at the 1865 Royal Academy, but observed that the sunset sky was Italian, while the scene and figures were British. F.T. Palgrave in 'English Pictures in 1865', *Fortnightly Review*, 1 August 1865, pp. 661 ff., compared Mason's 1865 paintings with contemporary French landscapes, particularly those of Jules Breton.

8 *Art Journal*, 1865, p. 171. Further reviews of LL 3146 appeared when it was exhibited again in 1873; the *Pall Mall Gazette*, 10 February 1873, p. 11 had extensive praise for the picture, particularly for its colour scheme.

9 William Coltart married Jonathan Tong's widow in 1881; both men were picture collectors; see *Thomas Armstrong, A Memoir*, ed. Lamont, 1912, pp. 10, 49. See F.G. Stephens, 'The Private Collections of England: Mr. W. Coltart's, *Athenaeum*, 26 September 1895, p. 408, with an extensive analysis of LL 3146; A. G. Temple, 'The Collection of William Coltart Esq.', *Art Journal*, 1896, p. 98.

10 F.W. Fox, Lever's usual adviser on the purchase of pictures, recommended LL 3146 to him very warmly – it was outside his usual rather classical taste; see Royal Academy, *Lord Leverhulme*, 1980, no. 24.

## **MOORE, Henry** (1831–1895)
## ***Rounding the Ness, Lowestoft***

LL 3706 (WHL 3403)
Canvas[1]: 21.5 × 45.8 cm
Signed: *H. Moore 1886*

Maclean[2] records a painting with the same title as this, but measuring 51 × 33 cm and painted in 1891; like this painting it was owned by Charles Winn and described as: 'churning sea with fishing boat in the centre

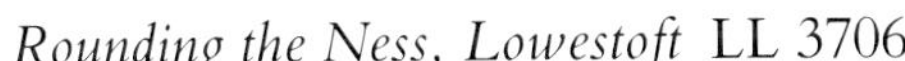
*Rounding the Ness, Lowestoft* LL 3706

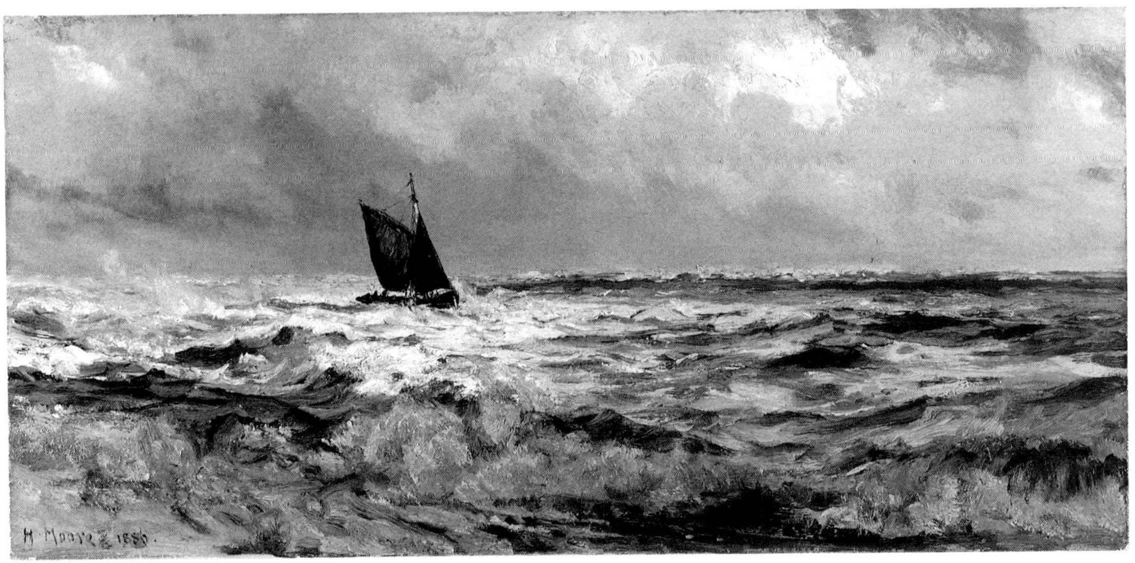

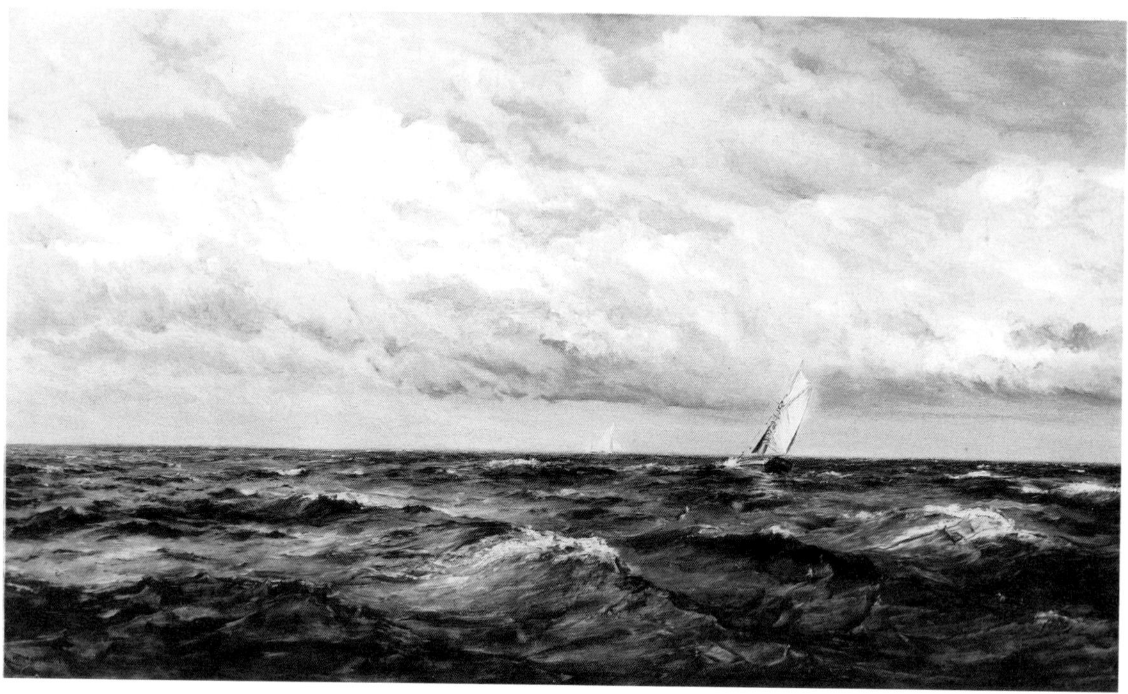

*A Breezy Day* LL 3626

foreground; fine silvery colour and light focussed on the middle of the picture'. Maclean's painting may have been another version of the Lady Lever Art Gallery painting, or it may have been that painting itself with an inaccurate date and measurements.

PROV: Charles Winn sale, Christie's 21 December 1917, lot 164, bought Gooden and Fox (£33.12*s*.) as *Rounding the Ness* for Lever (£34.9*s*.).

EXH: Institute of Painters in Oil Colours 1886–87 (252).

1 Canvas stamp: Winsor and Newton, 38 Rathbone Place, London.

2 F. Maclean, *Henry Moore*, 1905, p. 199. There was only one *Rounding the Ness* in the Charles Winn sale, Christie's 21 December 1917, and that was LL 3706; however, lot 165 was *Fishing Boats off the Coast*, 21.5 × 44.5 cm, dating from 1888.

## *A Breezy Day*

LL 3626 (WHL 15)
Canvas[1]: 90.5 × 155 cm
Signed: *H. Moore 1887*

This painting was not exhibited in 1887 or 1888 at the principal exhibitions to which the artist normally contributed – that is, the Royal Academy, the Grosvenor Gallery and the New Gallery.[2] It may have been commissioned by McCulloch (see provenance).

PROV: George McCulloch[3] sale, Christie's 29 May 1913, lot 169, bought Gooden and Fox (£504) for Lever (£516.12*s*.).

EXH: Royal Academy, *Winter Exhibition*, 1906 (153); Royal Academy, *Winter Exhibition*, 1909 (31).

1 Canvas stamp: *WINSOR & NEWTON / RATHBONE* —— [illegible]; also a label of W.R. Smith, carver and gilder of 20–22 Mortimer Street, London.

2 The artist's exhibits at these exhibitions are all reproduced or described in Henry Blackburn, *Academy Notes*, in *Royal Academy Pictures*, in Henry Blackburn, *Grosvenor Notes* and in Henry Blackburn, *New Gallery Notes* for the years in question. LL 3626 could just, however, have been *Fine Weather – Channel*, no. 38 at the 1888 New Gallery described in Henry Blackburn, *New Gallery Notes*, 1888 as 'sea and sky'.

3 McCulloch had acquired LL 3626 by 1897, see A.L. Baldry, 'The Collection of George McCulloch', *Art Journal*, 1897, p. 3.

## MORGAN, Frederick (1856–1927)
### *His Turn Next*

LL 3415 (WHL 2925)
Canvas: 88 × 62 cm
Signed: *Fred Morgan*
Inscribed: *PEARS*

This painting does not seem to have appeared at public exhibitions and may have been painted as an advertisement, as the inscription would indicate; its quality is certainly below that generally achieved by Morgan. A Pears advertisement of 1915 reproducing it has been traced[1] but the painting was probably used for this purpose well before that date.

PROV: Bought by A. and F. Pears from Grover and Co. May 1892 (£150);[2] bought by Lever August 1916; presented by Lever Brothers 1983.

1 M. Dempsey, *Bubbles: Early Advertising Art from A. and F. Pears Ltd*, 1978, p. 65 where the advertisement is reproduced in colour.

2 A. and F. Pears Ltd., *Inventory of Works of Art*, MSS Unilever Historical Archives, Port Sunlight, no. 144, p. 10.

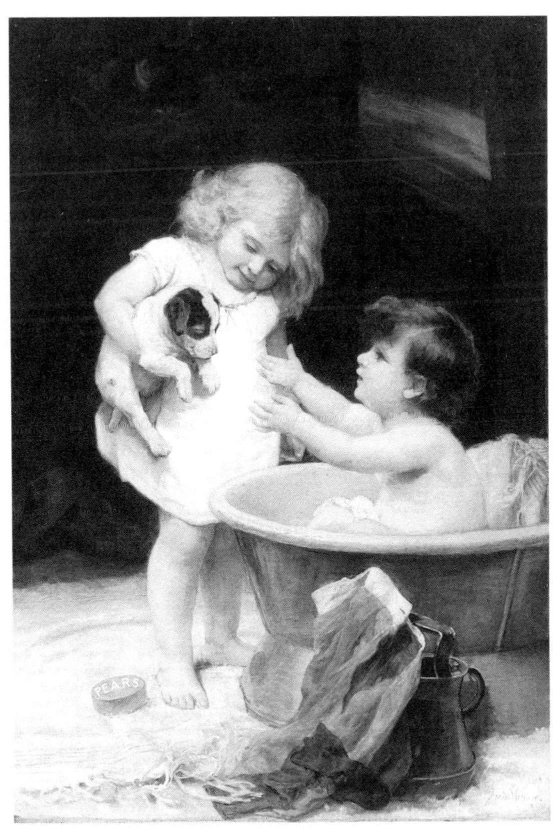


*His Turn Next* LL 3415

## MORRIS, Philip Richard (1836–1902)
### *Quite Ready*

LL 3615 (WHL 1176)
Canvas[1]: 138 × 92.5 cm
Signed: *Philip R. Morris*

The model used in this painting was Nansi Owen (*c.*1879–*c.*1885) whom the artist came across during a tour in North Wales; she was the daughter of a schoolmaster; the model's bonnet and dress were made by a women's clothes shop in Bethesda, called Compton House, and the setting was the staircase of that shop.[2]

The *Magazine of Art*[3] described this painting as a 'spirited and taking imitation of the child-pictures of Mr. Millais'. The *Spectator*,[4] however, reviewing the Royal Academy exhibition at which it was shown, wrote: 'Two years ago the desire of painting babies seized this artist, and since then he has produced more and bigger babies, more apple-cheeked, more brightly and expensively clothed, and altogether baby-er [*sic*] babies than any one painter we have ever seen.' Other reviews were generally favourable – the *Art Journal*[5] identified the girl as a bridesmaid.

REPR: H. Blackburn, *Academy Notes*, 1884, p. 16.

PROV: Proprietors of the *Graphic*[6] sale, Christie's 8 March 1889, lot 303, bought Lever[7] (£160.13*s*.).

EXH: Royal Academy 1884 (177); St. Jude's, Whitechapel 1888 (28); Hulme Hall, Port Sunlight, *An Exhibition to Celebrate the Coronation*, 1902 (2); Hulme Hall, Port Sunlight, *Autumn Art Exhibition*, 1902 (102).

*Quite Ready* LL 3615

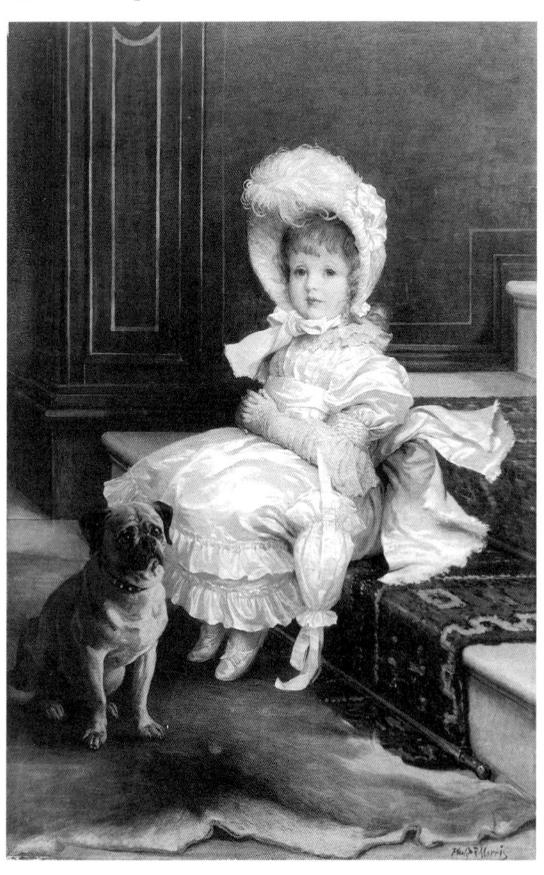

1 Label on stretcher: *Charles Roberson and Co., 99 Long Acre.*

2 Megan James Evans, 'Nansi Bach and her Portrait', *Country Quest*, May 1987, vol. 27, no. 12, p. 24 (published by North Wales Newspapers Ltd., Oswestry).

3 *Magazine of Art*, 1884, p. 351.

4 *Spectator*, 17 May 1884, p. 649.

5 *Art Journal*, 1884, p. 179; *Illustrated London News*, 17 May 1884, p. 490; Pall Mall Gazette, *Pictures of the Year, 1884*, p. 3.

6 The *Graphic* magazine had a gallery in the 1880s at 190 The Strand – there is a label on the back of LL 3615 referring to this gallery – see *Graphic*, 27 December 1884, p. 671; here paintings which had been bought by the magazine to be reproduced were on sale at prices lower than those set by the artists; LL 3615 was presumably reproduced either in the *Graphic* or as a separate print published by the *Graphic* but the reproduction has not been traced; it did not appear in the *Graphic* for 1884.

7 Lever presumably acquired LL 3615 for use as a soap advertisement; for his use of paintings as soap advertisements see p. xiii and Royal Academy, *Lord Leverhulme*, 1980, pp. 14 ff. No Lever Brothers advertisements using LL 3615 have, however, been traced (Ailsa Bowers, letter to the compiler, 5 November 1985).

**MOSTYN, Tom Edwin** (1864–1930)
***Silver and Gold***
LL 3686 (WHL 3591)
Canvas[1]: 175.5 × 236 cm
Signed: *T. Mostyn 1918*[2]

The artist seems at this time to have specialized in grand evocative semi-formal garden scenes very decoratively composed.[3]

PROV: Bought by Lever from the artist June 1918 (£350).

*Silver and Gold*
LL 3686

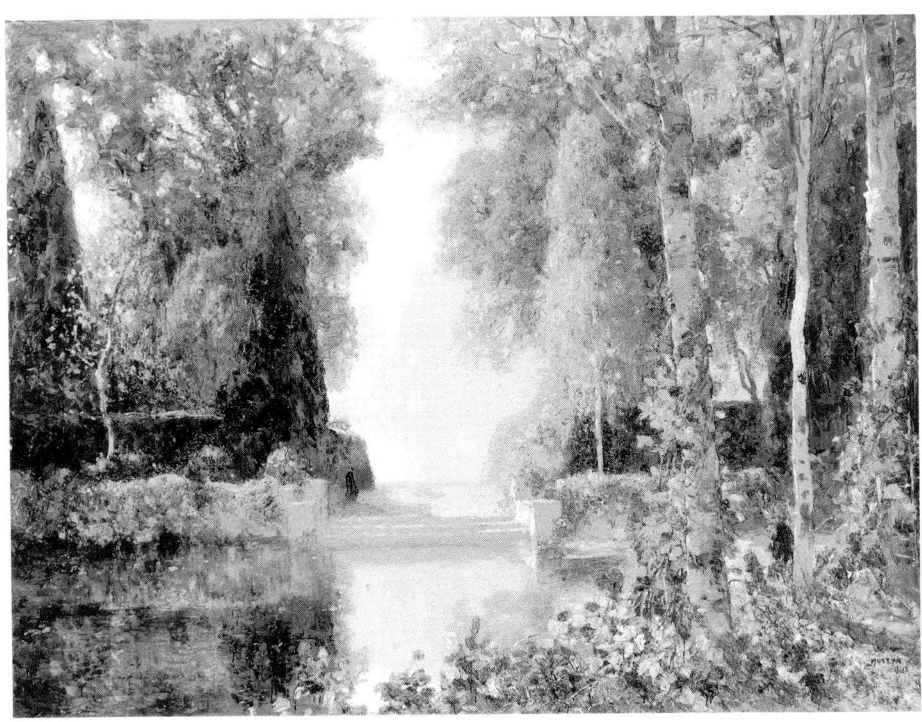

EXH: Royal Academy 1918 (380).[4]

1 Canvas stamp: G. Roberson and Co. Ltd., 89 Long Acre, London.

2 Not visible in 1991.

3 For example, *Enchanted* (see note 4), *An Elegy* and *A Garden of Memory*; for these two last paintings see *Royal Academy Illustrated*, 1917, pp. 46, 51. The critics in 1918 were, however, unimpressed; neither the reviews in *The Times* nor the long review of the Royal Academy landscapes in the *Connoisseur* (1918, vol. 51, pp. 116–17) mention LL 3686.

4 *Royal Academy Illustrated*, 1918, p. 36 printed an illustration of Mostyn's *Enchanted* instead of an illustration of LL 3686, although the reproduction was entitled *Silver and Gold* in the catalogue; this was due to a printer's error (letter from the artist dated 13 December 1918).

**MULLER, William James** (1812–1845)
***Stream With Peasants Driving Cattle***
LL 3573 (WHL 2812)
Canvas: 35.8 × 46 cm
Signed: *W. Muller / W. Muller 1840*[1]

The subject is probably Wickham Bridge, which crosses the River Frome at Stapleton just north of Bristol.[2]

PROV: J. Staats Forbes[3] sale, Christie's 2 June 1916, lot 135, bought Gooden and Fox (£39.18*s*.), for Lever (£41.10*s*.).

1 The second signature, *W. Muller 1840*, is incised rather crudely into the paint at the bottom right; it may not be genuine as LL 3573 seems substantially earlier.

2 Stapleton was very popular among Bristol artists in the 1820s – see Tate Gallery, *Francis Danby*, 1988, pp. 19–20; the example closest to LL 3573 is *Figures at Wickham Bridge, Stapleton* of about 1819–20 (Sotheby's sale 7 October 1981, lot 221,

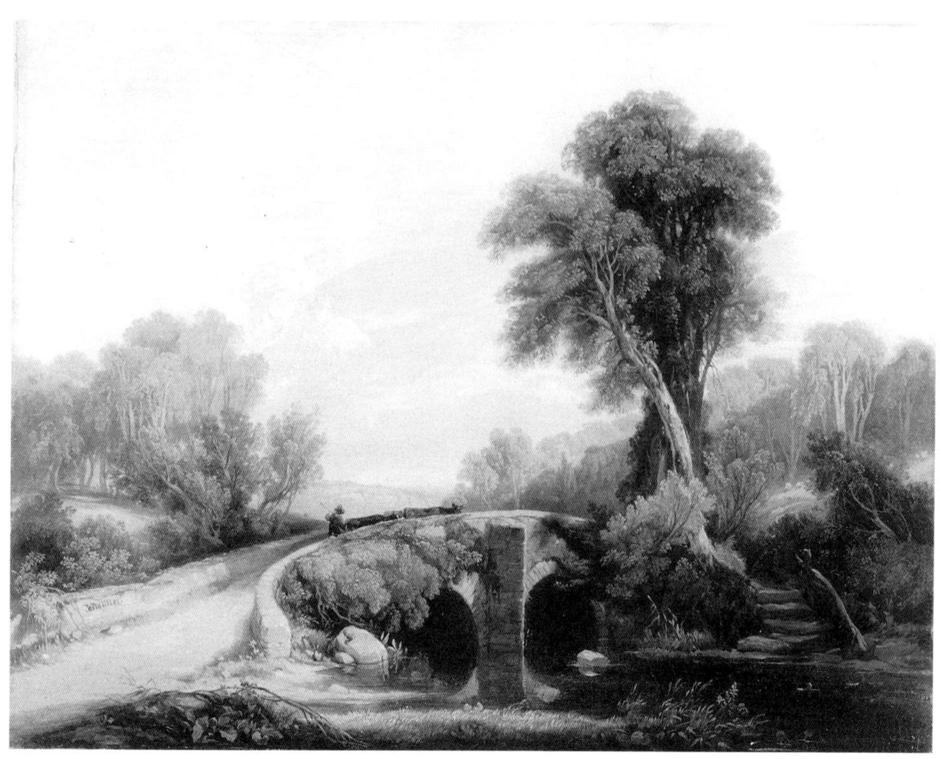

*Stream with Peasants Driving Cattle* LL 3573

there attributed to Thomas Creswick). I am indebted to Francis Greenacre for this suggestion. LL 3573 is listed in C.G.E. Bunt, *Life and Work of W.J. Muller*, 1948, p. 87.

3 A printed label on the back of LL 3573 reads *f 989*; perhaps this is a Staats Forbes inventory label.

**MULLER, William James** (1812–1845), **after**

## *Young Anglers*

LL 3687 (WHL 120, H 439)
Canvas[1]: 91.5 × 70.5 cm
Inscribed: *W. Muller 1845*[2]

This is a version of a well-known composition by Muller; other versions include the *Young Anglers* of 1843 formerly in the F.J. Nettlefold Collection,[3] the *Gillingham* of 1845 owned by the Mitchell Galleries in 1947,[4] the *Young Anglers* of 1843 or 1845 in the Walker Art Gallery, Liverpool, the *Young Anglers* formerly in the Lady Lever Art Gallery (WHL 2800)[5] and the *Gillingham on the Medway* of 1841 now in the Guildhall Art Gallery, London.[6] The Lady Lever Art Gallery version is probably not autograph. The church appears in other Gillingham views of this period by Muller; it may be identifiable with St. Mary Magdalene, Gillingham, but that church, even before its restoration in 1868, differed considerably from the church in Muller's painting.[7] Copies and forgeries of Muller's works were circulating as early as 1848.[8]

PROV: Bought by Lever[9] from James Orrock 1912.

1 Label: *R. Dolman and Sons, 6 New Compton Street, London, WC.*

2 Another possible reading of the date is 1842.

3 22 × 16 in.; C.R. Grundy and F.G. Roe,

*Catalogue of the Pictures and Drawings in the Collection of F. J. Nettlefold*, 1937, vol. 3, p. 114; this was presumably the *Gillingham: two children fishing in the foreground*, lot 321, in the Sam Mendel sale, Christie's 15 March 1875, bought Agnew (£630) for Sir William Armstrong; his sale, Christie's 24 June 1910, lot 81, bought Gooden and Fox (£210).

4 42 × 36 in.; reproduced in 'Souvenir of the Antique Dealer's Fair', *Connoisseur*, 1947, p. 48, and there stated to have been lot 181 in the John Heugh sale, Christie's 24 April 1874, bought Agnew (£2,152.10*s*.). The Heugh picture, however, was 33 × 54 in. according to the sale catalogue. The Mitchell picture was sold at Christie's 15 April 1988, lot 56.

5 41½ × 33½ in.; R.R. Tatlock, *A Record of the Collection in the Lady Lever Art Gallery, Port Sunlight*, 1928, vol. 1, p. 107 (there stated to have come from the collection of Lord Northwick and J.H. Standen); see C.G.E. Bunt, *Life and Work of William James Muller*, 1948, p. 87; it was also no. 79 (repr) in the 1896 Birmingham City Art Gallery *W.J. Muller* exhibition (there stated to have been formerly owned by Lord Northwick and George Wyatt) and lot 131 in the Joseph Standen sale, Christie's 26 May 1916, bought Gooden and Fox (£252) for Lever; then it was sold at Christie's 17 March 1961, lot 77, bought Davidge (£115.10*s*.). Lever liked buying various different versions of the same composition; indeed he owned yet another version signed and dated 1842 sold by his executors in 1926, see Appendix I and Alex Kidson, 'Lever and the Collecting of Eighteenth Century British Paintings', *Journal of the History of Collections*, 1992, vol. 4, pp. 201–9.

6 42 × 34 in.; Charles Gassiot Bequest. This was probably the version exhibited at the British Institution 1842 (112), 57 × 49 in. including the frame, as *Gillingham on the Medway*. Other *Young Anglers* and *Gillingham* paintings are listed by Bunt, *op. cit.*, and by N.N. Solly, *Memoirs of the Life of William James Muller*, 1875, but may refer to quite different compositions. The *View at Gillingham with Cottages* of 1841 in the Birmingham City Art Gallery (79 21) is very similar to LL 3687 but lacks the church and the anglers, while a copy after the composition without the anglers was made by Alfred Vickers (*Apollo*, 1934, p. iii – then owned by Vicars Brothers, 23 × 18 in.).

7 Russell Thomson, letter to the compiler, 8 May 1985; W.N. Yates, letter to the compiler, 25 June 1985.

8 See Bristol Museums and Art Gallery, *W.J. Muller*, 1991, p. 126, which argues that the composition reflects the demands of Muller's patrons, public and dealers, rather than his own ambitions.

9 MSS Orrock Inventory 1912, p. 13.

## *Young Anglers* LL 3687

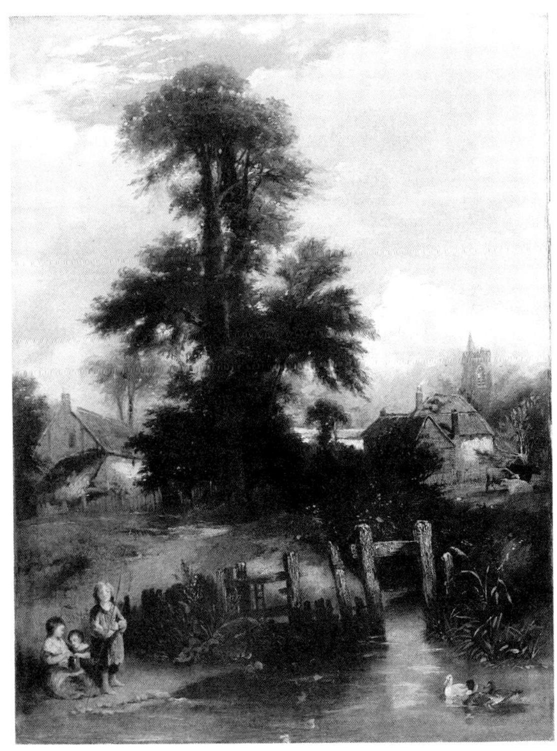

**MUNNINGS, Sir Alfred James**
(1878–1959)

### *The Friesian Bull*

LL 3915 (LP 69)
Canvas: 95.3 × 129 cm
Signed: *A.J. MUNNINGS*

In about 1920[1] the artist went to stay on the Devonshire farm of his friends and patrons, Mr. and Mrs. James Putnam, who lived at Home Farm, Farringdon, near Exeter. They had recently bought a Friesian bull called Ongar Vic Klaas for £2000; Munnings wrote in his autobiography:[2]

*One morning we had the bull taken out. Seeing the heavy, slow moving, black and white colossus led across the field was more than I could bear. The same afternoon, with the sun getting lower, I was at work on a large canvas. I still recall the picture of the placid, docile beast passing by with low, ominous roaring – which was friendly talk – and slow, rhythmic movement, led by the attendant with a long pole fixed to a copper ring in its nose. Beyond, as a background, the simple English landscape – hedges, fields and hedgerow oaks, not yet hacked down.*

Ongar Vic Klaas was born on 1 December 1913 and was bred by J.A. Palsma of Wirdum, from whom he was bought for £57 by the British Holstein Cattle Society, imported into England and sold by the Society at a sale conducted by John Thornton and Co. in the Clock House, Byfleet on 6 November 1914 (lot 21). There he was acquired by J.R. Furze for £157.10*s*., and early in 1919 the Putnams, then farming at Haydon Hill House, Aylesbury, bought him for £2000. Much of their famous herd was sold at auction on 4 September 1919 when they moved to Devonshire, but Ongar Vic Klaas went with them.

Munnings did not succeed in selling the painting – partly due to its subject – and before it was exhibited some twenty-seven years later at the Royal Academy he seems to have reworked it, adding in particular more finish and detail to the herdsman and to the foreground landscape.[3]

A sketch for this painting (or possibly a smaller version of it) was offered for sale by Richard Green (Fine Paintings) Ltd. in 1967;[4] Bert Smith, 'a handyman and jack of all trades' was the model for the herdsman.[5] The existence of this sketch and of the model, who seems to have lived, like the artist, in Dedham, indicate that the genesis of *The Friesian Bull* was not as spontaneous and immediate as the artist indicated in his account of its origin. Nor does the letter he wrote to the Curator of the Lady Lever Art Gallery in 1947[6] seem to have been entirely accurate: 'One of my few decent paintings and all done out of doors with the Bull held there. The background was done with the rest of it. Nothing altered.'

The importation of all live cattle into Britain was banned from 1896 onwards for fear of disease, but the rules were waived for a carefully controlled and very successful importation of 20 cows and 39 bulls (including Ongar Vic Klaas) in 1914. These were all pure-bred Friesian cattle – or Holstein as they were then called – and their numerous sons and daughters did much to popularize the breed in Britain; they provided a larger yield of milk[7] and more beef than the traditional English Shorthorn. Although in 1900 there were only some thirty or forty Friesian herds in Britain, by the middle of the 20th century they had become the dominant breed in British dairy farming. This painting can therefore be seen – like Stubbs's *Lincolnshire Ox* in the Walker Art Gallery, Liverpool – as an important symbol of a revolution in British farming.[8]

At the 1921 Alpine Club Gallery exhibition the *Connoisseur* critic[9] singled out only one painting for praise: *The Friesian Bull*. He described it as 'a study in stormy sunlight executed with a masterly comprehension of all the possibilities afforded by the subject'.

The most ambitious analysis of the painting was, however, provided by John Masefield in his introduction to the Alpine Club Gallery catalogue:[10]

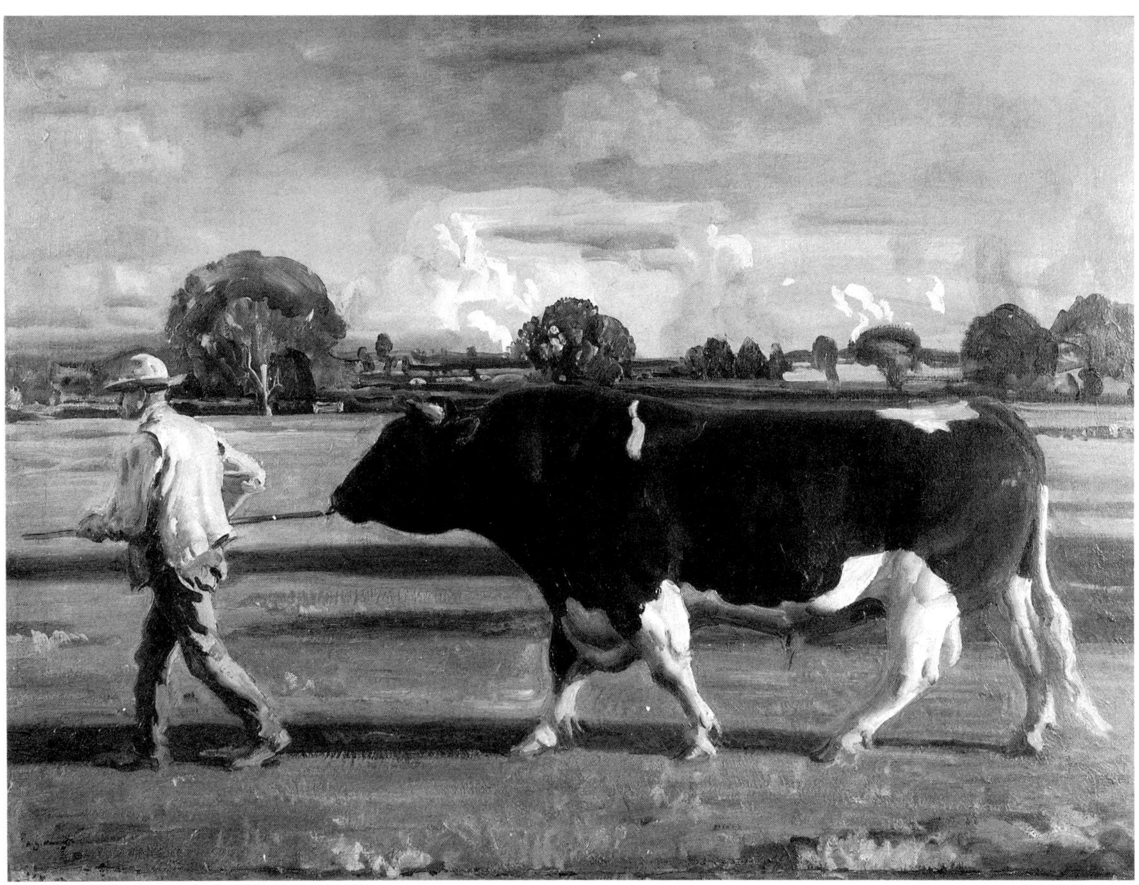

*The Friesian Bull* LL 3915

*The first [picture] is that of the foundation of civilization, and the rough ground on which we are built. It is that of a man leading a bull. The man leads the bull by a twitch hooked to a ring in the bull's nose. It is a picture of the elements of man's life on earth; his conquering of the beasts by which he lives. Without the bull man would be little indeed. He could hardly cultivate, he could hardly live. We here, living in this modern world of gas and God knows what, exist because somewhere, far enough out of sight of many, a man leads a bull thus.*

REPR: G.S. Davies, 'Mr. A.J. Munnings's Pictures at the Alpine Club Gallery', *Country Life*, 30 April 1921, p. 515.

PROV: Bought from the artist 1947 (£750).

EXH: Alpine Club Gallery, *Pictures of the Belvoir Hunt and other Country Scenes*, 1921 (12); Royal Academy, 1947 (221).[11]

1 The date comes from Royal Academy, *Sir Alfred Munnings*, 1956, no. 76, p. 10. Stanley Booth, *Sir Alfred Munnings*, 1978, p. 126 also dates LL 3915 to 1920.

2 Alfred Munnings, *The Second Burst*, 1951, pp. 211–12. Munnings does not here identify the bull or its owners, but a photograph of LL 3915 with Putnam's name written on the back is in the Sir Alfred Munnings Art Museum, Dedham, and J.K. Stanford in *British Friesians, a History of the Breed*, 1956, pp. 87–8 also names the Putnams as the owners. The distinguished ancestry and

progeny of Ongar Vic Klaas, together with details of their milk yields and his own history, can be obtained from the *Catalogue of Friesland Herdbook Cattle imported by the British Holstein Cattle Society* for sale by auction on 6 November 1914 by John Thornton and Co. at the Clock House, Byfleet, Surrey (lot 21); from the *Catalogue of British Friesian Cattle from the celebrated herd of Mrs. J. Putnam* for sale by auction on 4 September 1919 at Haydon Hill House, Aylesbury by John Thornton and Co., p. 22; and from British Friesian Cattle Society, *History of British Friesian Cattle*, 1930, pp. 438–9. The compiler is most grateful to Molly Garwood, Timothy Stevens and, most especially, to David Cleveland for these references.

3 Most of this work had been completed before 1927, see Lionel Lindsay, *A.J. Munnings*, 1927, plate VIII but the artist did more work to the foreground grass and to the upper areas of the sky between 1927 and 1947. This re-working may reflect the artist's change of style between 1920 and 1947 towards greater polish and finish or it may have been intended to circumvent the Royal Academy's ban on the showing in its annual exhibitions of pictures previously exhibited in London.

4 Reproduced in *Country Life*, 9 February 1967, Supplement; it measured 63.5 × 76 cm.

5 Munnings, *op. cit.*, pp. 133–4.

6 Letter to the curator, 16 May 1947.

7 The artist, in fact, disliked the breed because the cows gave 'quantities of thin milk' (Munnings, *op. cit.*, p. 134).

8 See particularly S.J.G. Hall and J. Clutton-Brock, *Two hundred years of British farm livestock*, 1989, pp. 87–9; Stanford, *op. cit.*, pp. 86 ff.; David Cleveland, 'The first 75 Years: Highlights of the Breed's History', *British Friesian Journal*, 1984, vol. 66, pp. 452 ff.; and British Friesian Cattle Society, *op. cit.* Predictably the *Country Life* critic at the 1921 Alpine Club Gallery exhibition was even more enthusiastic about the bull than about Munnings's rendering of it – see G.S. Davies, 'Mr. A.J. Munnings's Pictures at the Alpine Club Gallery', *Country Life*, 30 April 1921, p. 516.

9 *Connoisseur*, 1921, vol. 60, p. 184.

10 *Pictures of the Belvoir Hunt and other Scenes of English Country Life by A.J. Munnings*, Alpine Club Gallery, 1921, pp. 3–4. Whether Munnings's *Friesian Bull* can really sustain Masefield's rhetoric is not certain.

11 Where it was seen by a *Times* leader writer and used as part of a plea for more animal painting; see *The Times*, 7 June 1947.

## **MURRAY, David** (1849–1934)
## ***Scenting the Summer Air: Golden Gorse***

LL 3129 (WHL 3143)
Canvas[1]: 140 × 167.5 cm
Signed: *David Murray 1916*

The critic of the *Connoisseur*[2] described this painting as 'perhaps the artist's best work' and as 'a delightful embodiment of luscious early summer atmosphere glowing with delicate colour'. It shows the artist's increasing concern with elaborate design and monumental effect in his later years.[3]

REPR: *Royal Academy Illustrated*, 1916, p. 143.

PROV: Bought from the artist by Lever 1917 (£500).[4]

EXH: Royal Academy 1916 (358); Liverpool Autumn Exhibition 1916 (168).

1 Frame maker's label: *C.M. MAY AND SON, 134 Wardour Street, Soho.*

2 *Connoisseur*, 1916, vol. 45, p. 124. The critic of the *Studio* agreed; he found the artist 'at his best in his broad and expressive landscape' (*Studio*, 1916, vol. 68, p. 40).

*Scenting the Summer Air: Golden Gorse*
LL 3129

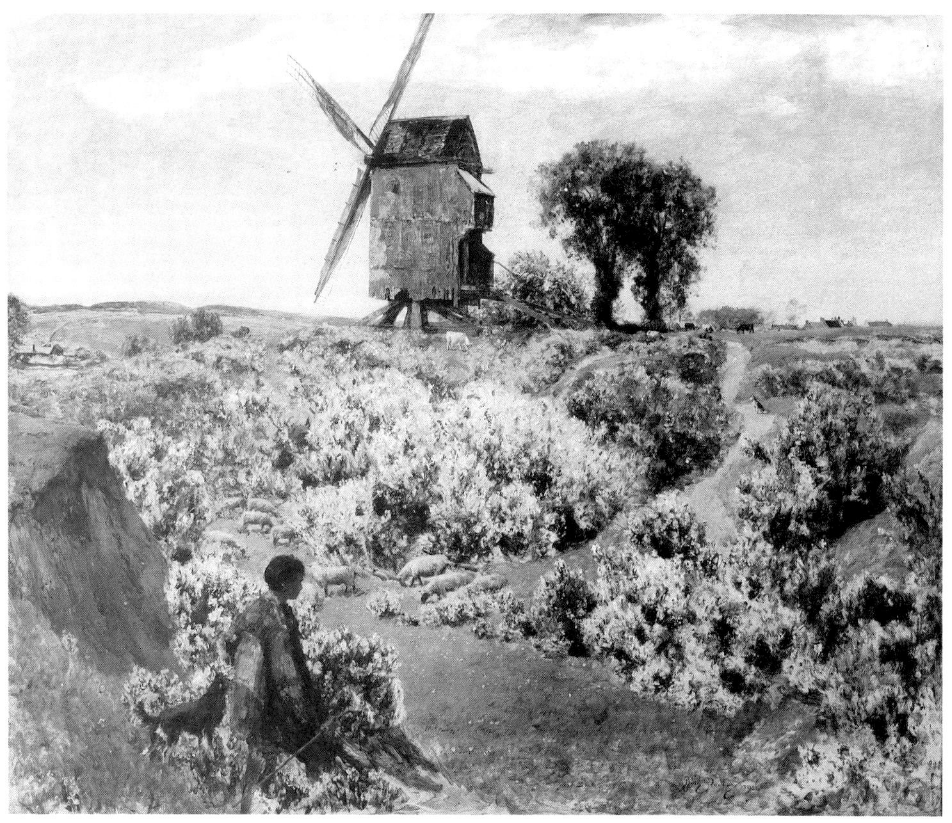

3 For this development see J.L. Caw, *Scottish Painting*, 1908, pp. 304 ff.

4 Murray spent two summer holidays as Lever's guest at Lews Castle on the Island of Lewis and consequently sent Hebridean subjects to the Royal Academy exhibitions of 1919, 1920 and 1921 (Viscount Leverhulme, *Viscount Leverhulme*, 1927, p. 281).

**NEALE, George Hall** (1863–1940)

***Sir William Hesketh Lever, Bart.***

LL 3916 (WHL 2757)
Canvas: 212 × 120.7 cm
Signed: *G. Hall Neale*

Lever wears court dress[1] and stands in one of the rooms of his London home, The Hill, at Hampstead.[2]

REPR: *Royal Academy Illustrated*, 1916, p. 53; *Liverpool Autumn Exhibition Catalogue*, 1916, p. 44.

PROV: Commissioned from the artist in 1916 by Lever (£399.3*s*.).[3]

EXH: Royal Academy 1916 (613); Liverpool Autumn Exhibition 1916 (191).

1 He became a baronet in 1911 and was raised to the peerage in 1917.

2 See the various illustrations of different rooms at The Hill reproduced in Anderson Galleries, *Art Collections of the Late Viscount Leverhulme*, Part 1, 9–13 February 1926. So many alterations were carried out to The Hill around 1916 that the exact room used by Hall Neale cannot be identified. Onslow Ford's *St. George and the Dragon* (now in the Lady Lever Art Gallery) is on the commode behind Lever. Lucy Wood has suggested to the

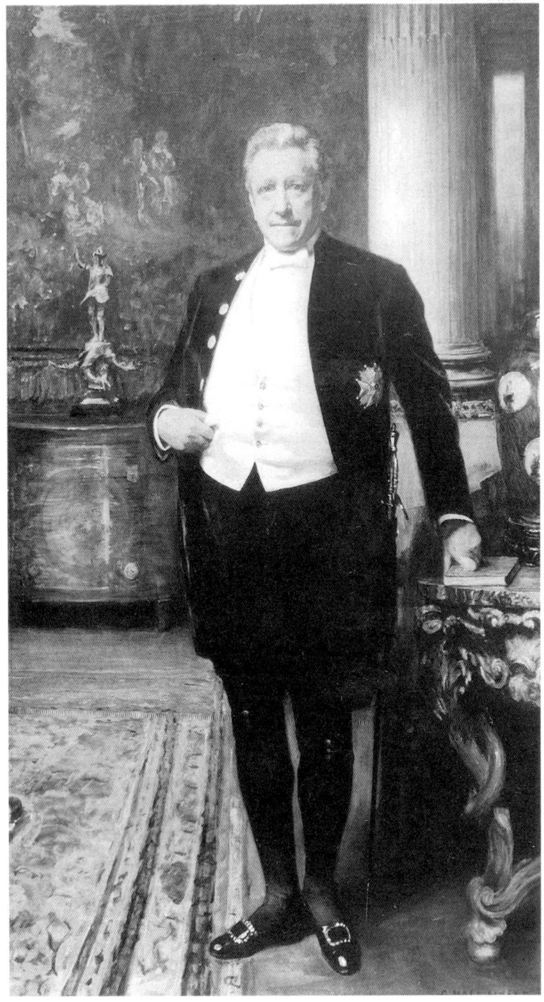

*Sir William Hesketh Lever, Bart.* LL 3916

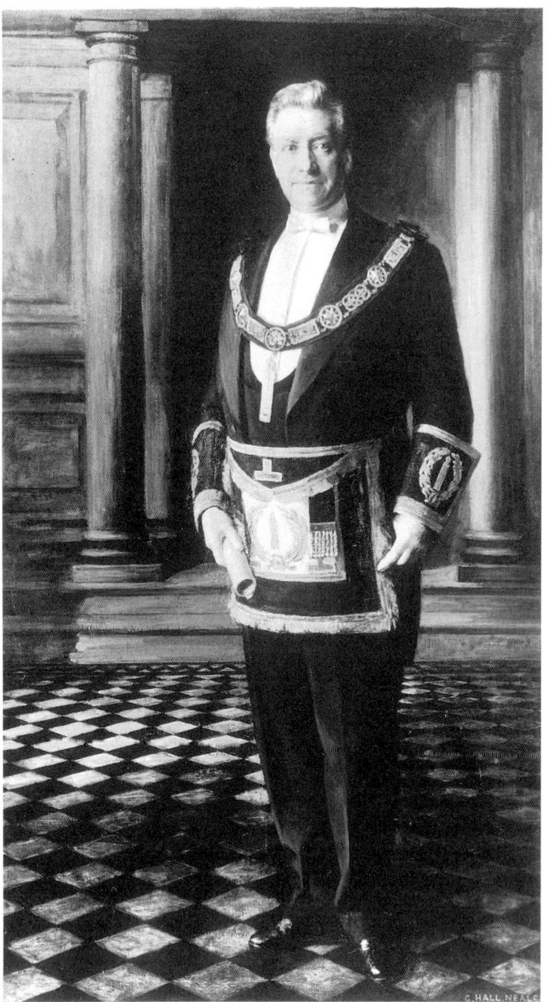

*William Hesketh Lever, Baron Leverhulme of Bolton-le-Moors, as Junior Grand Warden of England* LL 3747

compiler that the commode in the background was probably the 'segmental satinwood Adam commode' sold by Lever's executors at the Anderson Galleries (New York) 9–13 February 1926, lot 99, and that the table in the foreground may be the 'fine old Georgian carved and gilt side table of broken serpentine shape, the top surmounted by a green veined marble slab – the underpart with dragons and shaped stretcher' bought by Lever from D.L. Isaacs on 3 March 1915 and inventoried by Lever as X 212.

3 LL 3916 was probably commissioned to make a pair for LL 3649 (see p. 95).

## *William Hesketh Lever, Baron Leverhulme of Bolton-le-Moors, as Junior Grand Warden of England*

LL 3747 (WHL 3615)
Canvas: 213.8 × 120 cm
Signed: *G. HALL. NEALE*

Lever was an enthusiastic Freemason.[1] He was initiated in 1902; he founded a considerable number of lodges and in 1908 became Provinçial Senior Grand Warden of Cheshire; at national level in 1918 he was promoted to the rank of Past Junior Grand Warden of the United Grand Lodge of England and he wears the regalia appropriate to that post in this portrait. Lever gave to the Lady Lever Art Gallery an important Masonic collection mainly accumulated by Albert Calvert;[2] he encouraged the staff of Lever Brothers to become Freemasons and valued the movement's emphasis on self improvement and on high standards of conduct.

REPR: Photogravure for issue to Masonic lodges.

PROV: Commissioned by Lever 1918 (£399.3*s*.).

1 Viscount Leverhulme, *Viscount Leverhulme*, 1927, pp. 260–1; John Hamill, 'The Masonic Collection at the Lady Lever Art Gallery', *Journal of the History of Collections*, 1992, vol. 4, pp. 285–95.

2 Hamill, *op. cit.*

**NEALE, Maud Hall** (active 1889–1938)

***Lady Lever***

LL 3649 (WHL 1936)
Canvas[1]: 211 × 119.8 cm
Signed: *Maud Hall Neale*

Elizabeth Ellen Hulme married Lever in 1874 and died in 1913. Lever named the Lady Lever Art Gallery after her but she played no substantial part in the assembly of his collections. She was born in about 1851. The background shows the water garden at The Hill, Hampstead.[2] This is a posthumous portrait painted a year after the sitter's death. She is wearing court dress.

REPR: Rembrandt Intaglio Printing Co., Ltd.

PROV: Commissioned from the artist by Lever 1914 (£210).

1 Canvas stamp: *JOHN SMITH / 117 HAMPSTEAD ROAD N.W. / LONDON.*

2 See the illustration in *Country Life*, 1918, vol. 43, p. 192.

*Lady Lever* LL 3649

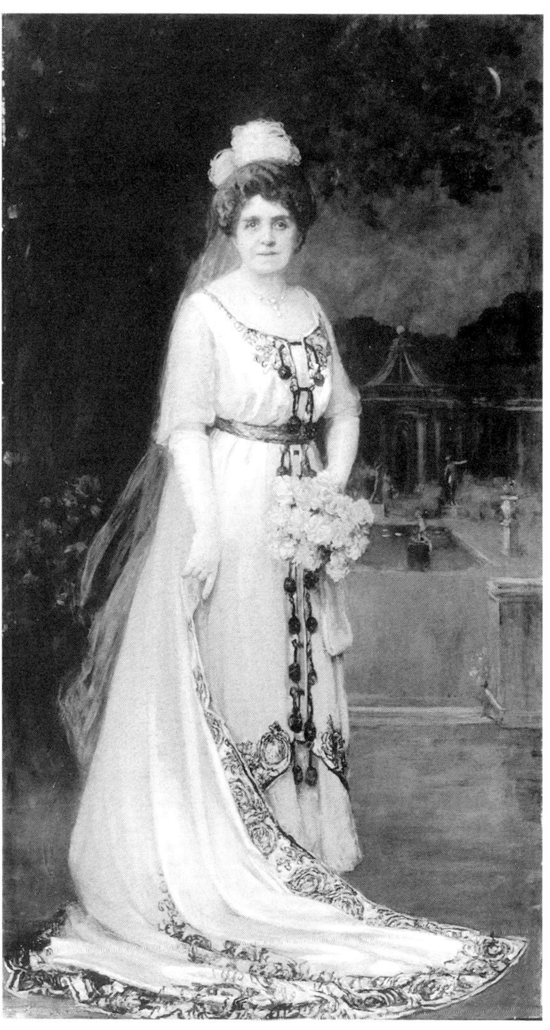

**ORCHARDSON, William Quiller** (1832–1910)

***The Young Duke***

LL 3612 (WHL 2872)
Canvas: 147 × 252 cm
Signed: *W.Q. Orchardson 88*

This painting represents an imaginary scene set in France during the reign of Louis XIV; a banquet to celebrate the young duke's coming of age has ended and his guests are drinking a toast to him.[1] As in his *Voltaire* of 1883 the artist is satirizing high society of the early 18th century; he was of course equally critical of the social behaviour of his own generation.[2] He may have been inspired by Augustus Egg's *Life of Buckingham* of 1853–5 (Yale Center for British Art, New Haven). This is another dissolute aristocratic drinking scene but set in 17th-century England.

The background was painted from the artist's studio built by him at 13 Portland Place;[3] the glass, plates and flower bowl belonged to the artist but he painted the silver nef from a smaller one lent by his friend Henry Gilbey;[4] Arthur Gilbey was the model for the young duke; the artist's servant, Tuke, and other professional models were used for the guests.[5]

At the 1889 Royal Academy, the *Young Duke* had the most favoured place – in the centre of the large room (gallery III) – where Leighton's pictures were normally hung[6] and from the critics it received considerable praise; the *Magazine of Art*[7] described it as 'the greatest work I venture to think that has appeared in the Royal Academy for many a year'. Praise was especially lavished on the artist's technical skill, particularly in the rendering of background, still life and accessories,[8] on his sense of colour and of colour harmony,[9] on the sinuous, rhythmical lines formed by the rows of figures[10] and on his moral purpose.[11] Some reservations were expressed about the prevailing hot yellow tonality of the painting,[12] about the relative triviality of the subject spread over so large a canvas[13] and about the monotonous repetition of a single facial type,[14] while the porcelain on the table was seen as too late for an early 18th-century setting.[15]

There are a considerable number of studies for the *Young Duke* in the large sketch books now at the Royal Academy (inv. 4B); they are mainly studies for the entire composition and one is inscribed, apparently by the artist: 'The king sleeps', indicating that the painting's title may have been an afterthought. A charcoal sketch for the *Young Duke* was lot 777 in the artist's sale, Gillow's

*The Young Duke* LL 3612 (colour plate 8)

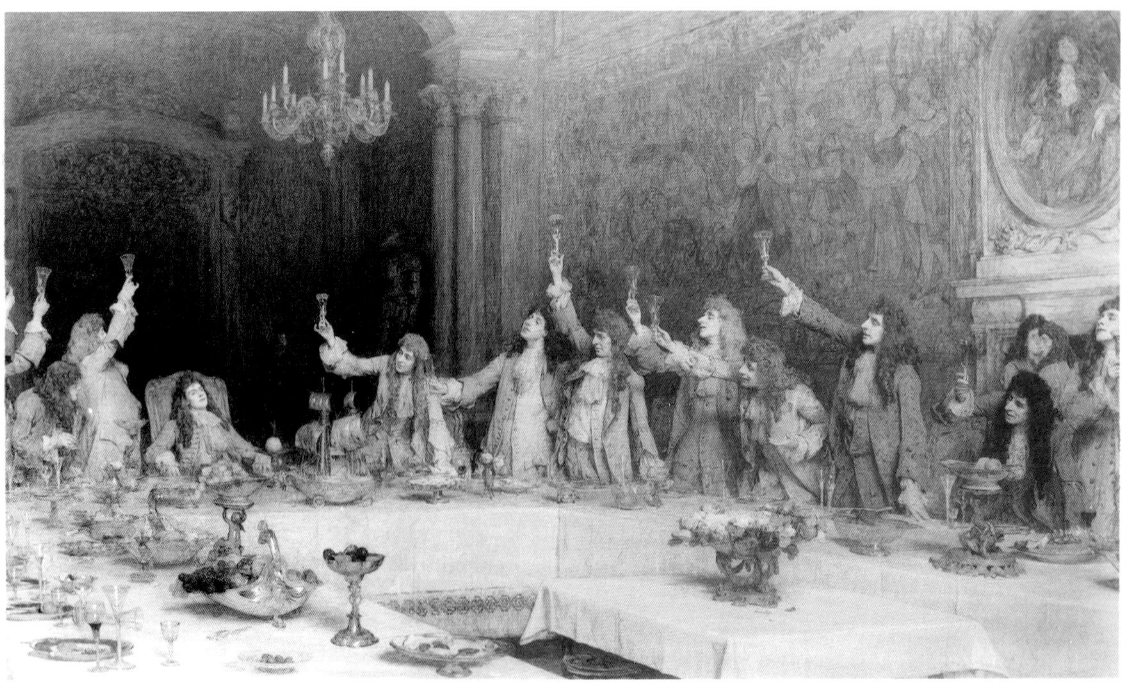

24–7 May 1910 (51 × 61 cm); Sir Thomas Glen-Coats lent a sketch for it (or possibly a version of it) to the *Scottish Exhibition of Natural History, Art and Industry*, Glasgow 1991 (48).

REPR: H. Blackburn, *Academy Notes*, 1889, p. 23; *Royal Academy Pictures*, 1889, p. 75; Pall Mall Gazette, *Pictures of the Year, 1889*, p. 4; Liverpool Autumn Exhibition catalogue, 1889, p. 98; F.A. Laguillermie (etching), 1891.[16]

PROV: Charles Neck;[17] George McCulloch (by 1897);[18] his sale, Christie's 29 May 1913, lot 178, bought A. Wertheimer (£4,620); T.J. Blakeslee sale, American Art Association (New York) 15 April 1915, lot 228; Knoedler; bought by Lever from Eugene Cremetti (or Thomas McLean), 17 July 1916 (£2,750).

EXH: Royal Academy 1889 (243); Liverpool Autumn Exhibition 1889 (1148);[19] Paris Salon, Société des Artistes français, 1896 (1520); Guildhall Gallery, *Pictures by Painters of the British School*, 1897 (33); Royal Scottish Academy 1905 (240); Royal Academy, *Winter Exhibition*, 1909 (77); International Exhibition, Rome, 1911 (69); Liverpool Autumn Exhibition 1922 (882).

1 H.O. Gray, *The Life of Sir William Quiller Orchardson*, 1930, pp. 273–4; W. Armstrong, 'Art of William Quiller Orchardson', *Portfolio*, 1895, pp. 52–3; Gray observed that the French critics described LL 3612 as an English scene. There are scenes in Disraeli's *The Young Duke* of 1829 not dissimilar to the one in LL 3612, but Disraeli has a contemporary setting for his novel. J.S. Little in 'W.Q. Orchardson', *Art Annual*, 1897, pp. 26–8, noted that the artist gradually abandoned illustration of particular historical and literary scenes in favour of more generalized and abstract subjects; *The Duke's Antechamber* of 1869 (Beaverbrook Foundations, Fredericton, New Brunswick) seems to have been an important precedent for LL 3612 (see Scottish Arts Council, *Sir William Quiller Orchardson*, 1972, no. 17).

2 In, for example, his *Mariage de Convenance* and in his *Mariage de Covenance – After!* of 1883 and 1886 (Glasgow Art Gallery and Museum and Aberdeen Art Gallery). *The Times*, 4 May 1889, saw LL 3612 as a companion picture to the earlier *Voltaire*.

3 Gray, *op. cit.*, p. 273; the studio is described by Gray, *op. cit.*, p. 118; it was hung with old tapestries and had the Italian marble columns visible in LL 3612; at the end not seen in LL 3612 was a large north window and sky light; the same studio seems to appear in Orchardson's *Voltaire* of 1883, although the artist built it in 1887 (Gray, *op. cit.*, p. 118) – was the studio built from the picture?

4 Gray, *op. cit.*, p. 273; the Gilbeys, who were wine merchants, were friends of the artist.

5 Gray, *op. cit.*, p. 273.

6 Luke Fildes and Marcus Stone were principally responsible for displacing Leighton; see Gray, *op. cit.*, pp. 271–2; *Illustrated London News*, 4 May 1889, p. 554; *The Times*, *op. cit.*

7 *Magazine of Art*, 1889, p. 271. Only the *Spectator*, 25 May 1889, p. 712, was hostile; it preferred the 18th-century paintings of Gérôme and Meissonier. The *Scottish Art Review*, 1889–90, p. 6, referred to 'aristocratic life in the time of the Georges, a period which his mannered but refined method of painting aids him so well in treating'.

8 *Academy*, 11 May 1889, p. 329 (by Claude Phillips); *Athenaeum*, 18 May 1889, p. 636; *The Times*, *op. cit.*; *Spectator*, *op. cit.*; *Magazine of Art*, *op. cit.*; the roses in their bowl received particular praise and the *Art Journal*, 1889, p. 188, stated that they were in the first part of the picture to be painted.

9 *The Times*, *op. cit.*; *Magazine of Art*, *op. cit.*

10 *Academy*, *op. cit.*, for this see also Little, *op. cit.*, who both praises the 'undulating curves' of the composition and finds 'that measure of diversity which avoids formality'.

11 *Athenaeum*, *op. cit.*

12 *Academy*, *op. cit.*; *The Times*, *op. cit.*

13 *Athenaeum*, *op. cit.*; *Academy*, *op. cit.*

14 *Academy*, *op. cit.*; *Illustrated London News*, *op. cit.* George Bernard Shaw in the *World*, 8 May 1889, p. 618, described LL 3612 as 'a large canvas containing an exquisite study of tablecloth and dessert service in the lower half, and a row of ludicrous figures, all exactly like one another, in the upper'.

15 *Academy*, *op. cit.*; *The Times*, *op. cit.*

16 An impression is in the Lady Lever Art Gallery (LP 39).

17 LL 3612 was not at the Charles Neck sale, Christie's 3 May 1890, but the Blakeslee sale catalogue states that it was owned by Neck until 1896.

18 See A.L. Baldry, 'The Collection of George McCulloch', *Art Journal*, 1897, p. 376.

19 Where it was reviewed by P.H. Rathbone in 'The Autumn Exhibition of 1889', *University College Magazine*, 1889, vol. 4, pp. 113–14.

## *St. Helena 1816: Napoleon dictating to Count Las Cases the Account of his Campaigns*

LL 3151 (WHL 4401)
Canvas: 125 × 204 cm

After his defeat at Waterloo, Napoleon was banished to St. Helena where Count de Las Cases wrote his *Mémorial de St. Hélène* based on Napoleon's conversations with him there; these conversations were effectively self-justification; their publication in 1823 was partly responsible for the growth of the Napoleonic legend and the creation of Bonapartism in France.[1]

Orchardson painted in 1880 another incident from Napoleon's life after his fall from power, *On board H.M.S. Bellerophon*. Reacting against the militarist paintings of Napoleon by Jacques Louis David and other artists of the First Empire, artists in France and Britain, led by Paul Delaroche, emphasized the domestic, intimate and reflective side of Napoleon's character.[2]

The psychological tension created by the artist's use of empty space was praised by the critics at the Royal Academy;[3] the *Academy* referred to the 'emptiness full of atmosphere which Mr. Orchardson so loves to depict', while the *Portfolio*[4] observed: 'he had often been twitted with his fondness for empty space but in truth his spaces are not empty . . . they are full of the infinity of nature'. The *Magazine of Art*[5] was more impressed by the artist's subtle colour scheme, describing the picture as a 'study in whites'; the critic of *The Times*[6] had especial praise for the painting of the accessories, particularly the maps on the floor. Critics were, however, divided over the artist's portrayal of Napoleon himself; the former emperor was seen variously as a 'stolid and almost brutal bourgeois',[7] as 'brutal and almost vulgar',[8] or as 'not fat enough';[9] but *The Times*[10] thought that his expression adequately reflected his defeats and disappointments, while the *Pall Mall Gazette*[11] found the figure of Napoleon 'impressive without being theatrical'.

David Murray recalled that parts of the canvas were completely unpainted on the day before it was due to go to the Royal Academy.[12] Gregory Jones, a friend of the artist John Pettie, was the model for the figure of Napoleon; the maps on the floor are alleged to be the very ones used by Napoleon, notably for his 1805 German campaign and were found by the artist at Stanford's, the well-known London map shop.[13]

There are studies for the composition in the large sketch books now at the Royal Academy (inv. 48). Other sketches for the painting included: (1) an oil sketch formerly owned by Lord Blyth,[14] (2) a chalk or charcoal study for the whole composition (125 × 216 cm) also formerly owned by Lord

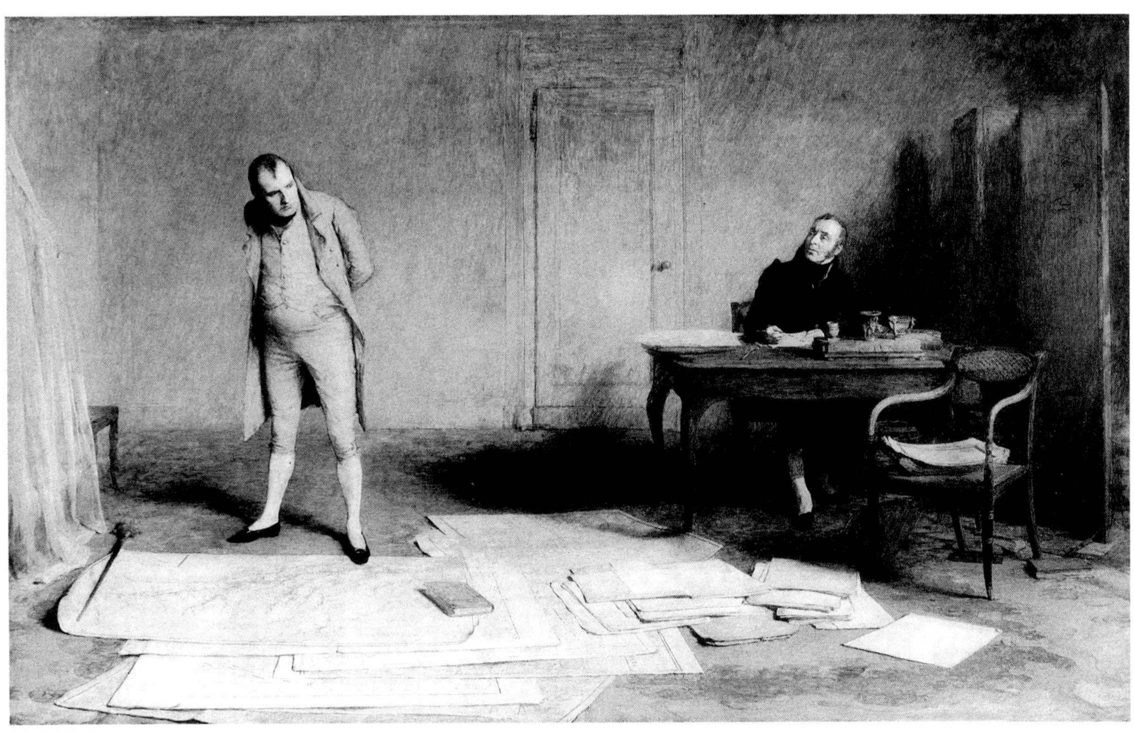

*St. Helena 1816: Napoleon dictating to Count Las Cases the Account of his Campaigns* LL 3151

Blyth,[15] (3) a study for the figure of Napoleon.[16] A charcoal drawing, *Head of Napoleon* (56 × 46 cm) was in the artist's sale, Gillow's 24–7 May 1910, lot 769.

REPR: *Royal Academy Pictures*, 1892, p. 149; Pall Mall Gazette, *Pictures of 1892*, p. 59.

PROV: James Keiller (by 1894);[17] the Keiller Trustees; bought by Lever from Barbizon House (D. Croal Thomson) 1923 (£750).[18]

EXH: Royal Academy 1892 (173); Royal Scottish Academy 1909 (318); Japan Exhibition 1910 (234).

1 Lever had a considerable collection of Napoleonic relics and paintings and was, like the artist, an admirer of Napoleon; see Royal Academy, *Lord Leverhulme*, 1980, no. 28, pp. 66–7.

2 See National Gallery of Scotland, *Masterclass*, 1983, no. 108, p. 98 for some French examples dating from the 1890s. The artist's library contained Antommarchi's *Last Days of Napoleon* and Bussey's *History of Napoleon* (Scottish Arts Council, *Sir William Quiller Orchardson*, 1972, no. 55). Orchardson might have known the prints by Maurin and after Chasselat showing Napoleon dictating to Las Cases – for further details about these prints see Castres, Musée Goya, *Las Cases et le Mémorial de Sainte Hélène*, 1967, nos. 63 and 63 *bis*. He was impressed by Napoleon's power and greatness and deplored the cruelty of his confinement in St. Helena at the end of his life; see H.O. Gray, *Life of Sir William Quiller Orchardson*, 1930, pp. 261, 276. For Scottish artists and collectors specializing in Napoleonic subjects, see Royal Scottish Museum, Edinburgh, *French Connection*, 1985, pp. 71 ff.

3 Like Orchardson's *Young Duke* (see above), LL 3151 had the place of honour in room III of the Royal Academy – see *Pall Mall Gazette*, 30 April 1892; the *Portfolio*, 1892, p. XI stated that LL 3151 was more or less the only narrative painting at the 1892 Academy.

4 *Academy*, 1892, vol. 41, p. 499 (by Claude Phillips), *Portfolio, op. cit.* The *Saturday Review* (14 May 1892, p. 569) was, however, less enthusiastic about the artist's empty spaces: 'The Impressionist is often empty; but although he is more natural in the quality of his emptiness even he dare not, we think, space these two sardines, as it were, so far apart in their box of oil.'

5 *Magazine of Art*, 1892, p. 254. The *Athenaeum*, 14 May 1892, p. 638 was also impressed by the 'chromatic scheme' of LL 3151 noting the black of Napoleon's shoes as 'an extremely telling chromatic accent'.

6 *The Times*, 30 April 1892.

7 *Art Journal*, 1892, p. 219.

8 *Academy, op. cit.*

9 *Magazine of Art, op. cit.*; *Portfolio, op. cit.*

10 *The Times, op. cit.*

11 *Pall Mall Gazette, op. cit.* Of the critics only George Moore was hostile – he preferred the artist's portraits; his reviews of LL 3151 appeared in the *Speaker*, 30 April 1892, p. 528 and in the *Fortnightly Review*, June 1892, reprinted in his *Modern Painting*, 1893, p. 114; this second review was the more severe:

*A great simplicity in the surroundings, and all the points of character insisted on, with the view of awakening the spectator's curiosity. From first to last a vicious desire to narrate an anecdote. It is strange that a man of Mr. Orchardson's talent should participate so fully in the supreme vice of modern art which believes a picture to be the same thing as a scene in a play. The whole picture conceived and executed in that pale yellow tint which seems to be the habitual colour of Mr. Orchardson's mind.*

12 Gray, *op. cit.*, p. 19.

13 Gray, *op. cit.*, p. 276; W. Armstrong, 'Art of William Quiller Orchardson', *Portfolio*, 1895, p. 73. The map visible in LL 3151 was identified by the *Athenaeum, op. cit.*, as a map of the Bay of Genoa; this seems plausible. Lot 374 at the artist's sale, Gillow's 24–7 May 1910, was a parcel of maps and plans by Jomini, etc., and entitled 'Napoleon's Campaigns' and stated to have been used in LL 3151.

14 Scottish Arts Council, *op. cit.*.

15 Executors of Viscount Leverhulme, Anderson Galleries, New York, 2 March 1926, lot 251; probably to be identified with the charcoal sketch of the same size in the artist's sale, Gillow's 24–7 May 1910, lot 828.

16 Reproduced in Armstrong, *op. cit.*, p. 46 as then owned by the artist and in J.S. Little, 'W.Q. Orchardson', *Art Annual*, 1897, p. 10.

17 See R.A.M. Stevenson, 'Mr. Keiller's Collection in Dundee', *Art Journal*, 1894, p. 60 (repr. opp. p. 58).

18 Barbizon House, *An Illustrated Record*, 1923, no. 34.

## **ORROCK, James** (1830–1913)
## ***Sandpits, Milford, Surrey***[1]

LL 3134 (WHL 2081, HH 331)
Canvas[2]: 61 × 91.3 cm
Signed: *J. Orrock 1907*

Lever bought from Orrock about sixty paintings and about one thousand drawings and watercolours by him between 1910 and 1913. Most of them were sold or given away after Lever's death in 1925. This is the only oil painting by Orrock to survive in the Lady Lever Art Gallery. For the importance of Orrock in the formation of Lever's collection,[3] see p. xv.

PROV: Bought from the artist by Lever 1910–11 (£75).[4]

1 This is the traditional title of LL 3134 but Orrock exhibited *Carting Sand on Danbury Common* at the

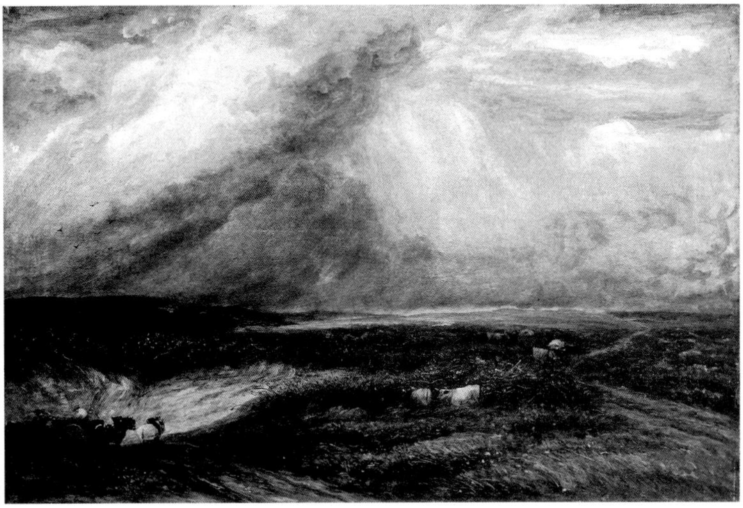

*Sandpits, Milford, Surrey*
LL 3134

1907 Institute of Oil Painters exhibition (no. 365); Danbury Common is in Essex.

2 Canvas stamp: *Winsor and Newton, 38 Rathbone Place, London, No. 417109.*

3 See also Royal Academy, *Lord Leverhulme*, 1980, pp. 22–5.

4 MSS Orrock Inventory, 1910, p. 67.

## **PATRICK, James McIntosh** (born 1907)
### *Glamis Village*

LL 3917 (LP 51)
Canvas[1]: 71.3 × 91.2 cm
Signed: *McINTOSH PATRICK / 39*

This is one of a series of paintings of notable houses, castles and historic buildings done with great topographical accuracy by the artist in the late 1930s;[2] very much less invention was involved than in his earlier work and this more literal approach found favour with patrons.[3] In the foreground is the saw mill and the cattle are pedigree poll Angus cows. In the distance is Kirriemuir.

The artist painted a quite different view of Glamis village in 1946 and this painting is now in the collection of Robert Fleming and Co., London.[4] His view of Glamis Castle was presented by the County of Angus to Princess Margaret and Mr. Antony Armstrong Jones as a wedding gift in July 1960; it had been commissioned by the County.[5]

Herbert Furst in his review of the 1939 Royal Academy exhibition listed the Lady Lever painting as a picture of interest both for its subject and for its aesthetic appeal, but H. Granville Fell in the *Connoisseur* failed to notice it.[6]

A watercolour sketch (24 × 33 cm) was owned by the Fine Art Society in 1991; it is very close to the Lady Lever painting except that it does not contain the trees in the left foreground.

PROV: Purchased from the artist 1939[7] (£262.10*s*.).

EXH: Royal Academy 1939 (357).

1 Canvas stamp: *WINSOR AND NEWTON'S / PREPARED ETC / PRIMED ETC.*

2 Colonel Cardwell Moore, letter to the compiler, 27 January 1992 confirms the accuracy of the depiction of Glamis village in LL 3917.

3 See Roger Billcliffe, *James McIntosh Patrick*, 1987, pp. 24–5. The artist in a letter (12 September 1993) to the compiler writes: 'The painting was

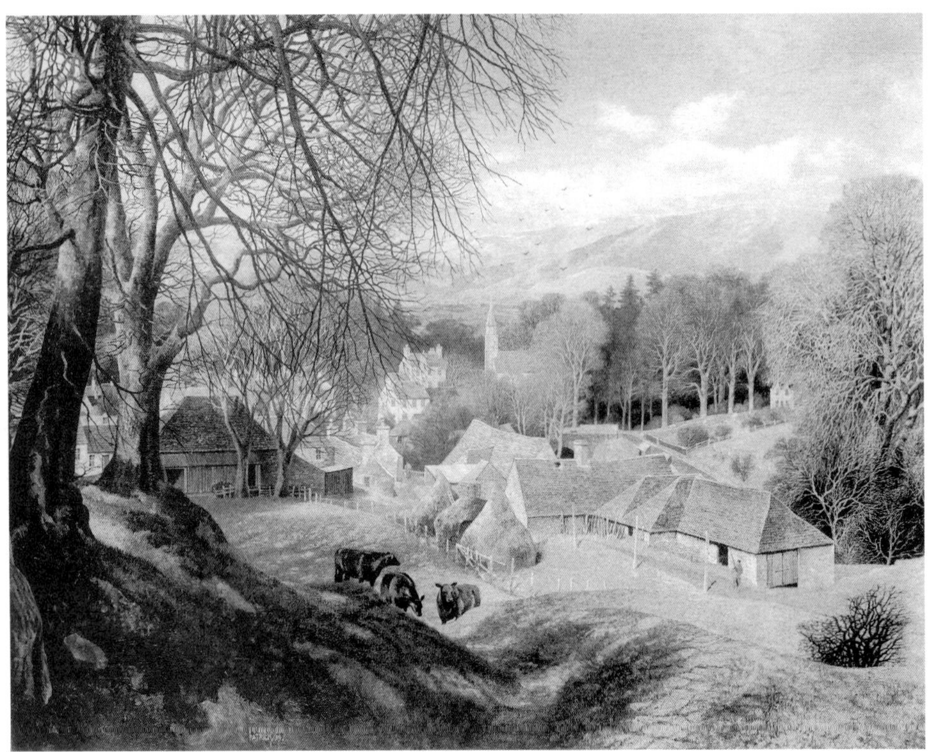

*Glamis Village*
LL 3917

done "on the spot" and so far as I remember only the foreground was "edited".'

4 Billcliffe, *op. cit.*, p. 27 notes that this 1946 view was painted in the open air in front of the subject whereas LL 3917 would have been partly painted in the studio; this new method of working led to a change in the artist's style. The 1946 view is reproduced in Billcliffe, *op. cit.*, plate 25.

5 Reproduced in Billcliffe, *op. cit.*, plate 36, and dated by him to 1960.

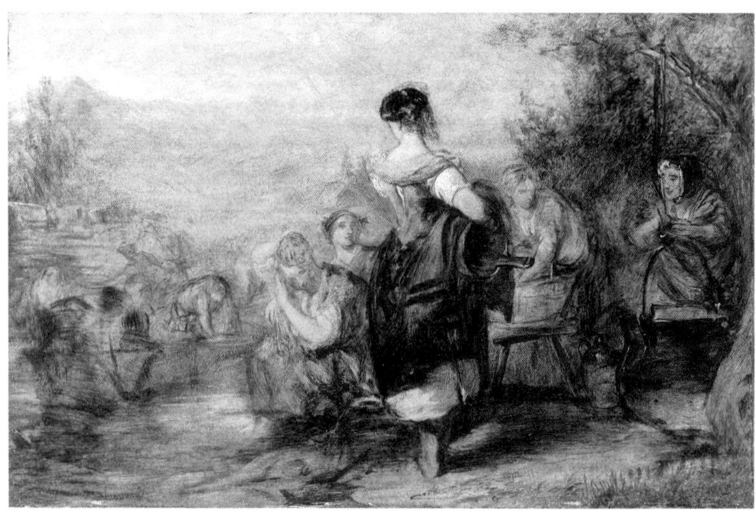

*Study for Scotch Washing*
LL 3918

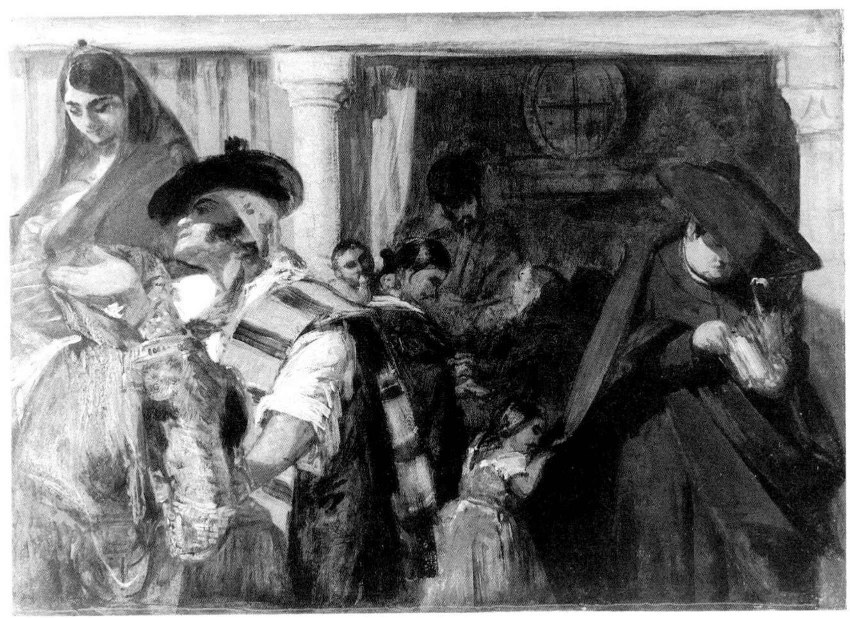

*Study for La Loteria Nacional: Buying the Tickets* LL 3743

6 *Apollo*, 1939, vol. 29, p. 302. *Connoisseur*, 1939, vol. 103, pp. 347–9.

7 A Fine Art Society label dated March 1939 is on the back of LL 3917.

**PHILLIP, John** (1817–1867)

***Study for Scotch Washing***

LL 3918 (WHL 2813)
Canvas: 31.7 × 47.5 cm

This is a study for the whole composition of Phillip's *Scotch Washing* dated 1850 and exhibited at the 1851 Royal Academy.[1]

PROV: J. Staats Forbes[2] sale, 2 June 1916, lot 145, bought Gooden and Fox (£5.15*s*.6*d*.) for Lever (£6).

1 This painting was last recorded at Sotheby's 10 November 1981, lot 3.

2 LL 3918 might have been the *Sketch for Heather Belles* by Phillip, lot 150 in the Edward Brooke sale, Christie's 4 March 1882 (bought Richardson £9.19*s*.6*d*.).

***Study for La Loteria Nacional: Buying the Tickets***

LL 3743 (WHL 176, H 145)
Paper, stuck down to canvas: 41 × 57.5 cm

This is a study for the whole composition of *La Loteria Nacional: Buying the Ticket* (now Dundee Art Gallery) which Phillip began in Seville in 1861 but left unfinished at his death.[1]

PROV: James Orrock sales[2], Christie's 25 April 1895, lot 104, bought in (£32.11*s*.) and 4 June 1904, lot 124, bought in (£73.10*s*.); bought by Lever from Orrock 1904–5.[3]

1 J. Dafforne, *Pictures by John Phillip*, n.d., p. 54; there is a long description of the Dundee picture in *Art Journal*, 1867, p. 153.

2 Lots 302 and 373 at the artist's sale, Christie's 31 May 1867 were *Three Figures from the Picture of the Lottery Office*, bought Smith (£31.10*s*.) and *Loteria Nacional: Buying the Tickets*, bought Massy (£115.10*s*); either lot might have been LL 3743. LL 3743 is reproduced in B. Webber, *James Orrock*, 1903, vol. 1, p. 16; Webber notes (p. 17)

that Phillip was a close friend of Orrock's master, Stewart Smith.

3 LL 3743 is listed as no. 22 in the 1904–5 MS inventory of the works of art bought by Lever from Orrock.

## **PHILPOT, Glyn** (1884–1937)

### ***Marchioness of Carisbrooke***

LL 3919 (LP 77)
Canvas: 117.7 × 87 cm
Signed: *Glyn Philpot*

Irene Frances Adza Denison (1890–1956) was the only daughter of the second Earl of Londesborough; she married the Marquess of Carisbrooke[1] in 1917; she was created Dame of Justice of the Order of St. John of Jerusalem and Dame Grand Cross of the Order of the British Empire.

This portrait was not described in the Royal Academy reviews of A.L. Baldry[2] and of C.R. Grundy[3] but D.H. Banner[4] wrote:

*The drawing of the portrait of Lady Carisbrooke is masterly, yet the construction is not forced in the common and anatomical way which is so unpleasant in the work of less artistic painters, nor is there any of that display of handling which is one element in the vulgarity of the average portrait. As in the work of Velasquez, any kind of handling seems to be used, according to the shape, the texture, the colour of the part, and its relation in accent to the scheme of the whole. Note, for instance, the handling of the hair and fur. The artist's mind is preoccupied with the fine realisation of truth usually rather intellectual than visual – if a distinction which is only one of degree may be allowed – for there is in truth no such thing as mere impression and effect, nor such a thing as mere intellectual reconstruction.*

Robin Gibson[5] noted that around 1924 the artist was at the height of his reputation as a fashionable society portrait painter and that this portrait characteristically combines 'Venetian opulence with restrained realism'.

*Marchioness of Carisbrooke* LL 3919

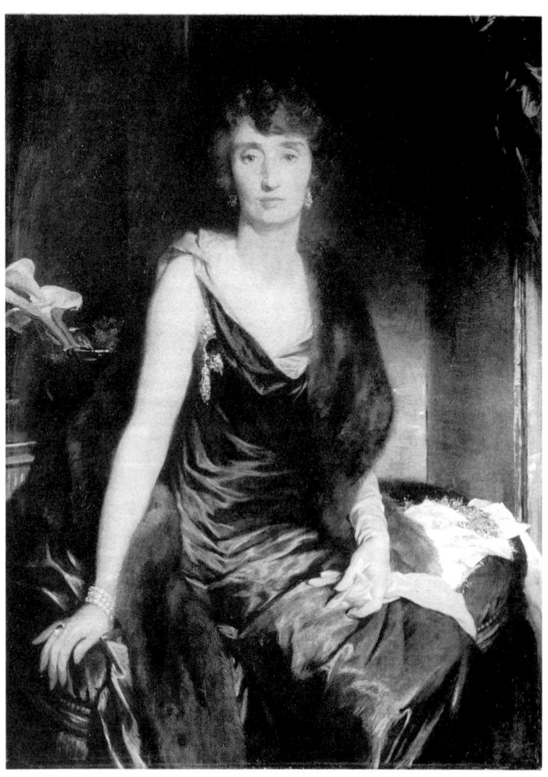

PROV: Presented by the Marquess of Carisbrooke 1952.

EXH: Royal Academy 1925 (122).

1 His mother was Princess Beatrice, youngest daughter of Queen Victoria; she formally opened the Lady Lever Art Gallery in 1922. His uncle was the father of Earl Mountbatten of Burma.

2 'The Royal Academy', *Studio*, 1925, vol. 89, pp. 308 ff.

3 'Reaction and the Royal Academy', *Connoisseur*, 1925, vol. 72, pp. 109–12.

4 'The Royal Academy', *Nineteenth Century*, 1925, vol. 97, p. 886. Similarly, Henry Scott Tuke found LL 3919 'very strong' ('The Diary of Henry Scott Tuke', 23 April 1925, MSS Tate Gallery).

5 National Portrait Gallery, *Glyn Philpot*, 1984, p. 65.

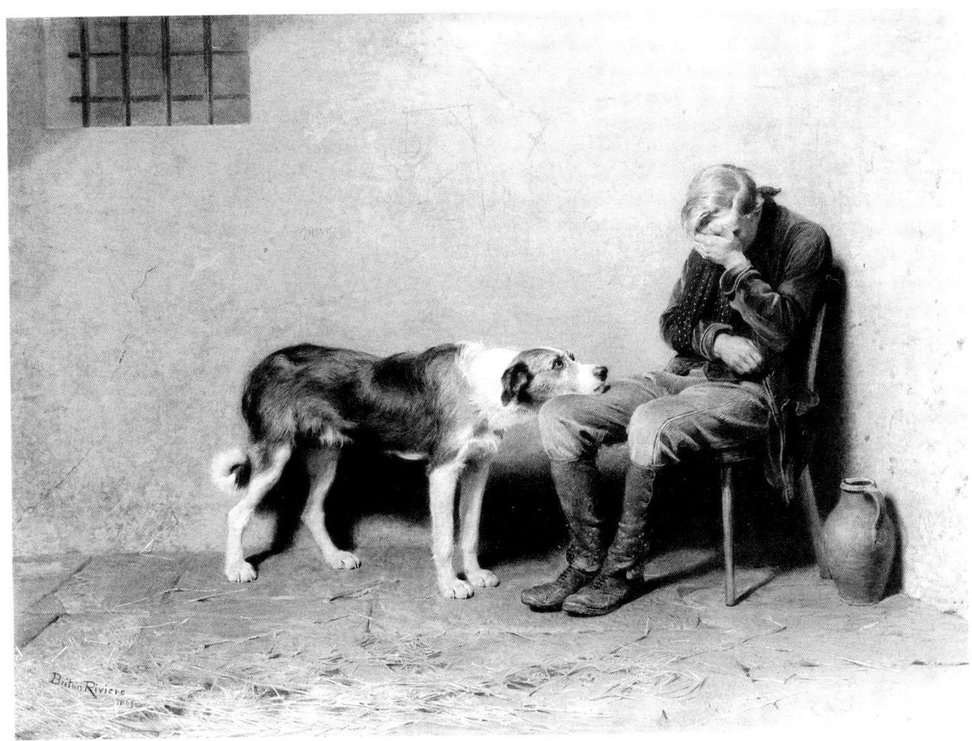


*Fidelity*
LL 3123

**RIVIERE, Briton** (1840–1920)

***Fidelity*[1]**

LL 3123 (WHL 109, TM 19)
Canvas: 80 × 115.5 cm
Signed: *Briton Riviere 1869*

This painting shows a poacher and his faithful dog awaiting trial.[2] The game laws against poaching were administered in the 19th century with great – but declining – severity and they were a favourite subject for Briton Riviere – for example, *The Poacher's Nurse* of 1866 and *The Poacher's Widow* of 1879; the 1879 picture showed a widow at the site of a poaching incident in which her husband had been killed and – with a quotation from Charles Kingsley – represented the mature social realism of the 1870s. By contrast *Fidelity* has more of the sentimentality of Landseer's famous *Old Shepherd's Chief Mourner* (Victoria & Albert Museum). The dog as a companion in adversity became a subject frequently treated by the artist; *His Only Friend* of 1871 is in the Manchester City Art Gallery; *Sympathy* of 1877 is at the Royal Holloway College; *Companions in Misfortune* of 1883 is in the Tate Gallery. *Imprisoned*, showing a girl unable to take her dog out for a walk due to the bad weather outside, was engraved by Samuel Cousins for Agnew's in 1880.

*Fidelity* was well received by the critics although *The Times*[3] objected to its lack of realism – prisoners are not locked up with their dogs, earthenware jars and loose straw. Writing in 1892, F.G. Stephens[4] overcame this objection by suggesting that the poacher and his dog are only temporarily locked up in the attic of a country house before being moved to the local jail. The *Art Journal*[5] critic particularly admired the dog: 'very admirable for the expression of sympathy and pity he bestows upon his master; the head is well studied and capitally painted.'

A drawing for *Fidelity* was exhibited at

the Fine Art Society, *Exhibition of Studies and Designs by Briton Riviere*, 1902 (6): *Design for Prisoners*.

PROV: Ernest Schuster. Bought by Lever from Gooden and Fox July 1903 (£800).[6]

EXH: Royal Academy 1869 (343).

1 LL 3123 was exhibited at the 1869 Royal Academy as *Prisoners*. The title was altered by Lever to *Fidelity* when he acquired it in 1903; no doubt for advertising reasons he wished to stress the sentimental rather than the punitive element in the painting.

2 For the subject see Martin Meisel, *Realizations*, 1983, p. 296; the dog, it appears, defines and symbolizes – or indeed stands in for – the domestic and family situation of the principal figure in the painting; other examples of this practice include Millais's *Order of Release* and Abraham Solomon's *Waiting for the Verdict* (both in the Tate Gallery).

3 *The Times*, 11 June 1869.

4 *Portfolio*, 1892, pp. 61 ff. W. Armstrong, 'Briton Riviere', *Art Annual*, 1891, p. 14 suggested that the scene is set in 'a J.P.'s upper room'.

5 *Art Journal*, 1869, p. 198.

6 Lever bought LL 3123 in order to make colour reproductions which could be exchanged for a number of soap wrappers or coupons as part of one of his soap advertising campaigns. Through his dealer F.W. Fox of Gooden and Fox, he contacted the artist about the scheme in 1905. Riviere remembered LL 3123 as one of his best paintings and was concerned about the rendering of the dog's expression which he regarded as the most important part of the picture; he did not, however, own the copyright so could not object – for further details see the Royal Academy Exhibition Catalogue, *Lord Leverhulme*, 1980, pp. 14, 73–4. See also above p. xiv.

**SADLER, Walter Dendy** (1854–1923)

## *The End of the Skein*

LL 3617 (WHL 680, TM 300)
Canvas: 96.5 × 127 cm
Signed: *W. Dendy Sadler*

This painting belongs to a category of Sadler's paintings of the 1890s designated by F.G. Stephens[1] as the pathetic group; sentimental renderings of couples in old age predominate with titles like *'Tis Fifty Years since* (1894), *Time and the Flowers* (1896) and *The Sweethearts* (1892), now Guildhall Art Gallery, London. The symbolism in *The End of the Skein* is, however, an unusual feature of Sadler's work.

The painting was not noticed by many critics at the 1896 Royal Academy, but the *Athenaeum*[2] noted:

*Quite as characteristic of him, and exhibiting almost at its best his peculiar vein of gentle humour, but not nearly so fresh and vivacious a subject as usual is 'The End of the Skein'. There is spirit as well as aptitude in the prim air and formal dress of each of the old couple introduced, who have nearly finished their lives' tasks together. Everything in the picture, from the faces and costumes to ornaments and decorations is in keeping with the chimney-piece of coloured marbles, the Gainsborough portrait on the walls, the clock, and the pattern of the carpet. It goes without saying of a leading picture by so careful a student of the properties of dress, furniture, and architecture, that the room itself and its fittings are of a somewhat older date than the furniture and nick-nacks which fill it, and older still than the dresses of the figures.*

The female portrait also appeared in Sadler's *Over the Nuts and Wine* of 1889.[3]

REPR: *Royal Academy Pictures*, 1896, p. 75; W.H. Boucher, etching published by L.H. Lefevre, 1897.[4]

PROV: Bought by Thomas Agnew and Sons from the artist 2 May 1896; bought by Lever 4 May 1896 (£350).[5]

EXH: Royal Academy, 1896 (439)

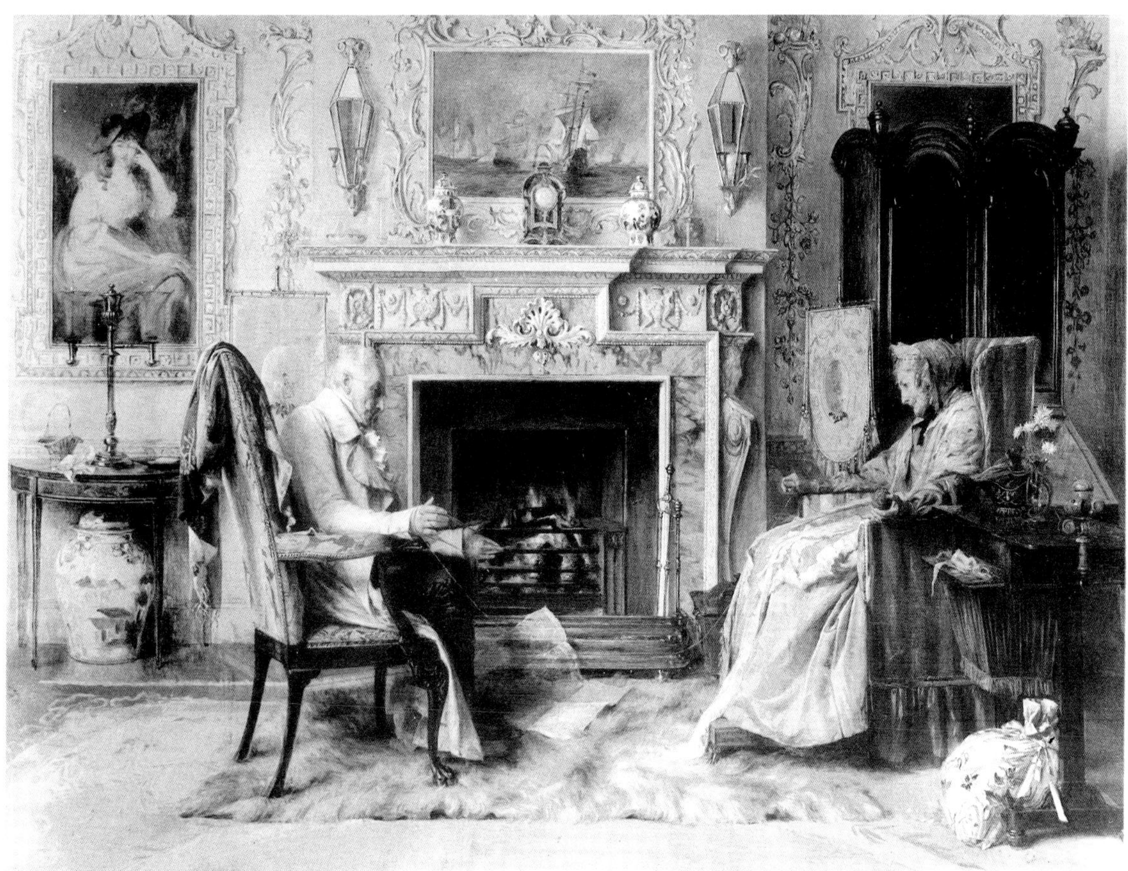

*The End of the Skein* LL 3617

1 F.G. Stephens, 'Walter Dendy Sadler', *Art Journal*, 1895, pp. 198 ff.

2 *Athenaeum*, 2 May 1896, p. 589. Lucy Wood has suggested to the compiler that the decoration, furniture, paintings and dress seem to span at least the entire 18th century; the chimneypiece and interior architecture date from around 1740–50 and the large bureau cabinet at the right might be even earlier; the coal box and work box appear to be the latest dateable items suggesting perhaps the 1820s; H. Blackburn in *Academy Notes*, 1896, p. 16, however, dated the old couple themselves to the 1830s.

3 Reproduced in Stephens, *op. cit.*, p. 199.

4 There is an impression in the Lady Lever Art Gallery, LL 3511; Lefevre published a number of large etchings after a selection of Sadler's work probably in the 1890s, see Arts Council of Great Britain, *Great Victorian Pictures*, 1978, p. 73.

5 It was around the late 1890s that Lever first became interested in collecting 18th-century works of art and this painting could be seen as transitional between his enthusiam for contemporary painting and his interest in the 18th century.

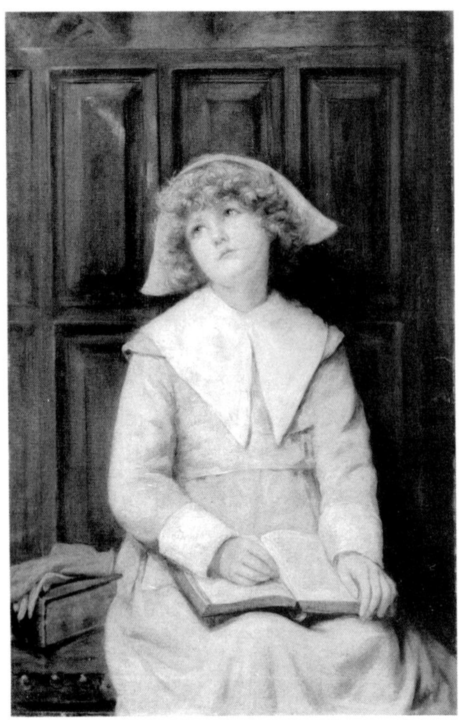

*The Puritan Maid* LL 3601

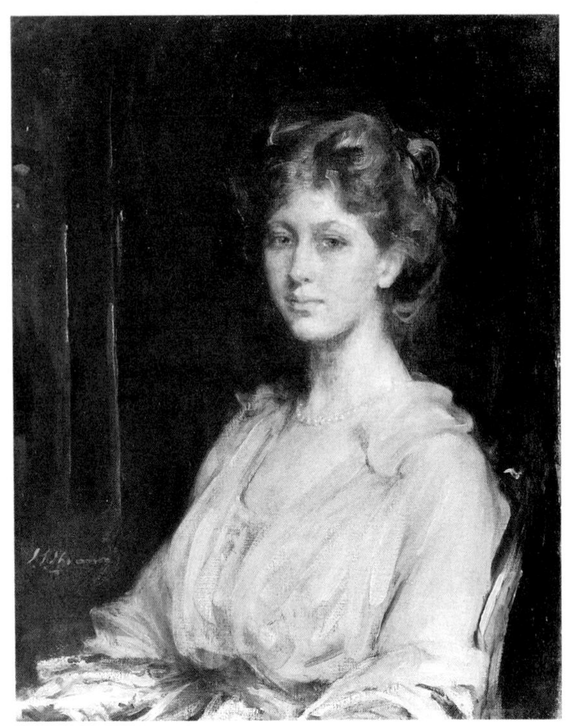

*Princess Mary* LL 3920

**SCANNELL, Edith** (active 1870–1921)
***The Puritan Maid***
LL 3601
Canvas: 91.5 × 61 cm
Signed: *Edith Scannell*

PROV: Found in the Gallery 1985.

**SHANNON, James Jebusa** (1862–1923)
***Princess Mary***
LL 3920 (WHL 2222)
Canvas: 78.5 × 64.7 cm
Signed: *J.J. Shannon*

Princess Mary (1897–1965) was the only daughter of George V; she married Viscount Lascelles, later the sixth Earl of Harewood, in 1922 and in 1932 was created Princess Royal.

The critic of the *Connoisseur*[1] at the Royal Society of Portrait Painters Exhibition described this painting as 'one of the few really attractive portraits of royalty' which would make a 'highly pleasing subject' for an engraving.

REPR: *The Princess Mary Gift Book* frontispiece, 1915; this reproduction shows LL 3920 not fully completed.

PROV: Commissioned for sale in aid of the Queen's Work for Women Fund[2] and bought from the artist 1915 by Lever (£525).

EXH: Grafton Galleries, *Royal Society of Portrait Painters*, 1915 (57); Leicester Galleries, *Princess Mary's Gift Book*, 1915 (1).

1 *Connoisseur*, 1915, vol. 42, p. 253. The reviewer for the *Studio*, 1915, vol. 65, p. 128 however, did not notice LL 3920.

2 See *Connoisseur, op. cit.*, and *Princess Mary's Gift Book*, 1915, Introduction; Princess Mary was conspicuous for her war work (see M.C. Carey, *Princess Mary*, 1922, pp. 72 ff.).

**SWAN, John Macallan** (1847–1910)

### *Orpheus*

LL 3138 (WHL 4744, LP 8)
Canvas[1]: 133 × 186 cm
Signed: *JOHN M SWAN / 1896*

Despite the date on this painting there seems to be no doubt that it was the *Orpheus* exhibited by the artist at the 1894 Royal Academy;[2] presumably the artist did additional work on it after its first exhibition and this extra work was only completed in 1896; a silver statuette, *Orpheus*, was shown by the artist at the 1895 Royal Academy (no. 1705) and this statuette[3] was closely based on the figure of Orpheus in this painting; possibly therefore, this figure was revised by the artist during 1895–6 in the light of the statuette.

The critics at the 1894 Royal Academy found the figure of Orpheus too realistic. *The Times*[4] wrote: 'Mr. Swan's Orpheus could never have loved Eurydice or felt any emotion but the overwhelming frenzy of the god who possesses him'; he was not 'the sedate Orpheus of convention but merely a "beast-charmer"'.

Similarly the *Athenaeum*[5] commented:

> *Mr. Swan contributes* Orpheus, *performing on the lyre, to the wonder and delight of the lions, leopards, and tigers whom the newly elected Associate paints with much originality and knowledge in a naturalistic manner, which seems quite out of keeping with the classic legend. The wild gestures of Orpheus (he is hardly adolescent) may be right, although they are a novelty, but he ought surely, according to the very conditions of the incident and subject, to possess the antique beauty, whereas he has only the beauty of a lithe and vigorous gipsy lad. In this respect he is out of harmony with the realistic animals.*

M.H. Spielmann[6] was disappointed by *Orpheus* and went on:

> *That this work contains many passages of the greatest beauty, whether of draughtsmanship or colour, none will deny – that sky, and beasts, and trees, and foreground are all admirable is beyond question. Yet it appears to us that the painter produced the picture while his artistic views were in a state of transition, the background and the figure being conceived in his earlier manner and the animals in the later. Nor is the figure of Orpheus himself – especially about the neck – entirely clear; nor the artist's view quite manifest in making so dignified and mournful a lover execute a sort of egg-dance among the panthers.*

Claude Phillips[7] was even more hostile: 'The movement and gesture of the naked Orpheus striking his lyre as he steps across the spotted pards, who roll cat like on the ground, are inexpressive and the composition lacks harmony.'

George Moore commented on the painting in his Royal Academy reviews of 1894 and 1895; in 1894 he observed:[8] 'Mr. Swan's "Orpheus" is not a good picture, I am afraid. It is very well done, the dancing figure and the leopards rolling on the sward, but the picture is not interesting. I failed to discover any artistic idea in it. The colour is harmonious, but it did not delight me; the drawing of the figure is correct, but it did not touch me.'

A year later he was even less polite:[9] 'Last year Mr. Swan sent a picture of Orpheus charming wild beasts with harp-playing, and the picture was a complete and disastrous failure: there was hardly a good thing about it; it was wrong, and Mr. Swan had expended upon it all the patience of his genius.'

R.A.M. Stevenson,[10] however, noted: 'The figure in Mr. J.M. Swan's Orpheus is full of grace and alive with movement. To see the masterly modelling you must stand fairly close to the canvas.'

Two other paintings by Swan illustrated the story of Orpheus; *Orpheus charming the Lions*, 43 × 66 in., was lent by Mrs. Florence Charlton to the 1911 Royal Academy Winter Exhibition (no. 17)[11] and *The Young Orpheus*, 22 × 16 in., was lent to the same exhibition by J. Martin White (no. 1); a chalk drawing *Orpheus*, 18½ × 9 in., was contributed to this exhibition by A.C. Ionides (no. 169).

PROV: George McCulloch (by 1896);[12] his sale, Christie's 23 May 1913, lot 89, bought Sampson (£1,732.10*s*.). W. Lawson Peacock.[13] D. Stoner Crowther sale, Christie's 2 May 1924, lot 47, bought Gooden and Fox (£1,522.10*s*.) for Lever (£1,560.11*s*.); bought from his executors 1925 (£1,560.11*s*.).

EXH: Royal Academy 1894 (222); Royal Academy, *Winter Exhibition*, 1909 (23); Royal Academy, *Winter Exhibition*, 1911 (24); Royal Academy, *Lord Leverhulme*, 1980 (38).

1 Label: *Charles Roberson, 99 Long Acre.*

2 Unfortunately, no reproductions of LL 3138 seem to have been published before 1896; in that year an illustration appeared in the *Art Journal*, 1896, opp. p. 350.

3 Reproduced in the *Art Journal*, 1895, p. 177. A silver *Orpheus* was lent to the 1911 Royal Academy *Winter Exhibition* by Mrs. Joseph (no. 173). A bronze *Orpheus* of 1907, 117 in. high, is now in the Manchester City Art Galleries and is a variant of the 1895 Royal Academy silver statuette; like LL 3138 it was formerly in the McCulloch collection.

4 *The Times*, 5 May 1894.

5 *Athenaeum*, 19 May 1894, p. 552. These critics were possibly suggesting that the artist was relying on current archaeological research indicating that Orpheus was a Dionysiac god.

6 *Magazine of Art*, 1894, p. 273.

7 *Academy*, 12 May 1894, p. 400. Phillips went on to criticize the picture's harmony of composition, its atmospheric effects and the dramatic significance of the particular event portrayed. It may have been felt that Swan was an animal painter attempting something outside his genre – but his *Prodigal Son* had been purchased from the Chantrey Bequest in 1889 and Swan was elected as an Associate of the Royal Academy in 1894.

8 *Speaker*, 5 May 1894, p. 500.

9 *Speaker*, 11 May 1895, p. 516.

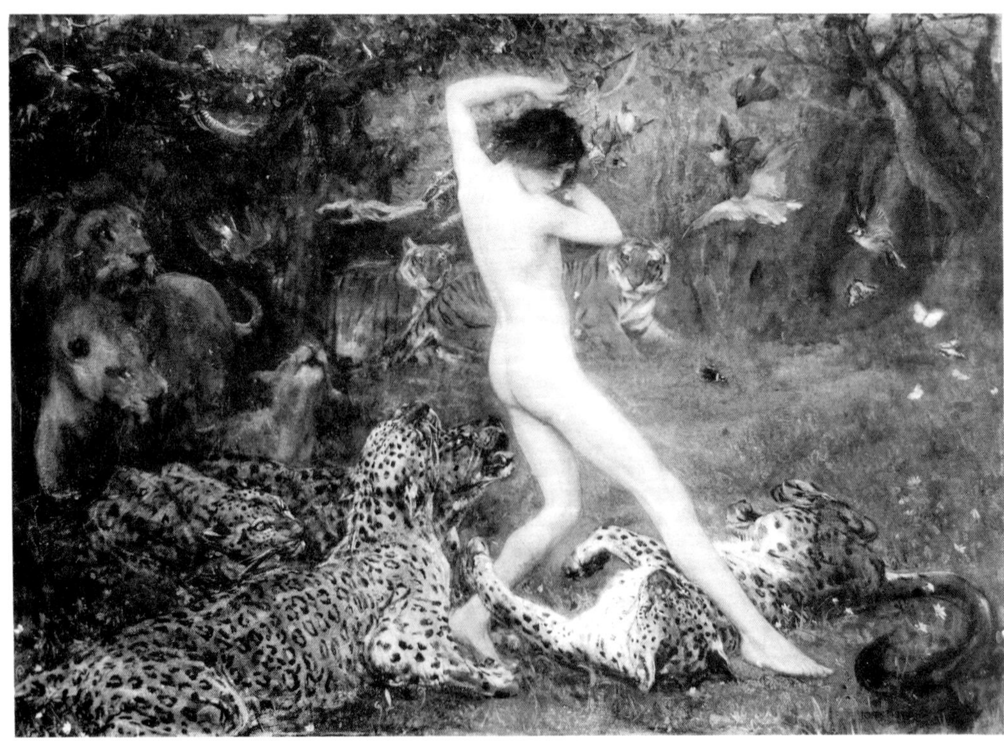

*Orpheus*
LL 3138

*A Dress Rehearsal*
LL 3409

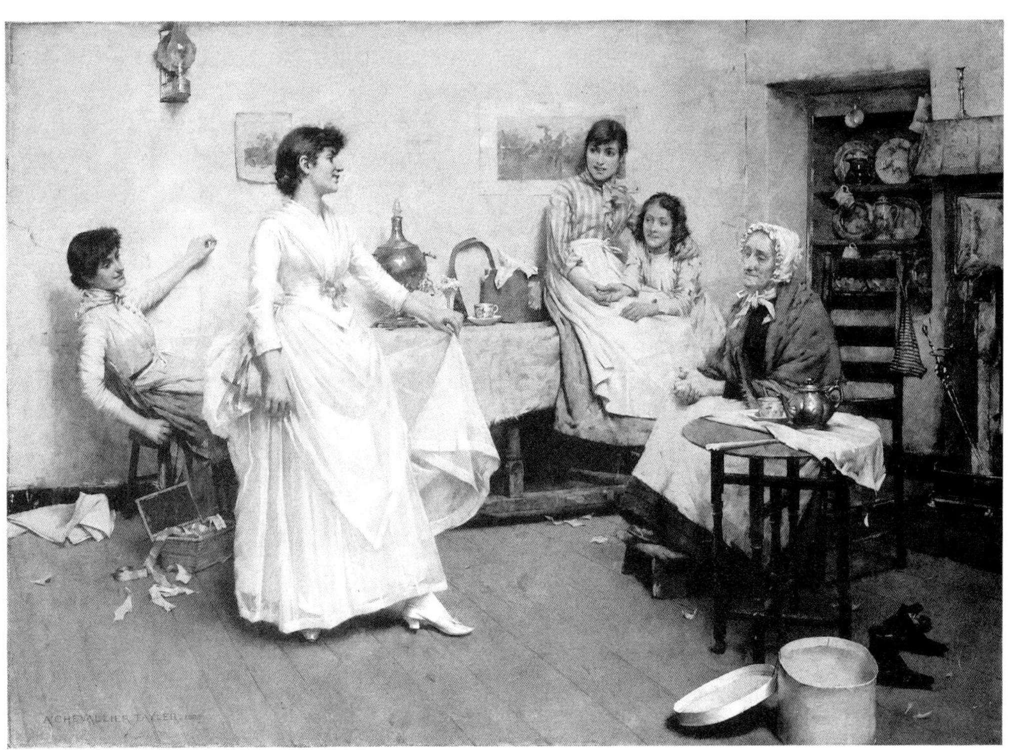

10 *Art Journal*, 1894, p. 211. The critic of the *Saturday Review* was also kind to LL 3138 (12 May 1894, p. 494): 'Not the most skillfully painted, but we think the most imaginative, work of the year is Mr. Swan's *Orpheus* which only wants a little more solidity to be a masterpiece.'

11 Reproduced in H.A. Guerber, *The Myths of Greece and Rome*, 1938, p. 68.

12 *Art Journal*, 1896, opp. p. 350.

13 *Studio*, 1918, vol. 73, p. 24. LL 3138 was not at the W. Lawson Peacock stock sales of 11–14 November 1921 and 6 February 1925 (Christie's).

## **TAYLER, Albert Chevallier** (1862–1925)
## ***A Dress Rehearsal***[1]

LL 3409
Canvas: 77.5 × 107.5 cm
Signed: *A. CHEVALLIER TAYLER 1888*

The artist was certainly in Newlyn early in 1888 and this painting with its slightly sentimental peasant subject matter (a bride trying on her wedding dress) is a typical and routine Newlyn School painting; this may explain why it failed to excite much interest among the critics at the 1888 Royal Academy exhibition; after 1888 Tayler began to concentrate on more middle class and specifically Catholic scenes.[2]

REPR: H. Blackburn, *Academy Notes*, 1888, p. 24.

PROV: Bought by Lever 1888[3]; presented by Lever Brothers 1983.

EXH: Royal Academy, 1888 (45); Laing Art Gallery, Newcastle, *Special Inaugural Exhibition*, 1904 (187).

1 Lever re-named LL 3409 as *The Wedding Dress.*

2 Newlyn Orion Galleries, *Artists of the Newlyn School*, 1979, pp. 145–7.

3 Lever made most of his purchases at the Royal Academy summer exhibitions and he began to use LL 3409 as an advertisement for his soap almost immediately; for example a Lever Brothers advertisement incorporating LL 3409 appeared in the *Graphic*, 10 August 1889, p. 187 with the motto: 'As good as new'. For further details of Lever's advertising policy see p. xiii. In 1889 Lever tried unsuccessfully to buy *The Health of the Bride* by Stanhope Forbes (now Tate Gallery) for use as a soap advertisement (W.P. Frith, 'Artistic Advertising', *Magazine of Art*, 1889, p. 422). Like LL 3409, this was a Newlyn School painting of a young bride and Lever may have been encouraged by his success with LL 3409 to try for *The Health of the Bride*.

## TAYLOR, Leonard Campbell
(1874–1969)

### *The Sampler*

LL 3921 (LP 33)
Canvas: 76.2 × 65.9 cm
Signed: *L. Campbell Taylor*

The artist[1] described at length his work on this painting. In June 1931 he was invited to lunch with a collector, Mr. W.B. Chamberlin of 37 First Avenue, Hove.[2] Chamberlin's drawing room with its 'veiled luminosity' and careful arrangement of works of art struck him as a good subject, and work began at Hove in November 1931. He made some preliminary sketches and selected a low viewpoint to suggest 'a sense of calm and repose'; these sketches involved some alterations to the actual appearance of the room with certain features eliminated but few added and with adjustments to spacing and proportions. The cerise-coloured old Italian damask hanging like a curtain at the right of the painting meant that the two figures had to be respectively dressed in green and grey to ensure colour harmony. The resulting drawing – inspired by the room but certainly not recording it – was then traced on to a canvas. A monochrome wash was next applied to the darker areas and further improvements to the design were made. The foreground chair was made larger and a chair in the background turned into a stool; some other chairs, sconces and pictures were discarded and the miniature chest of drawers lost one tier of its drawers; the panelling and dado of the room were changed into a more Italianate arcading. The artist then applied more paint in successive layers using petrol as his medium and working slowly and deliberately; he relied more on notes, sketches and drawings than on the room and objects themselves.

After some days in Hove he returned to London with the painting far from complete. Back in his studio he put on yet more layers of paint now using poppy oil as his medium and paying particular attention to tonal and colour relations. At the same time he traced on to the canvas the outlines of the figures from drawings and then painted the two women in from life, but afterwards varied the figures without reference to the models themselves.

He then revisited Chamberlin's home at Hove to compare his almost completed canvas with the original interior; there were striking differences but these were intended and he was able to finish the picture two or three days after his return from Hove.

In his long account of the genesis of *The Sampler* the artist frequently refers to the example of Vermeer, whose fastidious concern with arrangement and composition seems to have become with Taylor almost an obsession, while he also commends Vermeer's (apparently) slow and laborious technique. The atmosphere of refined but expensive domestic quietism was frequently cultivated by Campbell Taylor.[3]

The seated woman is embroidering on canvas using a tent stitch frame[4] The model for both figures was Marguerite Kelsey.[5] The painting was certainly Chamberlin's *Virgin and Child* then attributed to Antoniazzo Romano.[6] The cassone under the painting is more difficult to identify; it may have been the 'Italian walnut cassone with

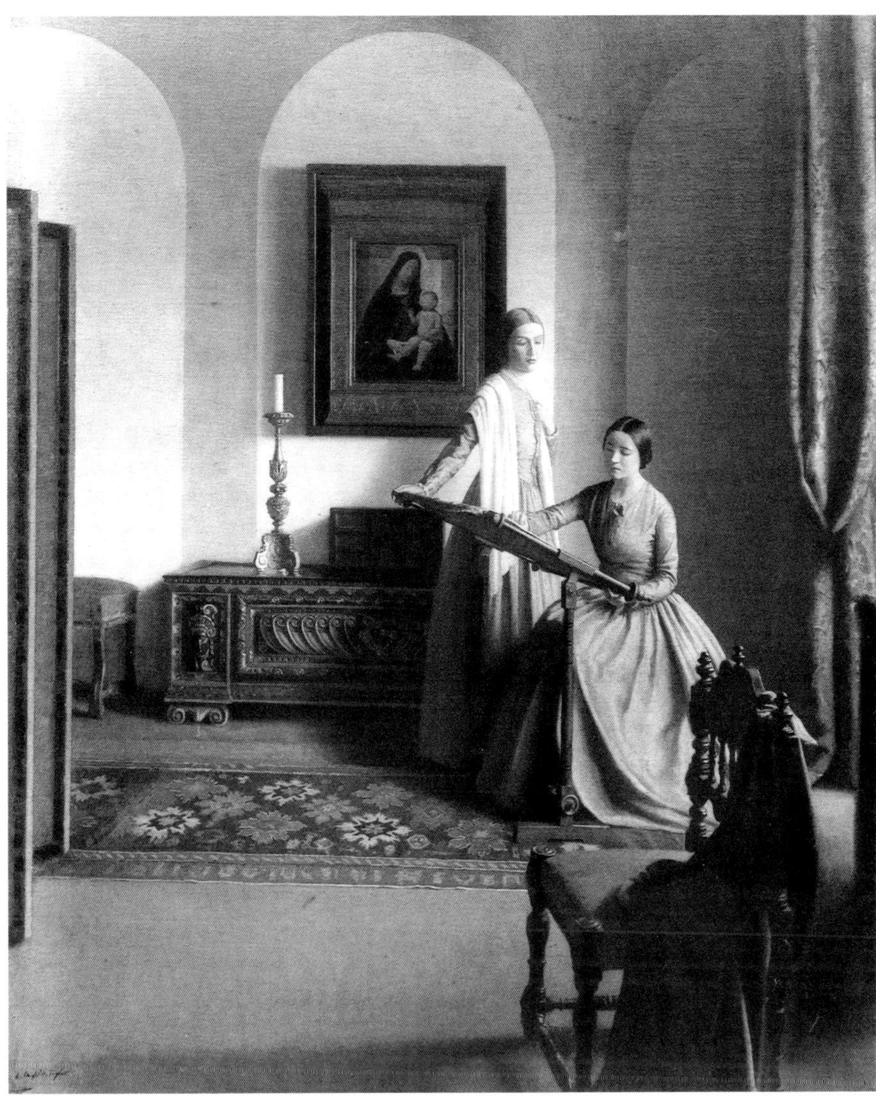

*The Sampler*
LL 3921

lifting top, the panelled front carved in relief with classical masks and symmetrical scrolls centring on a cabochon, bordered by foliage and flat flutes partly gilt, 64 ins. wide, 16th-century', lot 99 in the W.B. Chamberlin furniture sale,[7] but this cassone seems to have been acquired from the Mrs. Hornsby Drake sale of 17 March 1932[8] and by that date Taylor's painting was complete (or nearly complete).

At the 1932 Royal Academy F. Gordon Roe[9] wrote: 'Austerity, however, is not the term wherewith to convey the rich peace of *The Sampler* by Mr. L. Campbell Taylor. Here two of his early Victorian ladies find perpetuity in a grave room, with a painted Madonna, an elaborate candlestick and a carved cassone from Italy. The whole effect is admirably contrived.' Herbert Furst[10] saw *The Sampler* as one of a number of very good 'transcripts from nature' at the same exhibition but found it showing more 'creative design and a higher technical standard' than the others.

The artist's sketch for the whole composition, together with two studies for the figures in *The Sampler*, were reproduced by the artist in 1932.[11]

REPR: *Royal Academy Illustrated*, 1932, p. 18; *Apollo*, 1932, vol. 15, p. 255. A colour collotype was published by Frost and Reed in 1933.

PROV: Bought from the artist 1932 (£500).

EXH: Royal Academy 1932 (54).

1 L. Campbell Taylor, 'Interior Painting', *Artist*, 1932–3, vol. 4, pp. 64–5, 95–6, 126–7, 157–9. See also Herbert Furst, *Leonard Campbell Taylor*, 1945, p. 112 who emphasizes the artist's concern with abstract composition rather than with realism.

2 For Chamberlin see his obituary in the *Burlington Magazine*, 1937, vol. 71, p. 234; he was aged seventy-nine when he died on 8 October. His house at 37 First Avenue still survives but has been converted into flats (Timothy Wilcox, letter to the compiler, 17 December 1991).

3 Furst, *op. cit.*, refers to the 'impression of calm and repose' desired by Campbell Taylor. Young women doing needlework or posed among valuable furniture in lavish interiors often appear in his paintings.

4 Xanthe Brooke, conversation with the compiler, 1992.

5 Letter from Marguerite Kelsey to Richard Morphet of the Tate Gallery, 5 March 1982, kindly communicated by Richard Morphet 21 June 1982. Marguerite Kelsey was a professional model who worked for Campbell Taylor for some five years. There is a portrait of her by Meredith Frampton dating from 1928 (Tate Gallery, *Meredith Frampton*, 1982, no. 12, p. 48).

6 Burlington Fine Arts Club, *Pictures of the Umbrian School*, 1910, no. 47, p. 38 with the note that it was probably not by Antoniazzo Romano but rather Sicilian; W.B. Chamberlin sale, Christie's 25 February 1938, lot 45; there is a photograph of the painting in the Witt Library indicating that in fact Campbell Taylor copied it with great precision despite his belief that artists are entitled to adjust reality.

7 Christie's 14 December 1937, lot 99.

8 Christie's 17 March 1932, lot 122, bought Smith (£37.16*s*.). A cassone very similar to the one in LL 3921 is reproduced in Clelia Alberici, *Il Mobile Veneto*, 1980, fig. 74, p. 60; it is now in a private collection and is dated to 1590–1600. The compiler is indebted to James Yorke and Lucy Wood for help with the cassone.

9 'Dives and Lazarus at the Royal Academy', *Connoisseur*, 1932, vol. 89, p. 404.

10 H. Furst, 'The Royal Academy; The Bank Decorations and some other paintings', *Apollo*, 1932, vol. 15, p. 250.

11 Campbell Taylor, *op. cit.*, pp. 95–6.

## TENNANT, Dorothy (later Lady Stanley) (1855–1926)

### *Street Arabs at Play*

LL 3411
Canvas: 64.5 × 153.5 cm
Signed: *Dorothy Tennant 1890*

The artist[1] described at length how and why she painted poor London children; she noted that most such pictures of her own day showed children as unhappy and pitiable and she remarked: 'Murillo's Beggar Boys most nearly approached my ideal – but where was the modern Murillo? . . . Why go to Venice[2] when we have such pictures at home?' She used to sketch the children at play on Saturdays in St. James's Park or around the Embankment and then induce them to come to pose in her studio; they used often to come to her house looking too respectable for her purposes; 'the best thing', she suggested, 'is to keep your properties in the studio. A good supply of rags is essential (carefully fumigated, camphored and peppered) and you can then dress up your too respectable ragamuffin till he looks as disreputable as you can wish.'

This painting[3] shows the Surrey side of

the Thames looking south from Fresh Wharf in front of Adelaide House; the wharves visible on the Surrey side are, from west to east, Fenning's and Topping's, then Hay's, Cotton's and Chamberlain's.

*The Times*[4] described the artist as 'altogether modern in her excellent and amusing picture of *Street Arabs at Play* in which three little ragged urchins are swinging on a railing on the Embankment, while their two small sisters look on admiring, and with the evident intention to rival them'. Similarly, the *Art Journal*[5] commented:

*Miss Dorothy Tennant has done unusually well in her 'Street Arabs at Play', showing a company of ragged urchins, male and female, swinging and going through various unorthodox gymnastics on the Embankment railings. The figures of two little girls to the extreme right and left of the picture, who appropriately indulge in less exaggerated gyrations than their fellows, are especially well drawn and modelled. The background of bridge and river rendered in a grey evening light is, on the other hand, scenic and unreal, and might easily have been improved.*

REPR: Pall Mall Gazette, *Pictures of the Year*, 1890, p. 91.

PROV: Bought by Lever;[6] presented by Lever Brothers 1983.

EXH: New Gallery 1890 (170).

1 Dorothy Tennant, *London Street Arabs*, 1890, pp. 5 ff.; there are a number of illustrations in this book after drawings or paintings by the author, but LL 3411 is not reproduced; most of the illustrations are, however, very similar in character to LL 3411. Dorothy Tennant and Jules Bastien Lepage had together sketched London flower girls and shoeblacks in 1881 and 1882 (Dorothy Stanley, 'Bastien Lepage in London', *Art Journal*, 1897, pp. 53 ff.) but there is little evidence of his influence in LL 3411.

2 Presumably a reference to the Neo-Venetian school of Henry Woods, Luke Fildes and others.

3 Dr. C.A. Fox, letter to the compiler, 15 August 1984. H.D. Rodee in *Scenes of Rural and Urban Poverty in Victorian Painting 1850–1890*, 1975, p. 216 notes that Embankment scenes were generally of grim and unpleasant subjects such as Luke Fildes's illustration of 1878, *Found Dead on the Embankment*; in this context LL 3411 is unusual.

4 *The Times*, 23 May 1890.

5 *Art Journal*, 1890, p. 170. There is another brief review in the *Saturday Review*, 3 May 1890, p. 538.

*Street Arabs at Play* LL 3411

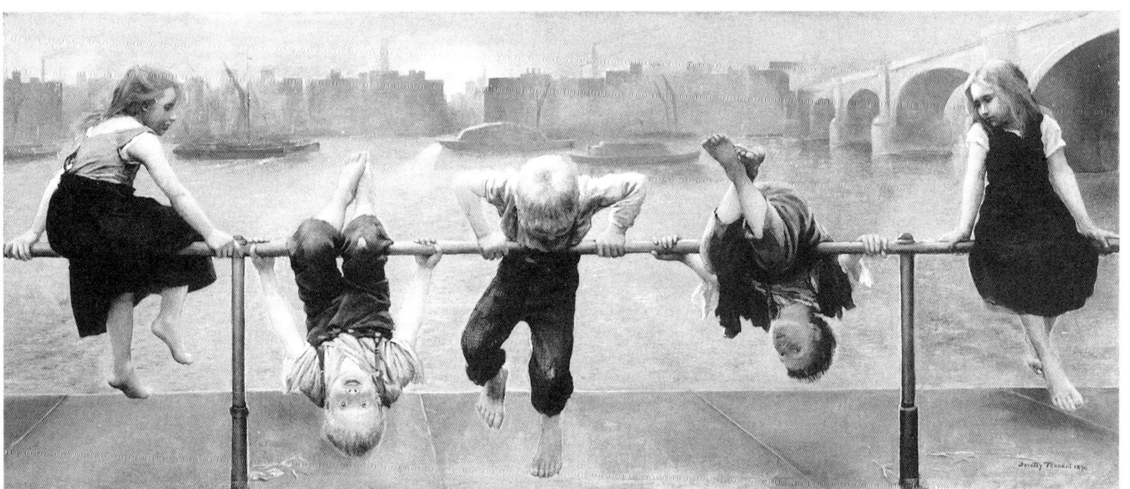

6 He bought LL 3411 for advertising purposes (*Port Sunlight News*, 1926, vol. 4, no. 20, p. 322) and renamed it *Head over Tails*. For his use of pictures for advertising purposes see p. xiii.

## THADDEUS, Henry Jones (or JONES, Henry Thaddeus) (1860–1929)

### *Father Anderledy*

LL 3922 (WHL 4508)
Canvas: 124.5 × 85.6 cm
Signed: *H.J. Thaddeus Rome 1886*

The artist had met Father Anderledy in Florence through a letter of introduction and thus was able to take advantage of the latter's visit to Rome in 1885 to paint him there; Thaddeus's studio in Rome during the winter of 1885–6 was in the Palazzo Savorgnan di Brazza.[1] Anthony Maria Anderledy was born in Switzerland in 1819, entered the Society of Jesus in 1839, was elected Vicar-General of the Society in 1883 and then assumed all the duties of General of the Society in 1887; in his administration of the Jesuits he was 'remarkable for great firmness of character'.[2]

*Father Anderledy* LL 3922

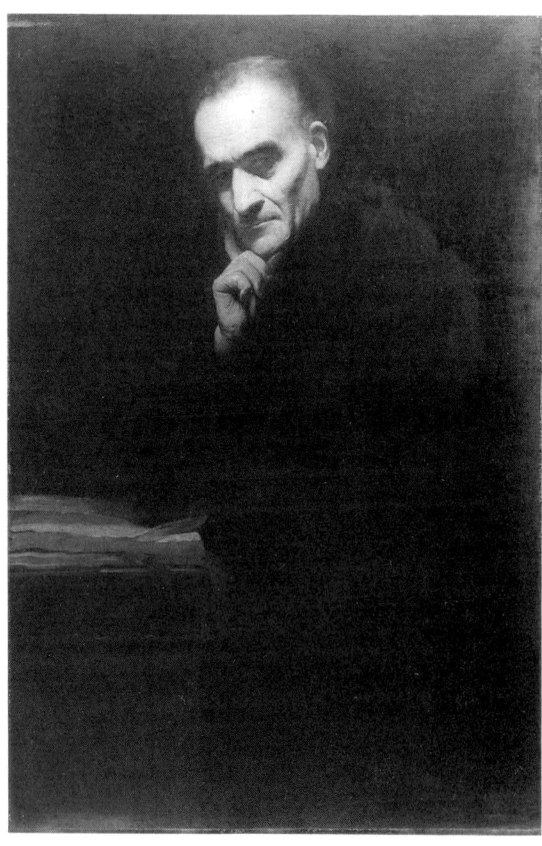

PROV: P. Naumann. Accepted by Lever as security for a loan which he made to Wilson Barrett[3] in 1916; acquired by Lever 1923.

EXH: Dublin, Irish International Exhibition, 1907 (111).[4]

1 H. Jones Thaddeus, *Recollections of a Court Painter*, 1912, pp. 131–4.

2 P.H. Kelly in *Catholic Encyclopaedia*, 1907, vol. 1, p. 466.

3 Wilson Barrett was later editor of the magazine *Colour* and a friend of Lever; he made the arrangements for Augustus John to paint his portrait of Lever in 1920.

4 There is an old torn label on the back of LL 3922 reading 'For the Salon / of the Champs' but it was not exhibited at the Société des Artistes Français in 1886.

## WALKER, Frederick (1840–1875)

### *The Bathers*

LL 3143 (WHL 3420)
Canvas: 92.7 × 214.7 cm
Signed: *F.W.*

*The Bathers* was widely recognized as the only work in which Walker departed from his usual realism to paint a scene ostensibly naturalistic, but permeated both with poses, gestures and expressions borrowed from classical art and with an ideal timeless mood divorced in feeling from everyday reality;[1] it is therefore a painting of exceptional importance within the development of the classical revival in English painting of the 1860s.[2]

The creation of *The Bathers* can be traced in detail.[3] The subject was developed from an illustration done for Dalziel Brothers in 1862 – two boys, one bathing in a river, the other undressing in order to bathe.[4] In April 1865 'the idea already simmering in his brain', Walker found the right background at Cookham on the Thames; in October 1865 he decided on a larger canvas, took it to a spot on the Thames near Marlow and painted the landscape directly onto the canvas in the open air until November; in January–March 1866 back in his London studio he did life drawings from models for the figures and painted them into the canvas. In February the great dealer Sir William Agnew saw the work in progress and liked it – his firm later bought the picture; two painters, John Phillip and Millais, gave advice and approval. As the weather improved in March, Walker returned to the Thames at Hurley with his partially completed canvas and one boy model 'to ascertain the truth of some of my flesh tones' in the open air, but he could not finish the work for the 1866 Royal Academy exhibition so he stopped work and left for Paris; in June and July he took the large canvas back to Cookham for more work from nature and in his London studio he worked on the figures throughout the autumn, winter and early spring – the two figures on the right in particular underwent considerable changes in size and pose;[5] the picture was hung unfinished and in a poor position at the 1867 Royal Academy exhibition.

Walker carried on working on the picture after its return from the Royal Academy and Agnew's did not get it until May 1868 – Walker in fact was still improving it in late 1869 when William Graham had already bought it. Indeed, the tortured surface of *The Bathers* is evidence of the artist's protracted battle to achieve naturalistic lighting, atmosphere and colour on a heroic and monumental scale.

Walker never reached the Life Class at the Royal Academy Schools and his first exhibited oil painting only dated from 1863,[6] two years before he started work on *The Bathers*; possible contemporary sources for the painting are therefore of some importance. He was in Paris in April 1863, May 1866 and April 1867, presumably to see the Salon exhibitions and the Exposition Universelle;[7] in 1863 he admired *Le Soir* (or possibly *Le Rappel des glaneuses*) by Jules Breton at the Luxembourg Museum,[8] but he could also have seen *Le Repos* and *Le Travail* by Puvis de Chavannes at the 1863 Salon (now Musée de Picardie, Amiens) and he was perhaps influenced by the monumental conceptions and rough chalky execution of Puvis de Chavannes.[9]

Contemporary critical opinion on *The Bathers* was broadly divided between those who saw it as an aberration within Walker's career, as a type of picture for which he was not qualified, and those who saw it as a unique synthesis of his usual genre realism and of a new instinctive grasp of classical, ideal form. John Ruskin[10] belonged to the first group, arguing that Walker had been seduced from unpretentious genre painting by the spurious lure of High Art: 'under which sorrowful terms being told also by your grand academicians that he should paint the nude and, accordingly, wasting a year or two of his life in trying to paint schoolboys' back and legs without their shirts or breeches'. Dafforne[11] sided with Ruskin: '*The Bathers* showed no ordinary talent but the subject was not agreeable neither were the figures generally good in drawing and colour; the nude was certainly never the artist's *forte*.' The *Art Journal* critic[12] at the 1867 Royal Academy wrote in a similar vein:

*Why in the name of all the arts, it may be asked, should Mr. Frederick Walker have painted 'The Bathers'? There are some pictures it were hard for even genius to justify. That no ordinary talent presides over this repulsive production few will deny. Yet why all so opaque and muddy, why so ungainly the figures*

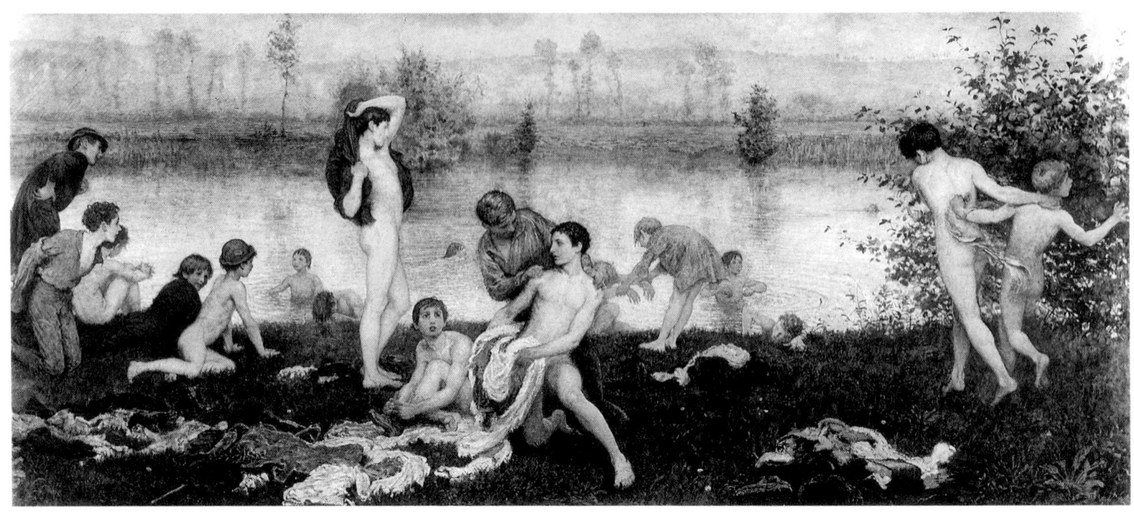

*The Bathers* LL 3143 (colour plate 9)

*of the bathers? Walker, but scarcely Apelles, might thus conceive of the human form divine. The best passages are the limpid water, and a line of landscape almost out of sight. The picture shows French influence.*

*The Times*[13] critic found the composition 'chaotic'; there was 'no artistic or imaginative purpose'; the picture was only 'a study of vulgar little boys bathing on the flat bank of say the Lea River not far from Tottenham'.

The opposite point of view was most eloquently expressed by J. Comyns Carr:[14]

*Nothing that he did is in this way more valuable than the picture of 'The Bathers', for although the execution will not compare with what came later, the design of this work, with its simple record of the unconscious grace of boyhood, is of most distinct originality. Here we are in the presence of a conception that has no sadness at all. There is no grave feeling to be expressed such as we find in the 'Ploughing' or the 'Harbour of Refuge'; and, so far as invention goes, the picture is no more than an attempt to see what could be done with a simple incident of boyish life. It is characteristic of Walker that he should have seized one of the few opportunities of modern life for dealing with nude designs, and that this should be the only study of the nude from his hand. For it seems to have been one of the fixed principles of his art not to disturb or depart from the realities of the world about him. With his feelings for grace in form it might have been thought that he would have been led to a class of subjects where the difficulties of modern costume would not have confronted him. But, rightly or wrongly, this was not a part of his scheme. He seems at no time to have been tempted to create for himself an ideal world; on the contrary, he took especial pleasure in using only such materials as lay near to his hand, fashioning them to shapes of beauty without sacrificing any of the realities of modern life. In this picture of boys bathing he was able for once, and once only, to reach the nude without departing from modern habit; and it is not surprising that he should have grasped the occasion, or that he should have turned it to good account. Some of these youthful figures prove very decisively that Walker's understanding of the sources of beauty in antique sculpture was no mere reminiscence of the masterpieces of antique art. He has found out for himself in these boy-figures a kindred grace; and here, at least, it may be said that the union of reality and refined beauty is successfully accomplished.*

A compromise between these two opposing judgments was suggested by Claude Phillips;[15] he found the two central nude figures, one standing and just removing his last garment and the other half kneeling with his shoulders held by a clothed figure, too obtrusively classical and devoid of any sincerity or spontaneity; in the other figures, however, he praised the combination of sculptural form and natural life.

Contemporary critics also felt that the intensely worked, rough surface of the painting reflected not the rugged grandeur appropriate to the classical pretensions of the subject, but rather an attempt to achieve in a naturalistic manner the effect of open air light on figures which had been studied by the artist with his canvas on the spot. F.G. Stephens,[16] for example, wrote:

> *Fred Walker's picture is . . . one of the best modern triumphs of that graceful sort of realism which aims to succeed in depicting human flesh, or, as skilled critics say, the carnations, from 'the life', according to Nature, and in sunlight. In this respect no one has succeeded better than the youth (for such was Walker when he painted 'The Bathers') who, with exquisite skill and delicacy of perception, and with indomitable patience to boot, put his nude models in the open-air when the atmosphere was surcharged with light, and, without sacrificing an iota of Nature's harmony, painted what he saw.*

The *Athenaeum* critic at the 1867 Royal Academy[17] (possibly Stephens again) praised 'the brilliancy of their [the boys'] bare flesh in various tints "coming" very strongly in that peculiar sunlight suffused with mist which the artist sometimes affects'; both this review and *The Times*[18] review observed that the technique, although offensive if studied in detail, becomes acceptable if the picture is seen from a distance; Claude Phillips[19] noted that the handling was broader than was usual in Walker's work but found the open air effects, the light playing on the flesh, produced tints of 'leathery brownness'.

The greatest impact of *The Bathers* was, however, reserved for two young artists; Hubert Herkomer while still a student at the South Kensington Schools was deeply influenced by it and Hamo Thornycroft was another admirer.[20]

REPR: R.W. Macbeth (etching) 1888; W.H. Hooper (wood engraving) reproduced in *L'Art* (see Leggatt Collection, *Works of Frederick Walker*, Department of Prints and Drawings, British Museum, p. 71, no. 474) and in E. Chesneau, *Artistes anglais contemporains*, n.d., p. 61.

PROV: Bought from the artist by Thomas Agnew and Sons, 27 April 1866; sold to William Graham 22 March 1869 (£1,050);[21] his sale, Christie's 2 April 1886, lot 84, bought Agnew (£2,625); Sir Cuthbert Quilter[22] sale, Christie's 9 July 1909, lot 84, bought Tooth (£3,045); K.M. Clark[23] sale, Christie's 22 February 1918, lot 143, bought Gooden and Fox (£2,205) for Lever[24] (£2,265.10*s.*).

EXH: Royal Academy 1867 (627); International Exhibition 1871 (389); Deschamps Gallery, 168 New Bond Street, *Frederick Walker*, 1876 (64); Glasgow 1888 (138); Royal Academy, *Winter Exhibition*, 1901 (7); Liverpool Autumn Exhibition 1922 (876).

1 Identifying precise sources for the figures in LL 3143 would be fruitless; the conception was probably indebted to Michelangelo's *Bathers*; the Elgin marbles and Greek sculpture generally were used for individual figures. Many of Walker's later works were widely (and probably correctly) given a symbolic meaning but this is quite different from the classicism of LL 3143.

2 For this revival see particularly P. Hook, 'The Classical Revival in English painting', *Connoisseur*, 1976, vol. 192, pp. 124 ff.; it was significant that LL 3143 hung in the same room of the 1867 Royal Academy exhibition as Frederic Leighton's *Venus Disrobing*, the first of Leighton's grand classical nudes (L. and R. Ormond, *Lord Leighton*, 1975, p. 87); Albert Moore's first full-length standing nude, *A Wardrobe* (Johannesburg Art Gallery) also dated from 1867.

3 J.G. Marks, *Life and Letters of Frederick Walker*, 1896, pp. 30 ff., and G.D. Leslie, *Our River*, 1881, pp. 17–18; Leslie reproduces (p. 17) a drawing by Walker of the artist working on the canvas near the bank of the Thames while a boy,

one of his models, rests in a boat moored to the bank.

4 Reproduced in Marks, *op. cit.*, p. 31; this drawing was eventually published in *A Round of Days*, 1866 (Routledge); it illustrated a poem entitled *Summer* by Dora Greenwell; drawing and wood block were no. 95 at the Deschamps Gallery, 168 New Bond Street, *Frederick Walker*, 1876; they were both lent by Messrs. Dalziel. Another early sketch (in watercolour) used by the artist for LL 3143 was no. 141 at the Deschamps Gallery, *op. cit.*, listed as *The Bathers*, watercolour, 4⅝ × 5⅝ in. lent by Thomas Agnew and Sons Ltd., see *Pall Mall Gazette*, 13 January 1876, p. 11; this was presumably lot 72, *Young Bathers* in the Frederick Walker sale, Christie's 17 July 1875, bought Agnew (£44.2*s*.); in 1912 it was owned by Sir George Agnew, Bart.; a copy by J.G. Bingley is in the Leggatt Collection, *Works of Frederick Walker* now in the Prints and Drawings Department of the British Museum, p. 11, no. 68.

5 A sketch for these two figures is reproduced in Marks, *op. cit.*, p. 90. Studies for LL 3143 probably included two lots in the Frederick Walker sale, Christie's 17 July 1875, lot 1, a pen and ink drawing, *The Bathers*, bought Stevenson (£3.3*s*.) and lot 86, a watercolour, *Study for the Bathers*, bought Stevenson (£11.0*s*.6*d*.). The Leggatt Collection (see note 4) contains (page 71, no. 473) a reconstruction of LL 3143 consisting of photographs of a nude boy posing in the various attitudes of the principal boys in LL 3143 stuck down over a watercolour of the background of LL 3143 painted in watercolour by J.G. Bingley; it is not clear what this reconstruction is supposed to demonstrate.

6 Marks, *op. cit.*, pp. 6, 34.

7 Marks, *op. cit.*, pp. 36–7, 80, 103. In 1867 Walker seems to have got ideas in Paris for the improvement of LL 3143.

8 Marks, *op. cit.*, pp. 36–7, where the picture by Breton is called *La fin de la journée*; see Grand Palais, *Le Musée du Luxembourg en 1874*, 1974, pp. 40 ff., for works by Breton at the Luxembourg Museum in 1863.

9 Claude Phillips, 'Frederick Walker and his Works', *Portfolio*, 1894, p. 32, and the *Art Journal*, 1867, p. 143, detected French influence in LL 3143. Philippe Burty in 'L'Exposition de l'Académie Royale de Londres', *Gazette des Beaux Arts*, 1867, pp. 84–96, noted paintings influenced by French art and praised LL 3143. There were reduced replicas of the two paintings by Puvis de Chavannes at the 1867 Exposition Universelle.

10 *Works of John Ruskin*, ed. Cook and Wedderburn, 1904, vol. 14, p. 341 (letter to Henry Stacy Marks published in *The Times*, 20 January 1876).

11 J. Dafforne, 'The Works of Frederick Walker', *Art Journal*, 1876, p. 299.

12 *Art Journal*, 1867, p. 143.

13 *The Times*, 14 May 1867.

14 J. Comyns Carr, *Essays on Art*, 1879, pp. 208–10. For the Irish artist George Joy, LL 3143 was 'an impression of happy innocent life and joyous freedom' (*Work of George W. Joy with an autobiographical sketch*, 1904, p. 42). Substantially Carr's opinions are expressed at even greater length in the *Pall Mall Gazette*, 13 January 1876, p. 11, and rather more briefly in the *Spectator*, 22 January 1876, p. 111. For the young Sidney Colvin LL 3143 'emphatically marked an era in English painting' ('Painting at the International Exhibition', *Dark Blue Magazine*, July 1871, p. 613) and Swinburne saw in it 'brilliant skill and swift sharp talent' (*Essays and Studies, Some Pictures of 1868*, 1911, p. 367). Similarly, W.B. Richmond described LL 3143 as Walker's best picture 'bringing a fresh glow of colour, of representation and design into the English school. Wholly uninfluenced by the Pre-Raphaelites indeed more Greek than English, is that amazingly beautiful design, so entirely fresh and healthy in feeling, if a little inefficient technically' (A.M.W. Stirling, *The Richmond Papers*, 1926, pp. 183–4). See also Marks, *op. cit.*, pp. 102–3, for favourable contemporary criticism of LL 3143.

15 Phillips, *op. cit.*, p. 32.

16 F.G. Stephens, 'The Collection of Mr. W. Cuthbert Quilter', *Magazine of Art*, 1897, pp. 121–2.

17 *Athenaeum*, 11 May 1867, p. 629.

18 *The Times*, *op. cit.*

19 Phillips, *op. cit.* S. Colvin in 'Frederick Walker', *Portfolio*, 1870, pp. 35–8, also criticized the 'spotty, broken' paint in 'little flicks and spots' of LL 3143.

20 *Autobiography of Hubert Herkomer*, 1890, pp. 28–9. See also Watford Museum, *Sir Hubert von Herkomer*, 1982, p. 20, and L.M. Edwards, *Hubert von Herkomer and the Modern Life Subject*, 1984, p. 12; for Herkomer LL 3143 was 'a new direction . . . a new light' – he admired its poetic realism, its shallow space and its chalky finish; Herkomer, having seen the picture, insisted on moving from the study of the antique to the life room. For Thornycroft, see Elfrida Manning, *Marble and Bronze: The Art and Life of Hamo Thornycroft*, 1982, p. 101; his *Mower* of 1884 was, like *The Bathers*, a synthesis of realistic observation and classical organization; the large bronze version is in the Walker Art Gallery. Walker's judgment was that LL 3143 was a 'partial success'; see Marks, *op. cit.*, pp. 110–11.

21 H.S. Marks in his *Pen and Pencil Sketches*, 1894, p. 79 noted that Agnew's were brave to purchase an apparently unappealing picture and that it remained with them unsold for some years – Sir William Agnew was, however, a friend of the artist and had seen the painting in progress (Geoffrey Agnew, *Agnew's*, 1967, pp. 28–9). Their sale of *The Bathers* to Graham must, however, have been facilitated by his friendship with the artist and no doubt it was thanks to this friendship that Graham was able to return the painting to the artist for the insertion of a towel (presumably the one held by the central foreground kneeling boy) when his evangelical friends in London objected to the nudity in the painting – the Reverend Samuel Martin, the Congregational Minister at the Buckingham Gate chapel where the Grahams worshipped, arbitrated in this delicate matter (see Frances Horner, *Time Remembered*, 1933, pp. 36–8, 43; see the *Dictionary of National Biography* for Samuel Martin (died 1878)).

22 *Sir Cuthbert Quilter's Pictures*, n.d., p. 85, where it is stated apparently wrongly that LL 3143 was painted for Thomas Agnew and Sons; Stephens, *op. cit.*, pp. 121–2; in 1886 at the Graham sale, T.J. Barratt and A. and F. Pears had attempted to acquire it for use in advertising soap but they were apparently unable to buy the copyright (*Pall Mall Gazette*, 19 July 1889, and A.C.R. Carter, *Let me tell you*, 1942, p. 234).

23 The young Kenneth Clark found LL 3143 too heavy when he practised hanging pictures with his father's collection, see Kenneth Clark, *Another Part of the Wood*, 1974, p. 47.

24 See Royal Academy, *Lord Leverhulme*, 1980, p. 80.

## WATERHOUSE, John William
(1849–1917)

### *The Decameron*

LL 3133 (WHL 2754)
Canvas[1]: 101 × 159 cm
Signed: *J.W. Waterhouse 1916*

### *The Enchanted Garden*

LL 3629 (WHL 4382)
Canvas[2]: 115.5 × 160 cm

Boccaccio's *Decameron* of about 1353 relates the stories told by a group of three young men and seven young women who retired into the country from the plague in 14th-century Florence; one of these stories is being told in Waterhouse's *The Decameron*. Boccaccio states that on each day one of the group was made king or queen and then directed the activities of the entire group for that day; this figure can be identified in Waterhouse's painting by her crown. *The*

*Enchanted Garden*, on the hand, relates an episode from one of the stories. The fifth story of the tenth day concerns Dianora who, pursued by Ansaldo, offers to yield to him if he can produce in January a garden with the flowers, foliage and fruits of May. With the help of a magician Ansaldo succeeds and in this painting he is showing the distraught Dianora the enchanted garden; Dianora then confesses all to her husband, Gilberto, who advises her that she must comply with Ansaldo's desires, but Ansaldo, moved by this display of honesty, releases Dianora from the reckless contract. Exactly the same episode is represented in a watercolour of 1889 by Marie Stillman entitled *The Enchanted Garden*.[3]

Although left unfinished by the artist's death in February 1917,[4] *The Enchanted Garden* is seen by Hobson as perhaps the most extreme example of the lyrical introspective symbolism of Waterhouse's late paintings; it is snowing outside the garden, but inside flowers are in bloom; the figures stare enigmatically out of the picture; the sense of enclosure and retreat into the realm of the imagination and away from the hostile world of reality is strong in both paintings.[5]

Understandably, escapist paintings like these did not attract much critical attention at the 1916 and 1917 Royal Academy exhibitions during the two worst years of the First World War; the *Studio* described *The Decameron* as a 'notable canvas' and mentioned Waterhouse's four paintings at the 1917 Royal Academy as evidence of the loss that art had sustained with his death; *The Times* critic did not notice the earlier painting in 1916, and in 1917 simply noted the later painting as Waterhouse's best picture at that Royal Academy exhibition.[6]

A large oil study (54 × 89 cm) for *The Decameron* was last recorded with the Owen Edgar Gallery, London;[7] a charcoal drawing for the same painting was in the artist's sale,

*The Decameron* LL 3133 (colour plate 10)

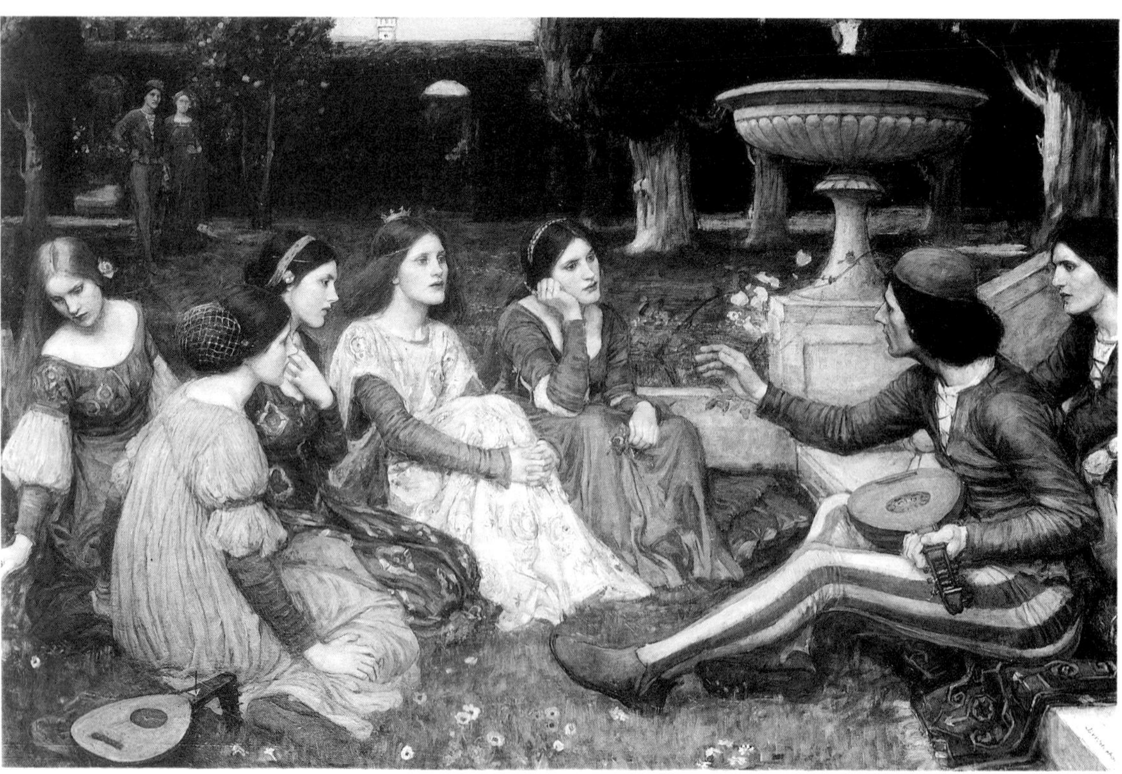

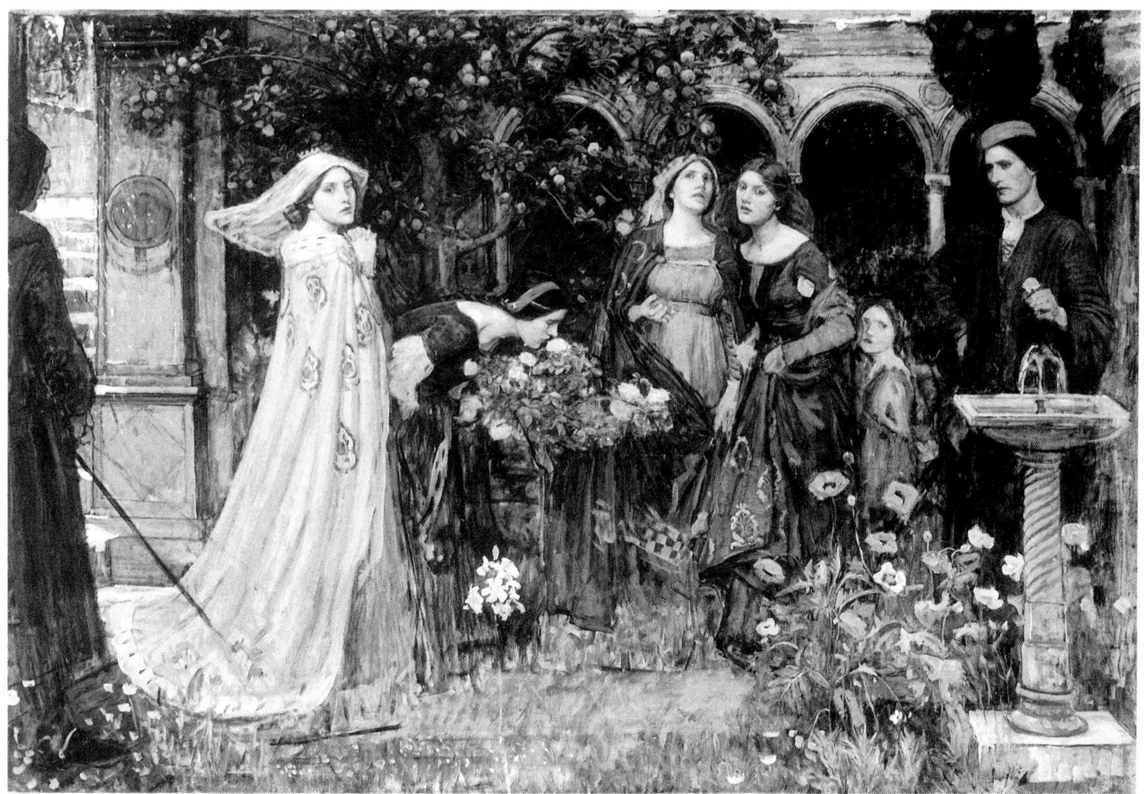

*The Enchanted Garden* LL 3629

Christie's 23 July 1926, lot 2,[8] and a pencil drawing for the whole composition was in the Christie's sale 8 February 1991, lot 11. An oil study for *The Enchanted Garden* was also in the artist's sale at Christie's, part of lot 69,[9] and a pencil study, 71 × 56 cm, is owned by Simon Williams.[10] A *Study of Lilies, Poppies and Carnations* for the same painting was exhibited in the *Victorian Age* exhibition at the Christopher Wood Gallery, 1990, no. 36. A *Study of a Seated Girl*, reproduced in 'Some Drawings by J.W. Waterhouse, R.A.',[11] may have been used by the artist for the crowned girl in *The Decameron*. An oil *Scene from Boccaccio* was in the artist's sale as lot 47 (62 × 85 cm) and might have been a study for either painting.[12] There are also preliminary drawings for both paintings in various of the artist's sketchbooks, notably one in the Victoria & Albert Museum (E 1112–1963), pages 8, 22, 24, 25, 40, 41, and one owned by John Physick.[13] The sketchbook in the Victoria & Albert Museum is dated July 1914–September 1915 and all the identified sketches in it are related to these two paintings.

PROV: LL 3133 bought by Lever from the artist through Arthur Tooth and Sons 4 April 1916 (£735); LL 3629 bought by Lever[14] from the artist's widow through Arthur Tooth and Sons 28 June 1922 (£500).

EXH: LL 3133 Royal Academy 1916 (363); LL 3629 Royal Academy 1917 (151).

1 The painted area of the canvas has at some time been re-attached to the stretcher about 5 cm higher than it was before.

2 Canvas stamp: *Leonard Sanders Artist's Depot, 1a Circus Road, St. John's Wood.*

3 For further details of the Stillman watercolour, see Barbican Art Gallery, *The Last Romantics*, 1989, no. 30, p. 87; her composition is strikingly similar to that of Waterhouse but her costume is more precisely localized to 15th-century Florence; the watercolour is owned by Pre-Raphaelite Inc.

4 On the back of the canvas of LL 3629 is inscribed: *J.W. Waterhouse 1916*. Similarly LL 3133 was begun well before it was first exhibited at the Royal Academy in May 1916; six figures were already painted in by 17 February 1915; see Royal Academy, *Lord Leverhulme*, 1980, p. 81.

5 See A. Hobson, *J.W. Waterhouse*, 1980, pp. 138 ff.; a similarly fanciful interpretation of LL 3629 appears in his later *J.W. Waterhouse*, 1989, p. 117; he seems to have been unaware of the exact subject of LL 3629. The artist's widow in a letter to Lever of 31 July 1922, described LL 3629 as 'The Enchanted Garden – from the Decameron' and stated that it was a companion to LL 3133. An MS label on the back of LL 3629 describes it as *The Enchanted Garden (from Boccaccio's Tales)*.

6 *Studio*, 1916, vol. 68, p. 40 and 1917, vol. 71, p. 18. *The Times*, 5 May 1917. The artist's widow, however, in her letter to Lever of 31 July 1922 stated that Poynter had written to her saying that he considered LL 3629 one of Waterhouse's most beautiful paintings.

7 Hobson, *op. cit.*, pp. 146 and 192, no. 215, plate 152.

8 Hobson, *op. cit.*, p. 197, no. 326.

9 Hobson, *op. cit.*, p. 193, no. 222.

10 Hobson, *op. cit.*, p. 197, no. 328.

11 *Studio*, 1980, vol. 44, p. 251.

12 Hobson, *op. cit.*, p. 192, no. 216.

13 Hobson, *op. cit.*, p. 200, nos. 387 and 392, plate 150.

14 Lever was an important patron of Waterhouse, particularly in the artist's later years (see Hobson, *op. cit.*, p. 148). As well as LL 3133 and LL 3629 he owned the *Alfresco Toilet at Capri* (1890), *The Siren* (1900) and *The Love Philtre* (1914). LL 3133, together with LL 3629, was, however, probably the last major contemporary painting which he purchased – see Royal Academy, 1980, *op. cit.*; as he grew older he became primarily interested in the art of the past. Lever's offer to purchase LL 3629, made to Arthur Tooth and Sons in a letter of 26 June 1922 (MSS Lady Lever Art Gallery) was unusual; he offered £400 if the picture was to go straight to the Bolton Art Gallery, but £500 if he was to retain it himself; Mrs. Waterhouse took the £500.

## **WATTS, George Frederic** (1817–1904)
## ***She Shall be Created Woman***

LL 3745 (WHL 4033)
Canvas: 78.3 × 31 cm

This is a small version of the first composition in Watts's *Eve* trilogy; the final large works are all in the Tate Gallery. The artist described the series, begun in the 1860s, as follows:[1] 'Eve in the glory of her innocence, Eve yielding to temptation and Eve restored to beauty and nobility by remorse – form part of one design and can hardly be separated.'

The Lady Lever Art Gallery painting is described by the artist's wife[2] as 'the first and most beautifully complete version of this subject' and she dated it to the early 1870s (probably); it lacks the symbolic flowers and birds of later versions; the large Tate Gallery version was not finished until 1892; other versions were sold at Sotheby's (Belgravia) 28 October 1978, lot 17 (86.5 × 35 cm), at Sotheby's (New Bond Street) 23 June 1981, lot 105 (60 × 26 cm – stated to date from the 1870s) and at Sotheby's (New Bond Street) 15 June 1982, lot 110 (86 × 35 cm – stated to date from the 1890s). This composition was intensely symbolic;[3] a shaft of light is set up between heaven and

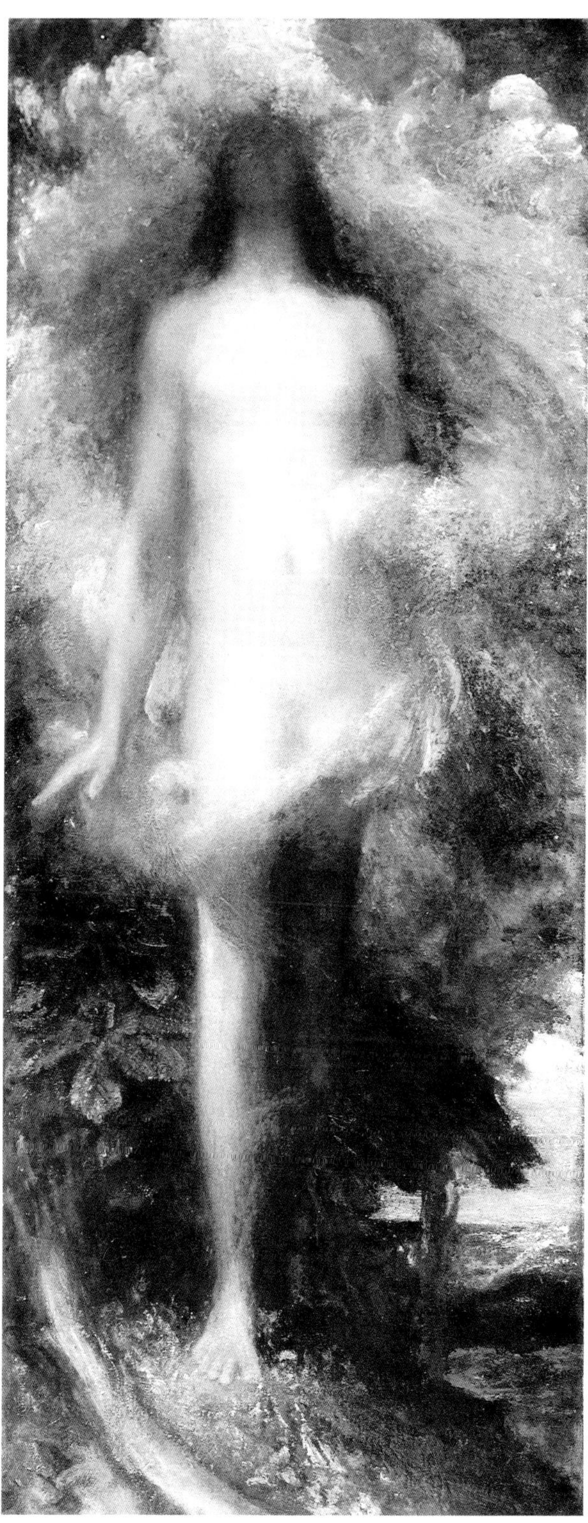

*She Shall be Created Woman* LL 3745

earth and the light is concentrated over the heart and breast as the seats of tenderness, goodness and love; the face is dark to suggest those areas of the human mind 'dark with excessive light'.

PROV: Sold by the artist through the dealer Robert Dunthorne to Sir George Drummond of Montreal in the autumn of 1899;[4] his sale, Christie's 26 June 1919, lot 161, as *Eve: The Creation Study for the large picture*, bought Gooden and Fox (£630) for Lever (£645.15*s*.).

EXH: Birmingham Musuem and Art Gallery, *G.F. Watts and Edward Burne-Jones*, 1885 (125) and *The Collection of Paintings*, 1886 (32).

1 M.S. Watts, *George Frederic Watts: Annals of an Artist's Life*, 1912, vol. 1, p. 262. Mrs. Russell Barrington in *G.F. Watts: Reminiscences*, 1905, p. 132, stated that the *Eve* trilogy together with another multi-figure *Genesis* series, were associated with Watts's *House of Life* scheme and Watts wrote to C.H. Rickards to the same effect on 6 June 1873, see Arts Council of Great Britain, *G.F. Watts*, 1954–5, p. 35 and Minneapolis Institute of Arts, *Victorian High Renaissance*, 1978, pp. 81–2. For the subject matter of the trilogy, see also Barrington, *op. cit.*, pp. 136–7 and M.S. Watts, *op. cit.*, vol. 2, pp. 138–9, 202–3. The date of the inception of the trilogy is very uncertain; the two large versions of the *Eve Repentant* (now Watts Gallery, Compton and Tate Gallery) are listed by the artist's wife as begun (respectively) in 1868 and in the 1860s, while the Walker Art Gallery, Liverpool, version of that composition is noted by her as also begun in 1868 (MS Catalogue, Watts Gallery, Compton); in her *George Frederic Watts*, 1912, *op. cit.*, vol. 2, p. 138, she states that the trilogy was designed 'some time in the sixties'; Mrs. Barrington, however (*op. cit.*, pp. 92–3), remarked that even by 1876 only rough sketches of the trilogy existed.

2 MS Catalogue, *op. cit.*

3 M.S. Watts, 1912, *op. cit.*, vol. 2, pp. 138–9, 202–3: 'It is not so much, or rather not at all, the Eve of Genesis, nor of Milton either. It is an

incarnation of the spirit of our own time, and a hope for the future etc.' Later versions of the composition owe much to theosophy; see David Stewart, 'Theosophy and Abstraction in the Victorian Era', *Apollo*, 1993, vol. 139, pp. 300–2.

4 MS Catalogue, *op. cit.*, Montreal Museum of Fine Arts, *Discerning Tastes: Montreal Collectors*, 1989, p. 162; see also pp. 23–5 for an assessment of Drummond as a collector.

**WHITTLE, Thomas** (flourished about 1845–1872)

### *Landscape with Horses and Cart*

LL 3709
Canvas[1]: 51.2 × 76.7 cm
Signed: *T. Whittle 1857*

PROV: Found in the Gallery 1991.

1 Canvas stamp: *PINNICE BROTHERS / HIGH STREET / CAMDEN TOWN*; label on stretcher: *JOHN CUMMINGS / 42 MOOR LANE / PRESTON.*

**WOOD, Emily Sara Stewart** (born about 1866, died 1937)

### *The Hill, Hampstead*

LL 3648 (WHL 2879)
Panel: 37.5 × 45.5 cm
Signed: *E. Stewart Wood*

The Hill was the house originally built in 1807 and bought by Lever as his principal London residence in 1904; he undertook a series of Neo-Georgian re-modellings;[1] the house was sold after his death in 1925. This painting shows the garden front[2] and part of the gardens laid out by Thomas Mawson.

PROV: Bought by Lever from the artist July 1916 (£8.8*s*.).[3]

1 See Royal Academy, *Lord Leverhulme*, 1980, pp. 183–4, 190. The house had been entirely rebuilt in about 1898 before Lever's remodellings.

2 For the same view see the illustration in *Country Life*, 1918, vol. 43, p. 187.

3 In her receipt the artist describes LL 3648 as *Sketch of the Hill.*

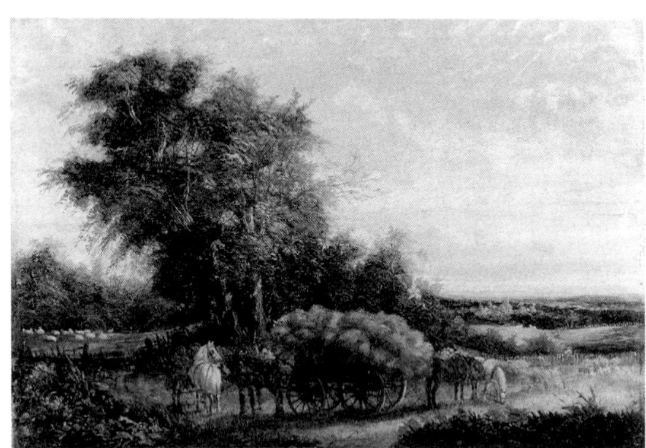

*Landscape with Horses and Cart* LL 3709

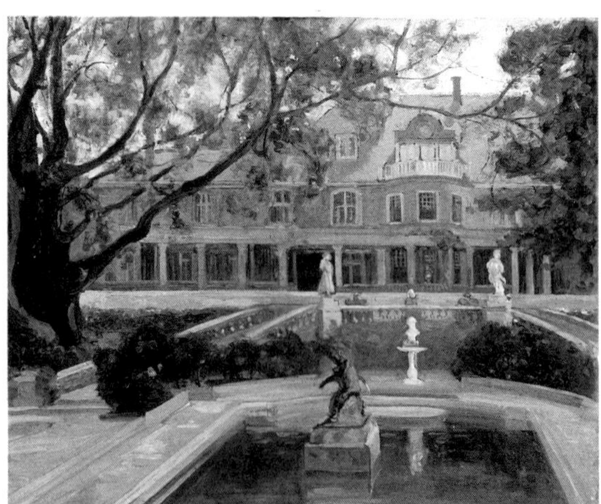

*The Hill, Hampstead* LL 3648

# APPENDIX 1:

## Victorian and Edwardian Paintings Collected by Lever but Sold by his Executors in 1925–1926

This list is taken from the sale catalogues at which the works were sold. Against each work in most cases appear Lever's inventory number (prefixed WHL), the dimensions in centimetres (where only one dimension is given it is the height) and details of the sale catalogue and lot number (the details in abbreviated form, see below). A small number of works of art from Lever's collection were neither dispersed at these sales nor passed to the Lady Lever Art Gallery but were given to other institutions and individuals; no attempt has been made to include them in this list.

### Abbreviations

AG 2 — Anderson Galleries, New York<br>17–19 February 1926<br>(Paintings)

KFR 1 — Knight, Frank and Rutley at the Bungalow and Rivington Hall, Horwich, Lancashire<br>9–17 November 1925

KFR 4 — Knight, Frank and Rutley, London<br>15–18 June 1926<br>(Pictures removed from Cheshire)

KFR 7 — Knight, Frank and Rutley, London<br>14–16 July 1926

### Paintings

Adams, William Dacres, *Cub Hunting* (WHL 4191), 68.6 × 60.9, KFR 1(1057)

Alexander, R., *Mrs. John Hope Holding a Book* (WHL 3322), 73 × 63.5, KFR 4(1)

Barber, Burton, *Suspense* (WHL 2921), 68.9 × 88.9, KFR 1(1060)

Barber, J.M., *The Bubble* (WHL 2964), 30.5 × 26.7, KFR 1(1062)

Brangwyn, Frank, *Cinerarias* (WHL 4760), 106.7 × 116.8, AG 2(10)

Brews, Edith Ruby, *The Newspaper Boy: The Coster Girl* (WHL 4800), 44.5 × 34.3, AG 2(11)

Brown, M., *Father Christmas* (WHL 2935), KFR 1(1061)

—, *Pluck* (WHL 2930), 66 x 43.2, KFR 1(1063)

Browne, A.K., *The Clachan, Highland Village* (WHL 4192), 38.1 × 116.8, KFR 1(1071)

Bundy, Edgar, *A Hearty Welcome* (WHL 2914), 60.9 × 91.4, KFR 1(1064)

Burgess, J.B., *Prayers* (WHL 1485), 41.9 × 29.2, KFR 4(13)

Burne-Jones, Edward Coley, *The Wheel of Fortune* (WHL 4016), 134.6 × 66, KFR 1(1066)

—, *Head of a Girl* (WHL 4014), 90.2 × 45.7, KFR 1(1067)

—, *The Passing of Venus* (WHL 4001), 57.2 × 24.8, KFR 1(1068)

—, *Mrs. Stillman* (WHL 4004), 67.3 × 45.7, KFR 1(1070)

—, *Saint John* (WHL 3997), 141 × 68.6, KFR 1(1072)

—, *Study for a stained glass window: St. Mark*, (WHL 3996) 165.1 × 95.3, KFR 4(15)

—, *Fortitude* (WHL 3999), 302.3 × 119.4, KFR 4(16)

—, *The Romance of the Rose* (WHL 4000), 155 × 305, KFR 4(17)

—, *The Sirens* (WHL 4002), 146.1 × 198.8, KFR 4(18)

—, *Meschach* (WHL 4005A), 152.4 × 48.3, KFR 4(19)

—, *Perseus and the Graiae* (WHL 4010), 152.4 × 132.1, KFR 4(20)

—, *Venus Concordia* (WHL 4011), 142.2 × 208.3, KFR 4(21)

—, *Venus Discordia* (WHL 4012), 116.8 × 208.3, KFR 4(22)

—, *Study for the Judgement of Paris* (WHL 4013), 105.4 × 67.3, KFR 4(23)

—, *The Rose Bower* (WHL 3301), 68.6 × 53.3, AG 2(12)

—, *The Princess Chained to the Tree* (WHL 3694), 104.1 × 94, AG 2(13)

—, *Hill Fairies* (WHL 4008), 182.9 × 61, AG 2(14)

—, *Wood Nymphs* (WHL 4009), 182.9 × 61, AG 2(15)

—, *The Garden of Pan* (WHL 4006), 152.4 × 185.4, AG 2(16)

—, *Spes* (WHL 4003), 213.4 × 81.3, AG 2(17)

Calderon, Philip Hermogenes, *Captain of the Eleven* (WHL 2974), 152.4 × 94, KFR 1(1073)

Carrington, James Yates, *An Out Patient at King's College Hospital, 31st July, 1887: Bob, Nell and Jack* (WHL 2918), 127 × 101.6, KFR 1(1074)

Cheston, Evelyn, *Creech Barrow, Dorset* (WHL 2829), 81.3 × 109.2, KFR 1(1078)

Clark, J., *Our Hearts' Delight* (WHL 2967), 66 × 45.7, KFR 1(1075)

Clausen, George, *Hayricks* (WHL 1159), 24.1 × 26.7, AG 2(19)

Cole, George Vicat, *Abingdon-on-Thames* (WHL 10), 110.5 × 180.3, AG 2(20)

Coleman, W.G., *Flowers of the East* (WHL 2941), 76.2 × 48.3, KFR 1(1076)

—, *Butterflies* (WHL 2963), 63.5 × 39.4, KFR 1(1077)

—, *Sunny South* (WHL 2940), 50.8 × 55.9, KFR 1(1079)

—, *Italian Girls* (WHL 2910), 44.5 × 63.5, KFR 1(1080)

—, *Oriental Colours* (WHL 2911), 71.1 × 33, KFR 1(1081)

Collier, Tom, *Cardigan Bay* (WHL 443), 49.5 × 64.8, KFR 4(34)

Colls, Katherine M., *Algeciras* (WHL 2828), 19.1 × 22.9, AG 2(22)

Crane, Walter, *The Lady of Shalott* (WHL 3304), 25.4 × 30.5, AG 2(53)

—, *Schwanen Jungfrauen* (WHL 4787), 148.6 × 113, AG 2(53A)

Cundell, Norah, *The Laundress* (WHL 4797), 36.8 × 29.8, AG 2(60)

Dawson, Henry, *A Coast Scene* (WHL 192), 19.1 × 29.2, AG 2(63)

Dawson, H. T., *The Old Guardship: Sunset* (WHL 649), 48.2 × 73.6, KFR 4(66)

—, *Moor Scene* (WHL 2299), 27.9 × 39.4, KFR 4(67)

—, *Carlisle Castle and Bridge* (WHL 2315), 49.5 × 73.7, KFR 4(68)

Dicksee, Frank, *The Redemption of Tannhauser* (WHL 3796), 172.7 × 271.8, AG 2(65A)

—, *The Symbol* (WHL 4102), 195.6 × 139.7, AG 2(65B)

Draper, Herbert James, *The Sea Nymph* (WHL 3751), 26.7 × 39.4, AG 2(66)

Duffield, William, *Parrot and Fruit* (WHL 2948), 55.9 × 41.9, KFR 1(1084)

East, Alfred, *Haru-No-Yuki* (WHL 1217), 102.9 × 154.9, AG 2(72)

—, *Autumn in Spain* (WHL 1218), 80 × 100.3, AG 2(73)

Elsley, Arthur John, *Surprised* (WHL 2926), 61 × 76.2, KFR 1(1085)

Faed, Thomas, *The Rendezvous* (WHL 149), 14.6 × 10.2, AG 2(93)

Fagan, B., *The Children's Bath* (WHL 2972), 170.2 × 127, KFR 1(1086)

Fanner, Alice, *A Windy Day, Shoreham Bridge* (WHL 1174), 71.1 × 101.6, KFR 1(1090)

Faustin, *Mischief* (WHL 2950), 54.6 × 39.4, KFR 1(1088)

—, *Peep-a-bo* (WHL 2936), 53.3 × 38, KFR 1(1089)

Fildes, Fanny, *Still Life – A Flower Painting* (WHL 4692), 19.7 × 27.9, AG 2(95)

—, *Still Life* (WHL 4691), 19.7 × 27.9, AG 2(96)

Forbes, Elizabeth, *June at the Farm* (WHL 4297), 125.7 × 101.6, AG 2(100)

Ford, Onslow, *Landscape* (WHL 1158), 24.1 × 40.6, AG 2(101)

Fowler, Robert, *Widnes: A Lancashire Epic* (WHL 4802), 152.4 × 182.9, KFR 4(74)

—, *Mist and Sunbeams in the Barmouth Estuary* (WHL 4666), 68.6 × 106.7, AG 2(102)

Frith, William P., *Evening Prayer* (WHL 2814), 34.9 × 24.7, KFR 1(1087)

George, Eric, *Flora* (WHL 4798), 101.6 × 96.5, AG 2(111)

Gregory, E.J., *Study for Boulter's Lock* (WHL 1495), 45.7 × 60.7, KFR 4(76)

—, *Study for Boulter's Lock* (WHL 676), 27.3 × 40.6, KFR 4(77)

Hacker, Arthur, *Porlock Church* (WHL 1154), 25.4 × 33, AG 2(120)

Haley, Henry, *The Sea Fairy* (WHL 3617), 90.2 × 44.5, KFR 1(1109)

Hardy, Heywood, *The Cab Fare* (WHL 2791), 17.8 × 30.5, KFR 1(1103)

Hare, *The Last Word* (WHL 2959), 53.3 × 33, KFR 1(1104)

—, *Reflection* (WHL 2937), 19.1 × 40.6, KFR 1(1113)

Hellaby, R.J., *Arundel Castle* (WHL 4821), 49.5 × 45.1, AG 2(133)

Hemy, Charles Napier, *The Old River Barge, Limehouse* (WHL 4656), 116.8 × 177.8, KFR 1(1105)

—, *The River Gloom, Limehouse* (WHL 4655), 119.4 × 180.3, KFR 1(1108)

Herkomer, Hubert von, *Haymaking and Lovemaking* (WHL 2811), 68.6 × 88.9, KFR 1(1102)

Hicks, George, *Playmates* (WHL 2953), KFR 1(1100)

Holden, Albert William, *Long Bill* (WHL 2907), 66 × 76.2, KFR 1(1094)

—, *A Boy Blowing Bubbles* (WHL 2943), 30.5 × 22.9, KFR 1(1095)

—, *Pounds, Shillings, Pence* (WHL 2947), 54.6 × 40.6, KFR 1(1096)

—, *Saluting Admiral* (WHL 2955), 76.2 × 48.3, KFR 1(1097)

—, *Naughty Polly* (WHL 2933), 50.8 × 58.4, KFR 1(1098)

—, *Old Dreadnought* (WHL 2965), 76.2 × 48.3, KFR 1(1099)

—, *The Five Senses* (WHL 2942), 30.5 × 22.9, KFR 1(1101)

Holl, Frank, *The Lord Giveth and the Lord Hath Taken Away* (WHL 3511), 52.1 × 74.9, KFR 1(1110)

Hollingsworth, Ruth, *Heron Pool on the Husk* (WHL 2696), 62.2 × 74.9, KFR 1(2)

—, *View from Bungalow, Rivington* (WHL 3850), 39.4 × 36.8, KFR 1(1106)

—, *Harewood Downs* (WHL 3848), 60.9 × 72.4, KFR 1(1111)

—, *The Lake, Thornton Manor* (WHL 2627), 52.1 × 47, KFR 4(85)

—, *Landscape with Steep Grassy Hill* (WHL 3172), 19.1 × 22.9, KFR 4(86)

—, *Still Life* (WHL 2835), 61 × 49.5, AG 2(139)

—, *The Shower* (WHL, 4672), 22.9 × 25.4, AG 2(140)

—, *Morning Mists* (WHL 2699), 35.6 × 40.6, AG 2(141)

—, *Primroses* (WHL 4674), 24.8 × 30.5, AG 2(142)

—, *Iceland Poppies* (WHL 4673), 34.3 × 36.8, AG 2(143)

—, *China Ducks* (WHL 2698), 38.1 × 35.6, AG 2(144)

Hornel, Ernest Atkinson, *Through the Woods to Fairyland* (WHL 3419), 48.3 × 60.9, AG 2 (151)

Jack, Richard, *Whither* (WHL 4749), 83.8 × 109.2, AG 2 (152)

Jacomb-Hood, George Percy, *When the World was Young* (WHL 3309), 101.6 × 100.3, KFR 1(1107)

Jutsum, Henry, *A Woodland Scene with Children* (WHL 653), 22.2 × 17.1, KFR 4(109)

Kilburne, George Goodwin, *Shy* (WHL 2952), 60.9 × 88.9, KFR 1(1114)

—, *The Bashful Lover* (WHL 672), 42 × 59.6, KFR 4(112)

Knowles, George Sheridan, *A Peep en Route* (WHL 2971), 88.9 × 58.4, KFR 1(1115)

Kricheldorf, Carl, *Peace* (WHL 1481), 13.3 × 17, KFR 4 (114)

La Thangue, Henry Herbert, *Provençal Forge* (WHL 4280), 76.2 × 88.9, KFR 1(1168)

Ladell, E., *Dessert* (WHL 2960), KFR 1(1118)

Landseer, Edwin Henry, *Black Dog* (WHL 2014), 25.4 × 29.2, KFR 4 (115)

Lavery, John, *The Weaver* (WHL 4634), 52.1 × 36.8, KFR 1 (1123)

Leader, Benjamin William, *Evening, Worcestershire* (WHL 1413), 40.6 × 60.9, AG 2(163)

—, *Worcester Cathedral* (WHL 692), 134.6 × 227.3, AG 2(164)

Leighton, Frederic, *Antigone* (WHL 3198), 59.7 × 50.8, AG 2 (166)

—, *Mecca Donkey with Arab Attendant* (WHL 3791), 19.1 × 19.1, AG 2(167)

—, *A Mecca Donkey* (WHL 3792), 19.1 × 19.1, AG 2(168)

—, *Madonna and Child* (WHL 2761), 26.7 × 17.1, AG 2(169)

Lewis, John Frederick, *The Bezestein Bazaar, Cairo* (WHL 3793), 111.8 × 86.4, KFR 1 (1119)

Lillie, *A Witch* (WHL 2944), KFR 1(1120)

Linton, James Drongole, *The Surrender* (WHL 3847), 124.5 × 221, AG 2(176)

Lipscombe, Mabel, *The Harbour, St. Ives, Moonlight* (WHL 4202), 76.2 × 106.7, KFR 4(190)

Lucas, Edward George, *Of Such is the Kingdom of Heaven* (WHL 2957), 26.7 × 44.5, KFR 1(1117)

Lucas, John Seymour, *A Lively Measure* (WHL 2902), 26.7 × 44.5, KFR 1(1116)

MacWhirter, James, *The Valley by the Sea* (WHL 3402), 45.7 × 74.9, AG 2(177)

Mitchell, *Happy as a King* (WHL 2969), 71.1 × 91.4, KFR 1 (1132)

Moore, Albert, *The Marble Seat* (WHL 2641), 47.6 × 73.7, KFR 4(192)

—, *Lilies*, (WHL 4125), 29.2 × 47, AG 2(182)

—, *Cherry Blossom* (WHL 4128), 76.2 × 24.1, AG 2(183)

Morgan, Frederick, *Over the Garden Wall* (WHL 2968), 86.4 × 50.8, KFR 1(1127)

—, *Sweethearts* (WHL 2954), 81.3 × 60.9, KFR 1(1131)

—, *Ring a Ring o' Roses* (WHL 4651), 63.4 × 83.8, KFR 1(1136)

Morley, H., *Fellow Prisoners* (WHL 4395), 41.9 × 52.1, KFR 1(1135)

Morley, T.W., *Winter* (WHL 2962), 36.8 × 27.3, KFR 1(1126)

Mostyn, Tom, *The Rondel* (WHL 4652), 101.6 × 152.4, KFR 1 (1134)

—, *The Forest Lovers* (WHL 3177), 73.7 × 152.4, KFR 4(191)

Muirhead, David, *Head of a Girl* (WHL 2798), 76.2 × 63.5, KFR 1(1128)

Muller, William James, *Venice: Canal Scene* (WHL 4528), 63.5 × 54.6, KFR 1(1133)

—, *Angers, France* (WHL 61), 63.5 × 105.4, AG 2(201)

—, *The Young Anglers* (WHL 4122), 92.7 × 77.5, AG 2(202)

—, *Whitchurch* (WHL 3199), 78.7 × 127, AG 2(203)

Mullock, *The Board of Guardians* (WHL 2924), 96.5 × 78.7, KFR 1(1124)

Murray, David, *In the Bay of Stornoway* (WHL 4429), 114.3 × 130.8, AG 2(204)

Nichol, Erskine, *Common Pleas* (WHL 4040), 29.2 × 24.1, KFR 1(1137)

—, *Irish Stew* (WHL 3801), 45.7 × 137.2, AG 2(208)

Noble, Robert, *A Sunlit Stream* (WHL 3378), 50.8 × 76.2, KFR 4(117)

Orpen, William, *Portrait of Lady Rocksavage* (WHL 4389), 119.4 × 94, AG 2(210)

—, *The Old Cabman* (WHL 4750), 73.7 × 60.9, AG 2(211)

Orrock, James, *Sands of Chapel* (WHL 179), 29.2 × 44.5, KFR 4(118)

Philip, John, *Friar Tuck at Supper* (WHL 595), 91.4 × 66, KFR 1(1141)

Pinwell, George John, *The Enchantress* (WHL 4747), 26.7 × 38.1, AG 2(214)

Poynter, Edward John, *Sweet is the Breath of Man* (WHL 32), 57.2 × 57.2, AG 2(216)

—*A Suppliant to Venus* (WHL 3313), 71.1 × 41.9, AG 2(217)

—, *At Low Tide* (WHL 2903), 81.3 × 55.9, AG 2(218)

Priestman, Bertram, *A Suffolk Valley, Autumn* (WHL 4281), 81.3 × 127, AG 2 (219)

Prinsep, Valentine Cameron, *Rosina* (WHL 3354), KFR 4 (123)

Rathbone, Harold Stewart, *Primavera* (WHL 2644), 49.5 × 59.7; KFR 4(125)

Reilly, *A Girl's Head* (WHL 2945), 41.9 × 31.7, KFR 1 (1146)

—, *Suspense*, KFR 4(126)

Richmond, William Blake, *Phidyle* (WHL 4434), 64.8 × 38, KFR 1(1142)

Riviere, Briton, *The Wounded Adonis* (WHL 3459), 53.3 × 95.3, KFR 1(1145)

Shannon, James Jebusa, *White Lilies* (WHL 4653), 208.3 × 102.9, AG 2(240)

Shaw, John Byam, *The Woman, the Man and the Serpent* (WHL 2132), 182.9 × 121.9, AG 2(241)

—, *Purity* (WHL 4214), 91.4 × 45.7, AG 2(242)

—, *Hope* (WHL 4213), 91.4 × 45.7, AG 2(243)

—, *Love, Strong as Death, is Dead* (WHL 3315), 40.6 × 30.5, AG 2(244)

Shayer, William Joseph, *Landscape with Mill* (WHL 1439), 24.1 × 29.2, KFR 4(138)

Storey, George Adolphus, *Pan and Syrinx* (WHL 4555), 73.6 × 125.7, KFR 1(1153)

—, *Choice of the Beautiful* 101.6 × 160, KFR 1(1154)

—, *A Country Girl* (WHL 4539), 59.7 × 49.5, KFR 1(1155)

—, *Painter and the Connoisseurs* (WHL 4530), 100.3 × 160, KFR 1 (1156)

— *The Wounded Captain* (WHL 4044), 88.9 × 63.5, KFR 1(1157)

— *The First Letter* (WHL 4021), 45.7 × 58.4, KFR 1 (1158)

—, *Chrysantheal* (WHL 4536), 64.8 × 49.5, KFR 1 (1159)

—, *In Evening Shade* (WHL 4546), 81.3 × 114.3, KFR 1(1160)

—, *Summer Days* (WHL 4532), 59.7 × 44.5, KFR 1(1161)

—, *Fotis* (WHL 4550), 64.8 × 36.8, KFR 1(1163)

—, *Olivia* (WHL 4541), 81.3 × 44.5, KFR 1(1164)

—, *Armida in the Enchanted Wood* (WHL 4531), 57.2 × 81.3, KFR 1(1165)

—, *Pamela* (WHL 1178), 91.4 × 63.5, AG 2(253)

—, *In Time of War* (WHL 4565), 87.6 × 69.8, AG 2(254)

—, *A Young Prodigal and His Friends* (WHL 3074), 96.5 × 157.5, AG 2(255)

—, *The Shy Lover* (WHL 4556), 44.5 × 34.3, AG 2(256)

—, *The Captive* (WHL 4560), 7.6 × 43.2, AG 2(257)

—, *The Pink Sunshade* (WHL 4551), 57.2 × 40.6, AG 2(258)

—, *Follow My Leader* (WHL 4549), 69.9 × 90.2, AG 2(259)

—, *The Brigand* (WHL 4554), 58.4 × 47, AG 2(260)

—, *Paris and Oenone* (WHL 4543), 83.8 × 111.8, AG 2(261)

—, *Venus Lamenting Adonis* (WHL 4544), 90.2 × 64.8, AG 2(262)

Strang, William, *The Wife of a Picador* (WHL 3372), 90.2 × 73.7, AG 2(263)

Stretton, P., *The Mate's Watch* (WHL 2961), 36.8 × 48.3, KFR 1(1150)

—, *Cheek* (WHL 2956), 63.5 × 58.4, KFR 1(1148)

Tarpey, K., *Fowey Harbour* (WHL 2831), 71.1 × 81.3, KFR 1(1169)

Unknown, *An Oriental Tournament* (WHL 2272), 86.4 × 127, KFR 1(1)

—, *Bowl of Roses* KFR 1(3)

Varley, John Jnr., *Road in Shiba, Tokyo* (WHL 1488), KFR 7(43)

Vigor, Charles, *He Who Lives a Good Life is Sure to Live Well* (WHL 2927), 63.5 × 81.3, KFR 1(1171)

Walker, Frederick, *Peaceful Thames* (WHL 4515), 40.6 × 61, AG 2(279)

Ward, Edward Matthew, *Washing Day at Liverpool Docks* (WHL 2966), 19.7 × 17.8, KFR 1(1172)

Waterhouse, John William, *The Love Philtre* (WHL 1395), 91.4 × 61, AG 2(280)

—, *An Alfresco Toilet at Capri* (WHL 8), 85.1 × 73.7, AG 2 (281)

Waterlow, Ernest Albert, *The Silent Wood* (WHL 1400), 121.9 × 86.4, AG 2(282)

Weguelin, John Reinhard, *The Bathers* (WHL 24), 81.3 × 12.7, AG 2(283)

Wetherbee, George, *Land of Romance* (WHL 2753), 50.2 × 75.6, KFR 1(1175)

Williams, Haynes, *The Toast* (WHL 2929), 60.9 × 44.5, KFR 1(1172)

Wimperis, Edmund Morison, *A Stream through the Marshes* (WHL 689), 26.7 × 43.2, KFR 4(163)

Wood, E. Stewart, *In Parham Wood* (WHL 2827), 99.1 × 121.9, KFR 1(1177)

Woods, Henry, *Venezia Bendetta* (WHL 5), 76.2 × 38.1, AG 2(294)

Wylie, R., *Mendicants* (WHL 4028), 52.1 × 38.1, KFR 1(1176)

Wyllie, William Lionel, *Spithead in Peace*, (WHL 4270), 43.2 × 99.1, KFR 1(1174)

# APPENDIX 2:

## Victorian and Edwardian Paintings Collected by Lever but Sold from the Lady Lever Art Gallery in 1958–1961

Against each work in most cases appear Lever's inventory number (prefixed WHL), the dimensions in centimetres (where only one dimension is given it is the height) and details of the sale catalogue and lot number.

### Paintings

Appleyard, Fred, *A Pergola*, (WHL 2412) 62.2 × 74.9, Christie's 6 June 1958 (94)

Bundy, Edgar, *Finance* (WHL 685), 129.5 × 243.8, Christie's 6 June 1958 (97)

Burne-Jones, Edward Coley, *Cupid Delivering Psyche* (WHL 3998), 73.7 × 90.2, Christie's 6 June 1958 (99)

—, *The Garden of Pan* (WHL 3333) 76.2 × 116.8, Christie's 6 June 1958 (98)

Burton, Arthur, *A Sleeping Nymph* (WHL 1437) 33 × 106.7, Christie's 6 June 1958 (100)

Carelli, Conrad, *Capri with Fishing-Boats on a Calm Sea* 34.3 × 59.7, Christie's 7 April 1961 (139)

Dawson, Henry, *Windsor Park* (WHL 2310), 88.9 × 104.1, Christie's 6 June 1958 (112)

—, *Sunset at Sea* (WHL 45), 68.6 × 100.3, Christie's 6 June 1958 (109)

—, *Dovedale, Derbyshire* (WHL 625), 72.4 × 90.2, Christie's 6 June 1958 (110)

—, *Virginia Water* (WHL 2300), 49.5 × 73.7, Christie's 6 June 1958 (111)

—, *The Boat in the Lock* (WHL 2310), 48.3 × 74.9, Christie's 6 June 1958 (112)

—, *Cattle by Ruins* 30.5 × 40.6, Bonham's 20 April 1961 (150)

East, Alfred, *On thė Upper Thames* (WHL 1434), 80 × 100.3, Christie's 6 June 1958 (114)

— *Rivington Water* (WHL 1441), 68.6 × 88.9, Christie's 6 June 1958 (115)

Farquharson, David, *Winter* (WHL 3), 149.9 × 241.3, Christie's 6 June 1958 (121)

Ford, Onslow, *The Hills of Scotland* (WHL 1210), 40.6 × 94, Christie's 6 June 1958 (122)

Gallon, Robert, *The Sunset Hour* 29.2 × 44.5, Christie's 7 April 1961 (127)

Gilbert, John, *Don Quixote at the Castle of the Duke* (WHL 2900), 94 × 119.4, Christie's 6 June 1958 (123)

Hoggatt, William, *Sunny Manxland* (WHL 2680), 90.2 × 120.5, Christie's 6 June 1958 (127)

Holmes, G.A., *The Pet Puppy* (WHL 684), 30.5 × 22.9, Christie's 6 June 1958 (131)

Jacomb-Hood, George Percy, *Spring* (WHL 682), 149.9 × 101.6, Christie's 6 June 1958 (132)

Jacques, Jules, *Travellers Preparing To Depart* 44.5 × 59.7, Christie's 7 April 1961 (133)

Knight, Laura, *Marsh Mallows* (WHL 2168), 73.5 × 61, Christie's 6 June 1958 (134)

Leighton, Frederic, *Cimabue's Madonna in Procession through Florence* (WHL 1173), 26.7 × 62.2, Christie's 6 June 1958 (135)

Moran, Thomas, *The Puebla Laguna, New Mexico* (WHL 679), 30.5 × 58.5, Christie's 6 June 1958 (140)

Muller, William James, *A River Scene, Milking Time* (WHL 77), 84 × 132, Christie's 6 June 1958 (142)

—, *A Stormy Day* (WHL 105), 24.1 × 29.2, Christie's 6 June 1958 (143)

—, *The Young Anglers, Gillingham* (WHL 2800) 104.1 × 86.4, Christie's 17 March 1961 (77)

Murray, David, *Ullswater, Moonlight* (WHL 3572) 36.8 × 44.5, Christie's 6 June 1958 (144)

Nichol, Erskine, *The Children Fairing* (WHL 3797), 85.1 × 69.9, Christie's 6 June 1958 (145)

Niemann, Edmund John, *Richmond Castle, Yorkshire* 74.9 × 125.7, Christie's 7 April 1961 (134)

Parry, John, *The Fortune Teller* (WHL 1429), 87.6 × 67.3, Christie's 6 June 1958 (146)

Phillip, John, *A Highland Lassie Reading* (WHL 683), 68.6 × 52.1, Christie's 6 June 1958 (148)

—, *La Señora* (WHL 569), 33 × 27.9, Christie's 6 June 1958 (149)

—, *The Gleaners* 38.1 × 30.5, Christie's 31 July 1958 (134)

Pollentine, Alfred, *Italian Coast Scene* 44.5 × 80, Christie's 7 April 1961 (130)

Reid, John Robertson, *A Woman Seated on a River Bank* (WHL 2024), 49.5 × 29.2, Christie's 6 June 1958 (151)

—, *The Haymaker* (WHL 2302) 29.2 × 49.5, Christie's 6 June 1958 (152)

—, *A Stream* (WHL 2306), 24.1 × 34.2, Christie's 6 June 1958 (153)

—, *A Fishing Port* (WHL 2292), 25.3 × 35.5, Christie's 6 June 1958 (153)

Richmond, William Blake, *Dionysus and the Bacchantes* (WHL 2848), 44.5 × 90.2, Christie's 6 June 1958 (154)

Riviere, Briton, *The Lions Roaring After Their Prey, Do Seek Their Meat From God* (WHL 3404), 25.4 × 40.6, Christie's 6 June 1958 (155)

Robb, William George, *Music by the Lake* 49.5 × 59.7, Christie's 7 April 1961 (128)

Robins, Thomas Sewell, *At the Well* 57.2 × 44.5, Christie's 7 April 1961 (129)

Robinson, Evelyn Fothergill, *The Beech Pool, River Usk* (WHL 3060), 63.5 × 74.9, Christie's 6 June 1958 (156)

Solomon, Solomon Joseph, *The Judgement of Paris* (WHL 7) 243.8 × 160, Christie's 6 June 1958 (158)

Stone, Marcus, *The Gambler's Wife* (WHL 23), 94 × 152.4, Christie's 6 June 1958 (160)

Storey, G.A., *A Type of Beauty* (WHL 673), 58.4 × 48.3, Christie's 6 June 1958 (161)

Strang, William, *Danae* (WHL 3413), 121.9 × 121.9, Christie's 6 June 1958 (163)

—, *Sketch of Danae* (WHL 3418), 43.2 × 43.2, Christie's 6 June 1958 (164)

Topham, Frank William Warwick, *Stepping Stones; The Strayed Lamb* (WHL 2347), 58.4 × 68.6, Christie's 6 June 1958 (165)

Varley, John Jnr., *A Temple Gate, Tamachi, Tokyo* (WHL 1487), Christie's 6 June 1958 (166)

—, *Maple Trees, Mujajima* (WHL 1489), Christie's 6 June 1958 (166)

Waterhouse, John William, *The Siren* (WHL 3314), 78.7 × 50.8, Christie's 6 June 1958 (167)

Watson, George Spencer, *The Fountain* (WHL 2901), 73.7 × 60.9, Christie's 6 June 1958 (168)

Watts, George Frederic, *Una and the Red Cross Knight* (WHL 4676), 134.6 × 152.4, Christie's 6 June 1958 (170)

Wells, G., *Arranging the Flowers* (WHL 1482), 26.7 × 19.6, Christie's 6 June 1958 (140)

Wimperis, Edmund Morrison, *A Marshy Common near Penzance* (WHL 2321), 21.6 × 29.2, Christie's 6 June 1958 (173)

Wingfield, *Portrait of a Young Woman with a Rose*, 91.5 × 71, Bonham's 20 April 1961 (144)

Woods, Henry, *The High Street, Serra Valle* (WHL 681), 66 × 43.2, Christie's 6 June 1958 (174)

—, *Serra Valle* (WHL 697), 26.7 × 15.9, Christie's 6 June 1958 (175)

# *APPENDIX 3:*

## ***Victorian and Edwardian Paintings Recorded as still in the Lady Lever Art Gallery but now not Locatable***

Against each work appear Lever's inventory number and the dimensions in centimetres.

### Paintings

Tarpey, Mr. or Mrs. J. Toler Kingsley, *A Highland Girl* (WHL 3169), 46.4 × 33.6

—, *View from a Florentine Terrace Garden* (WHL 3170), 35 × 45.1

# INDEX

*Bold type indicates a catalogued artist; all works of art are indexed in italic type; numbers in italic refer to illustrated pages or colour plates; references to notes are indicated by* n. *Exhibitions, galleries and museums are indexed under their their town or city of location.*

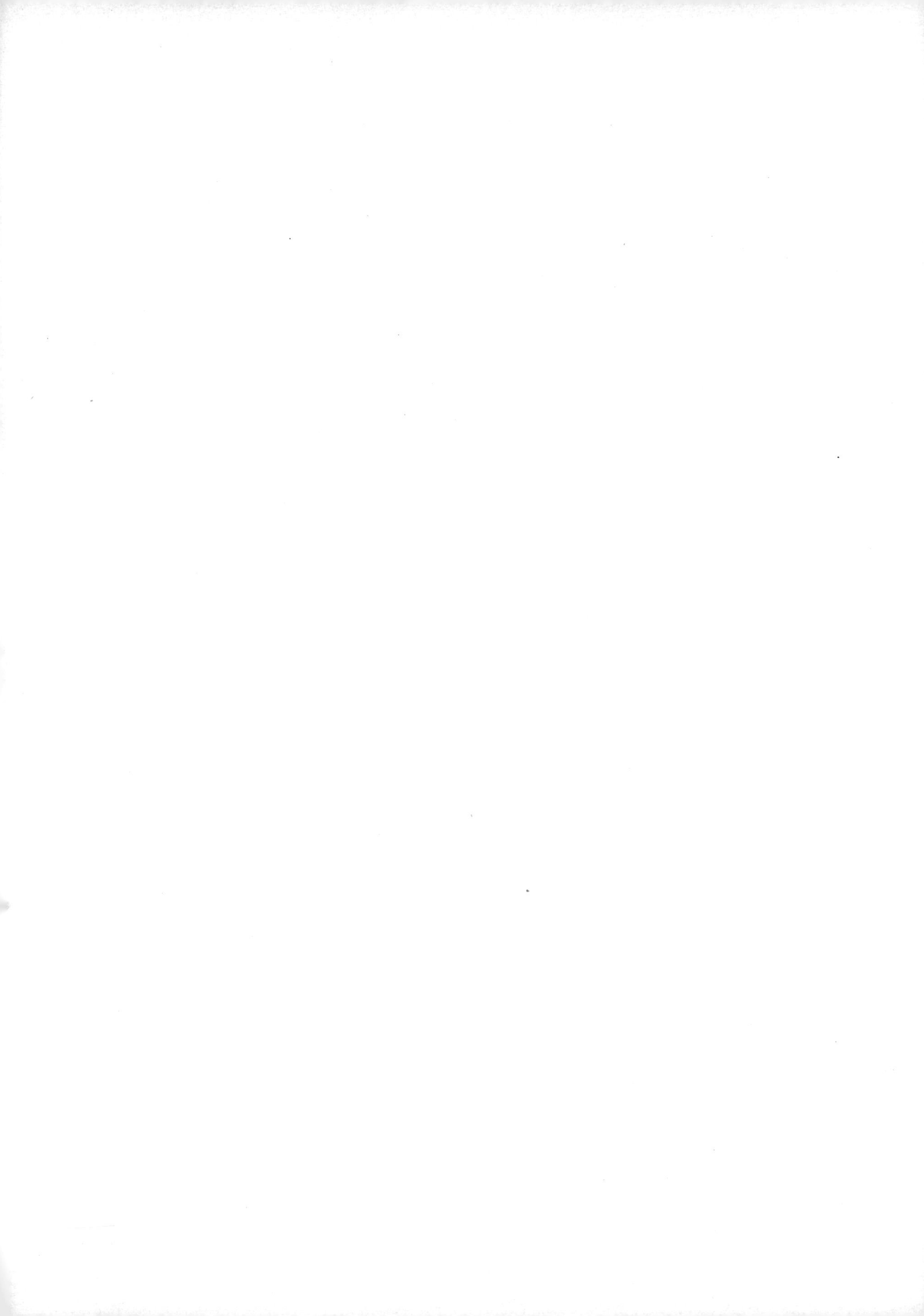